**Wesoła, Kleparz
and Biskupie**
Pages 130–141

QUARTER

WESOŁA, KLEPARZ
AND BISKUPIE

0 metres   400
0 yards   400

OKÓŁ
AND STRADOM
QUARTERS

**Okół and Stradom
Quarters**
Pages 76–89

KAZIMIERZ
QUARTER

Kazimierz Quarter
Pages 120–129

EYEWITNESS TRAVEL

KRAKOW

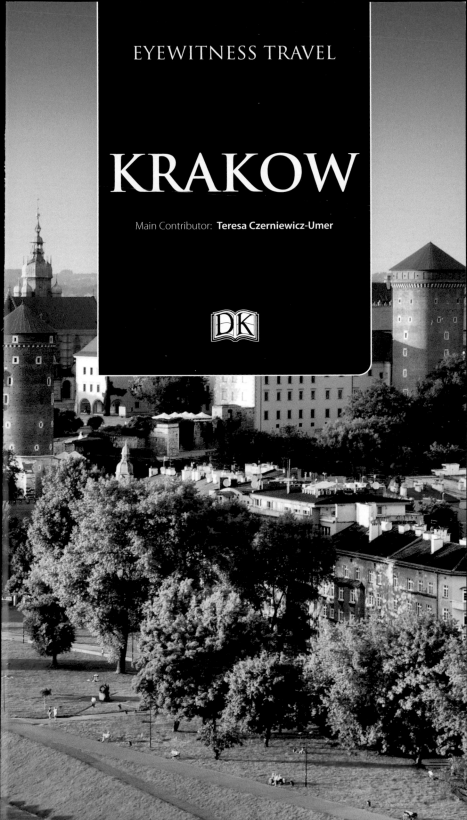

EYEWITNESS TRAVEL

KRAKOW

Main Contributor: **Teresa Czerniewicz-Umer**

LONDON, NEW YORK,
MELBOURNE, MUNICH AND DELHI
www.dk.com

Produced by Wydawnictwo Wiedza i Życie, Warsaw

Managing Editor Ewa Szwagrzyk
Series Editor Joanna Egert
DTP Designer Paweł Pasternak
Consultant Jan Ostrowski
Production Anna Kożurno-Królikowska

Contributors
Teresa Czerniewicz-Umer, Andrzej Betlej, Piotr Krasny,
Robert Makłowicz, Craig Turp

Photographers
Andrzej Chęć, Wojciech Czerniewicz, Piotr Jamski,
Dorota and Mariusz Jarymowicz

Illustrators
Andrzej Wielgosz, Piotr Zybrzycki, Paweł Mistewicz

Printed and bound in China

First American Edition, 2000

15 16 17 18 10 9 8 7 6 5 4 3 2 1

Published in the United States by
DK Publishing, 345 Hudson Street, New York, New York 10014

Reprinted with revisions 2003, 2007, 2010, 2013, 2015

Copyright 2000, 2015 © Dorling Kindersley Limited, London
A Penguin Random House Company

Published in Great Britain by Dorling Kindersley Limited.

A catalog record for this book is available from the Library of Congress.

ISSN 1542-1554

ISBN 978-1-46542-663-5

MIX
Paper from
responsible sources
FSC
www.fsc.org   FSC™ C018179

**The information in this
DK Eyewitness Travel Guide is checked regularly.**
Every effort has been made to ensure that this book is as up-to-date as possible at
the time of going to press. Some details, however, such as telephone numbers,
opening hours, prices, gallery-hanging arrangements and travel information are
liable to change. The publishers cannot accept responsibility for any consequences
arising from the use of this book, nor for any material on third-party websites, and
cannot guarantee that any website address in this book will be a suitable source of
travel information. We value the views and suggestions of our readers very highly.
Please write to: Publisher, DK Eyewitness Travel Guides, Dorling Kindersley,
80 Strand, London, WC2R 0RL, UK, or email: travelguides@dk.com

Front cover main image: Krakow Cathedral on Wawel Hill

◀ View of the Wawel Royal Castle from across the Vistula River

Contents

The side arcade of Cloth Hall *(see pp104–5)*

Introducing Krakow

Icon of the Virgin of the Rosary
in the Dominican Church *(see pp118–19)*

Town Hall in Kazimierz, housing the Ethnographical Museum *(see p125)*

Pickled herrings

Musicians wearing regional Krakow costumes

Krakow Cathedral on Wawel Hill *(see pp66–7)*

HOW TO USE THIS GUIDE

This Eyewitness Travel Guide is intended to help you make the most of your stay in Krakow. It provides detailed practical information and expert recommendations. *Introducing Krakow* tells you about the geographical location of the city, establishes Krakow in its historical context and guides you through the succession of cultural events. The section on *Krakow at a Glance* takes you through the tourist attractions in the city. *Krakow Area by Area* describes the most important sights with photographs, maps and illustrations. It recommends short excursions out of Krakow and offers three walks around the city. Information about hotels, restaurants, shops and markets as well as cafés, bars, entertainment and sport can be found in the section called *Travellers' Needs*. The section headed *Survival Guide* has advice on everything from posting a letter to using public transport to getting medical assistance.

How to Use the Key Indicators

Each of the six quarters has been colour coded for your convenience. Each section gives an introduction to the area, its history and character. The *Street by Street* map shows the most interesting parts of the quarter. Finding your way round is made easy by the numbering system. This reflects the order in which the descriptions are presented.

Each area has its colour coded thumb tabs.

1 Area Map
For ease of reference, sights in each area are located and numbered on the area map. Sights of particular interest are listed together: churches, museums and galleries, streets and squares, historic buildings, parks and monuments.

Stars indicate the features that no visitors should miss.

Locator map

A locator map places the quarter in relation to the surrounding area.

A suggested route takes you through the most interesting streets in the area.

2 Street-by-Street Map
The most interesting part of each sightseeing area is given from a bird's-eye view. On the area map the most interesting sights are indicated and given a full description on the following pages.

Krakow Area Map

This colour-coded map *(see pages 18–19)* indicates the six main sightseeing quarters described in this guide. Each of these quarters is more fully covered in the *Area by Area* section *(pages 58–153)*. In *Krakow at a Glance* this same colour coding allows you to locate the most interesting places. You will also be able to orientate yourself during the three suggested walks *(page 166)*.

Numbered circles locate the listed sights on the area map and within the descriptive boxes.

Practical information provides everything you need to know to visit each sight. Map references pinpoint the sight's location on the *Street Finder* map *(see pp228–37)*.

3 Detailed Information
Each of the most interesting sights is described in depth. You will find them listed in order following the numbering on the area map. Practical information, including map references, opening hours and telephone numbers is also provided.

The visitors' checklist provides useful information you may need to plan your visit.

The boxes contain detailed information on a particular subject related to the sight.

Numbered circles point out key features of the sight listed in a key.

4 Krakow's Main Sights
Historic buildings are dissected to reveal their interiors. Museums and galleries have colour-coded floor plans enabling you to find important exhibits.

A timeline indicates important dates in the history of the building.

The Prussian Homage (1882) by Jan Matejko ▶

INTRODUCING KRAKOW

GREAT DAYS IN KRAKOW

There are three themes that define the most visited city in Poland – its royal past, Judaism and culture. Some of Krakow's most important sights are along the Royal Route to the Wawel Castle, while the Kazimierz district, home to the city's Jews since the 14th century, is seeing a welcome revival after the tragedy of the Holocaust. As Poland's cultural capital, many museums here house artistic treasures. Krakow is also a surprisingly green city, full of grottoes and parks particularly suited to children. The four days on pages 10–11 are designed to uncover the city from these different viewpoints; the price guides include travel, food and admission fees. The itineraries on pages 12–13 show visitors how to make the most of their time based on length of stay.

Walking the Royal Route

Two Adults allow at least 340zł

- **Explore Krakow's Old Quarter**
- **Great views from the Town Hall Tower**
- **Authentic Polish cuisine**
- **Impressive churches and a cathedral**

Morning
Starting early to avoid the crowds, especially in summer, there is no better way to enter Krakow's Old Quarter than through the 700-year-old **St Florian's Gate** *(see p113)*, one of the few remnants of the city's original defences. Stroll along **Floriańska Street** *(see p116)*, once Krakow's main commercial thoroughfare and still very much a thriving bazaar where artisans and hawkers sell all sorts of souvenirs – look out for watercolours depicting the best of the Old Quarter. Krakow's **Market Square**

St Florian's Gate

(see pp100–103) is both the geographical and spiritual heart of the city, and is surrounded on all sides by historic treasures; **St Mary's** *(see pp94–7)* and **St Aldabert's** *(see p99)* churches are worth a look. Climb the **Town Hall Tower** *(see p99)* for superb panoramic views and wander around the market inside the 14th-century **Cloth Hall** *(see pp104–5)*. For lunch, enjoy some classic Polish dishes at Krakow's oldest restaurant, **Wierzynek** *(see p192)*.

Afternoon
One of Krakow's oldest streets, **Grodzka** *(see p80)* is a cobbled route of different, but harmonious, architectural styles. Admire the **Royal Arsenal** *(see p81)* and the modest but charming **Church of St Giles** opposite *(see p81)*. A little further down, don't miss the **Church of St Martin** *(see p81)*, set slightly back from the street, or the impressively preserved Romanesque **Church of St Andrew** *(see p80)*. Take a look inside the **Church of Saints Peter and Paul** *(see pp82–3)*, an early Baroque masterpiece. At the end of the Royal Route is **Wawel Hill** *(see pp62–3)*, and late in the afternoon, after the majority of visitors have gone, you can stroll the hill at leisure. Be sure to visit the wonderful **Krakow Cathedral** *(see pp66–71)*, and to wander around the Renaissance-style inner courtyard of the **Wawel Royal Castle** *(see pp72–3)*.

Interior of the Old Synagogue

Jewish Krakow

Two Adults allow at least 180zł

- **The history of Krakow's Jewish population**
- **Great kosher food**
- **World War II Jewish ghetto**
- **The famous Schindler factory**

Morning
Start your day at the **Old Synagogue** *(see p124)*, damaged during World War II, but now restored to its original 16th-century design. The exhibition inside serves as a good introduction to the history of Jews in Krakow. Nearby are two cemeteries: the **New Jewish Cemetery** *(see p125)*, created in the 19th century as a resting place for the city's wealthiest Jews, and **Remu'h Cemetery** *(see pp124–5)* in the courtyard of the Remu'h synagogue. For a kosher lunch head to **Klezmer Hois** *(see p192)*.

Afternoon
Stroll over the Kładka Ojca Bernatka footbridge to the Podgórze district. The Nazis moved the Jews here from Kazimierz in 1941, squeezing them into a ghetto in the area around Bohaterów Getta and Rynek Podgórski. One Polish man, Tadeusz Pankiewicz, owner of the Pharmacy Under the Eagle at Bohaterów Getta 18, stayed on in an attempt to help the city's Jews. Here today, an exhibition portrays life in the ghetto. At Lipowa 4 is the former **Schindler's Factory** *(see p158)*, featured in the film *Schindler's List*. An exhibition details stories from Krakow's Polish and Jewish inhabitants during World War II.

Flowers in bloom in Planty Park

City of Culture

Two Adults allow at least 230zł

- **Admire the only Leonardo da Vinci painting in Poland**
- **Visit the former home of Pope John Paul II**
- **Explore the Collegium Maius**
- **Beautiful Secessionist architecture**

Morning
The **Czartoryski Museum** *(see pp114–15)* is currently undergoing renovations. During this time, its most famous work of art, Leonardo da Vinci's *Lady with an Ermine*, can be admired at the **Wawel Royal Castle** *(see pp72–3)*. Next, head over to the **Szołayski House** *(see p112)* to admire the talents of

Jagiellonian University

Stanislav Wyspiański, Poland's leading Secessionist painter. Jump on the No. 124 bus for the short ride to the **Archdiocesan Museum** *(see p84)*, home of Poland's finest collection of ecclesiastical art. Today the building is also popular with pilgrims interested in the life of Pope John Paul II; he lived in the building in the 1950s. For lunch, head to **Smak Ukraiński** *(see p190)* for outstanding Ukrainian food.

Afternoon
A walk through the southern part of **Planty Park** *(see pp168–9)*, past the statue of Copernicus, to the Jagiellonian University and Museum in the **Collegium Maius** *(see pp108–9)* is the perfect post-lunch stroll. Enjoy the glorious courtyard and take the 30-minute guided tour of the building, then take a quick peek inside the **Church of St Anne** *(see pp110–11)*. If you have an appetite for more art, head to the **"Bunker of Art"** *(see p107)*, home to cutting-edge exhibitions. Next pay a visit to the **Słowacki Theatre** *(see p117)*. It is officially closed unless there is a performance on, but the doorman may just let you in to admire the lovely Secessionist interior. Round off this cultural day with dinner at **Jazz Club U Muniaka** *(see p206)*, Krakow's best jazz café.

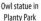
Owl statue in Planty Park

A Family Day

Family of Four allow 545zł

- **The magical and mysterious Dragon's Lair**
- **Picnic lunch in the park**
- **Shopping in the Cloth Hall**
- **Cycle round the city**

Morning
Few children will fail to be intrigued by the **Dragon's Lair** *(see p65)* on Wawel Hill, a warren of tunnels, nooks and crannies. They can then shop for chocolate at **Wawel** *(see p201)* before you head next door to the deli to buy bread, sausage and cheese for a picnic lunch. Then visit the **Cloth Hall** *(pp104–105)*, which sells excellent wooden toys.

Afternoon
Tram 20 will take you out to the family-friendly Jordan Park, where you can enjoy your lunch while the kids take a paddle-boat on the lake. If you still have some energy, take a bike tour around the sights of the city with Krakow Bike Tour (www.krakowbiketour.com). The tour starts from ul. Grodzka 2 at 3pm. After such an active afternoon, you might want an early dinner; try **U Babci Maliny** *(see p191)*, a cosy basement restaurant serving traditional Polish fare.

2 Days in Krakow

- Stroll around the buzzing main Market Square
- Admire the tombs of Poland's kings in the Krakow Cathedral
- Explore the mixed Jewish-Christian heritage of the Kazimierz Quarter

Krakow's Market Square, with St Adalbert's Church to the left

Day 1

Morning Start with a circuit of the **Market Square** (pp92–3) before exploring the covered stalls of the Renaissance **Cloth Hall** (pp104–105). Join the crowds milling around at the foot of the **Mickiewicz Statue** (p93), then head for the sumptuously decorated **Church of St Mary** (pp94–7). Try to arrive by 11:50am to observe the ritual unveiling of Veit Stoss's **High Altar** (pp96–7).

Afternoon Walk south through the Okół district along **Grodzka Street** (p80) to **Wawel Hill** (pp60–75), site of the **Krakow Cathedral** (pp66–71) and **Wawel Royal Castle** (pp72–3). Admire the stunning views from the ramparts before taking the spiral steps down to the **Dragon's Lair** cave (p65). Finish the day with a stroll on the Vistula riverbank just below.

Day 2

Morning Explore the multi-cultural past of the **Kazimierz Quarter** (pp120–29) with a stroll around its atmospheric streets and piazzas, notably the former market square of **Szeroka Street** (pp122–3). Visit the **Old Synagogue** (p124) and the **Remu'h Synagogue** (p124) for an evocative taste of Jewish Krakow, then stop at one of the area's many restaurants for lunch.

Afternoon Cross the footbridge at the end of Mostowa Street to reach **Schindler's Factory** (p158), now a moving museum recalling the fate of many Krakovians during World War II. Head back northwards via the western half of Kazimierz,

with its churches of **Corpus Christi** (p125) and **St Catherine** (p128). In the evening, stay in Kazimierz to enjoy the numerous cafés and bars of this bohemian quarter.

3 Days in Krakow

- Step back into Krakow's Middle Ages with a visit to the Rynek Underground
- Tour the former royal apartments of Wawel Royal Castle
- Spend a day at the Auschwitz-Birkenau memorial museum

Day 1

Morning Soak in the sights of the **Market Square** (pp92–3), including the subterranean history museum **Rynek Underground** (p99). Enjoy the rich interior of the **Church of St Mary** (pp94–7) before

The statue of Apollo topping the façade of the Palace of Art

strolling up **Floriańska Street** (pp116–17) towards the **Barbican** (p116), pausing to admire the 19th-century paintings and furnishings at the **Matejko House** (p116). From here, walk west through **Planty Park** (pp168–9) towards Szczepański Square.

Afternoon Delve into Krakow's Art Nouveau heritage with a visit to the ornate **Palace of Art** (p107) and the inspirational **Szołayski House** (p112). Walk south through the atmospheric University quarter to the **Collegium Maius** (pp108–109) and the Baroque splendour of the **Church of St Anne** (pp110–11). Finish at the **Franciscan Church** (pp88–9), famous for its beautiful Art Nouveau frescoes by Stanisław Wyspiański.

Day 2

Morning Devote a few hours to **Wawel Hill** (pp60–75). Explore the royal tombs in the **Krakow Cathedral** (pp66–71) before choosing to see at least one of the many museum collections located in **Wawel Royal Castle** (pp72–3).

Afternoon Take a stroll around the former Jewish quarter of **Kazimierz** (pp120–29), calling in at renovated synagogues such as the **Tempel** (p124), the **Isaak's** (p124) and the **Remu'h** (p124). Walk through the **Remu'h Cemetery** (pp124–5) and the **New Jewish Cemetery** (p125), filled with reminders of Kazimierz's rich Jewish past. If time allows, cross the river and visit **Schindler's Factory** (p158).

Day 3
Morning Take the bus to Oświęcim for a guided tour of the former **Auschwitz** concentration camp *(pp162–3)*.

Afternoon Visit the nearby killing fields of **Birkenau** *(pp164–5)* before returning to Krakow by bus.

5 Days in Krakow

- Immerse yourself in Krakow's monument-packed Old Town
- Descend into the amazing underground world of the Wieliczka Salt Mines
- Enjoy woodland walks in Las Wolski forest

Day 1
Morning Explore the **Market Square** *(pp92–3)*, touring the Gallery of Polish Art on the top floor of the **Cloth Hall** *(pp104–105)* before climbing the **Town Hall Tower** *(p99)* for views of the Old Town skyline. Admire the altars of the **Church of St Mary** *(pp94–7)*, then take a peek at **St Barbara's Church** *(p98)* just behind it. Stand beneath the towers of the Church of St Mary on the hour to hear a trumpeter playing the *hejnał* bugle-call *(p94)*.

Afternoon Walk south along **Grodzka Street** *(p80)*, pausing to examine the churches of **St Andrew** *(pp80–81)* and **Saints Peter and Paul** *(pp82–3)*.

Royal Wawel Castle at Wawel Hill seen from across the Vistula River

Detour into pretty **Kanonicza Street** *(p81)*, where you can visit the medieval art collections of the **Archdiocesan Museum** *(p84)* and the **Palace of Bishop Erazm Ciołek** *(p84)*. Afterwards, spend a leisurely hour or two walking the complete circuit of leafy **Planty Park** *(pp168–9)*.

Day 2
Morning Devote the morning to as many museum collections within **Wawel Royal Castle** *(pp72–3)* as you have time for. If time is at a premium, prioritize the State Rooms and the Private Royal Apartments. Try to arrive early, since there may be queues for tickets.

Afternoon Head for **Kazimierz** *(pp120–29)* and visit the area around **Szeroka Street** *(pp122–3)*, site of the original Jewish quarter. Afterwards, visit the western part of the Kazimierz district, with the **Church of**

St Catherine and the **Paulite Church "On the Rock"** *(p128)*.

Day 3
Morning and afternoon Reserve the whole day for a bus trip to the **Auschwitz-Birkenau** memorial museum *(pp162–5)*, taking time to walk through the extensive Birkenau site.

Day 4
Morning Catch a swift suburban train to **Wieliczka** to take a guided tour of the spectacular man-made caverns of the **Salt Mines** *(p158)*.

Afternoon Return to Krakow by train and take the tram to **Nowa Huta** *(p156)*. You can then stroll from the centre of this 1950s-era suburb to the medieval **Mogiła Monastery** *(p156)* nearby. Again taking the tram, call at the **Polish Aviation Museum** *(p156)* on your way back to the city centre.

Day 5
Morning Explore the extensive art and history collections of the **National Museum in Krakow** *(pp150–51)*. Be sure to leave enough time for the modern paintings on the top floor.

Afternoon Walk, cycle or catch a bus to the Zwierzyniec district in order to scale the **Kościuszko Mound** *(p171)*. Follow this up with a stroll or mountain-bike ride around the **Las Wolski** forest *(pp172–3)*, pausing to visit either **Krakow Zoo** *(p173)* or the **Camaldolese Monastery** *(p172)*.

Kościuszko Mound and the fortification surrounding it

Putting Krakow on the Map

The old part of Krakow (Kraków), with the Royal Castle on Wawel Hill, is regarded as a fascinating historic town rich in heritage. The historic quarters constitute only a small part of present-day Krakow, the largest urban development in the Lesser Poland (Małopolska) region. The geographical position makes Krakow an ideal base for excursions to the Polish mountains, Auschwitz or the picturesque Krakow-Częstochowa Valley. The town is also well positioned for international connections to Prague, Brno, Bratislava, Vienna and L'viv.

Europe

Key

▬▬ Motorway
or dual carriageway

= = Motorway under construction

— Major road

— Railway line

— National border

--- Provincial border

0 kilometres 100

0 miles 50

For keys to symbols see back flap

Krakow and Environs

RUSSIAN FEDERATION (KALININGRAD)

Gulf of Danzig

Miechów
Olkusz
Słomniki
94
7
Proszowice
Trzebinia
79
79
See next page
Wisła
Kaliningrad
Alwernia
Kraków
KRAKOW
75
Niepołomice
Lidzbark Warmiński
51
Wisła
Wieliczka
94
A4
75
Elbląg
S22
Skawina
Bochnia
Pasłęk
7
WARMIŃSKO-MAZURSKIE
44
Raba
Kwidzyn
Ostróda
Olsztyn
Szczytno
Wadowice
28
52
Dobczyce
16
Nidzica
53
7
Myślenice
7
52
Brodnica
Mława
Ostrołęka
Łomża
Białystok
PODLASKIE
Ciechanów
60
MAZOWIECKIE
Zambrów
8
Bielsk Podlaski
Pružany
Lipno
10
Narew
Ostrów Mazowiecka
19
Włocławek
Płońsk
Wyszków
Bug
63
BELARUS
Płock
61
S8
Warsaw Modlin
Wisła
Warsaw
Siedlce
Biała Podlaska
Brest
Kobryn
2
Kutno
Pruszków
Warsaw Chopin
63
Międzyrzec Podlaski
Łęczyca
A2
A1
Garwolin
19
A2
Łódź
Łódź
Tomaszów Mazowiecki
17
Kock
Włodawa
Kovel'
ŁÓDZKIE
S8
S7
Puławy
Volodymyr-Volynsky
Bełchatów
Piotrków Trybunalski
12
Radom
12
Wisła
Lublin
Lublin
Chełm
74
Iłża
82
Skarżysko-Kamienna
7
LUBELSKIE
1
9
Ostrowiec
Kraśnik
Zamość
74
Częstochowa
Kielce
Opatów
74
ŚWIĘTOKRZYSKIE
19
17
ŚLĄSKIE
78
Jędrzejów
Tarnobrzeg
Nisko
A1
Zawiercie
7
73
9
Katowice
Mielec
77
Zhovkva
Katowice
See map above
Rzeszów-Jasionka
Lviv
Kraków
KRAKOW
A4
Tarnów
Rzeszów
Radymno
1
MAŁOPOLSKIE
PODKARPACKIE
Przemyśl
S1
Bielsko-Biała
98
Krosno
98
Sambir
Rabka
Nowy Sącz
19
Sanok
UKRAINE
Čadca
Trstená
98
87
Žilina
Zakopane
Svidník
Stryi
Ruzomberok
D1
Poprad
Presov
Ivano-Frankivsk
SLOVAKIA
Košice
Mukacheve

Krakow and its Environs

Until the early 20th century the conurbation of Krakow occupied a relatively small area on the banks of the Vistula (Wisła) River and was made up of several small towns (Kleparz, Kazimierz, Garbary and Podgórze). Greater Krakow was established in 1910 after the incorporation of the extensive lands of Rakowice, Prądnik, Czarna Wieś, Krowodrza, Bielany, Dębnik, Płaszów and Prokocim. A new industrial district of Nowa Huta was constructed outside Krakow after World War II. Long walks in Krakow are always interesting as all the historic quarters have their own unique character.

Kielce

Garlica

Bibice

Zielonki

Węgrzce

Dąbrowa Górnicza

Witkowice

794

Prądnik

Bronowice Małe

Prądnik Biały

Górka Narodów

774

79

Wielkie Pola

57

Rząska

Balice

Krowodrza

Olsza

Katowice

Mydniki

Rudawa

Łobzów

Rakowice

John Paul II International Airport

Warszawskie

Olszanica

Nowa Wieś

Balice

Wola Justowska

Główny

Błonia

Krakow

Grzegórzki

Piłsudski Mound

Zoo Las Wolski

Kościuszko Mound

780

Dębniki

Kryspinów

Bielany

780

Podgórze

Płaszów

Bodzów

Vistula

Krakus Mound

Pychowice

Kostrze

Zakrzówek

Heltmana

Bonarka

Piekary

Cegielniana

Wola Duchacka

A4

Tyniec

Skotniki

Kobierzyn

Borek Fałęcki

Kurdwanów

Kliny Zacisze

Jugowice

Sidzina

Swoszowice

44

Opatkowice

Wilga

Wróblowice

Skawina

Skawina

Korabniki

Libertów

Lusina

Gołkowice

Oświęcim (Auschwitz)

Skawinka

7

Wrząsowice

953

Ochojno

Zakopane

Proszowice

776

Więcławice

Baranówka

Młodziejowice

Książniczki

Luborzyca

Głęboka

Zastów 🚉 Zastów

776

Raciborowice

Krzysztoforzyce

Batowice

Kantorowice

Węgrzynowice

Łuczanowice

🚉
Batowice

Mistrzejowice

Grębałów

Lubocza

Wadów

79

Bieńczyce

🚉
Lubocza

Ruszcza

776

Dłubnia

Sendzimir Steelworks

Nowa Huta

79

Sandomierz

Czyżyny

*Wanda
Mound*

Pleszów

Wyciąże

Dąbie

Branice

Mogiła

Łęg

776

Vistula

Rybitwy

Brzegi

Podgrabie

Płaszów

Grabie

Podłężanka

🚉
Bieżanów

Wielkie
🚉

Niepołomice

Bieżanów

Podłęże

A4

Węgrzce
Wielkie

964

Tarnów

Rżąka

964

Zakrzów

A4

57

94

Kosocice

Krzyszkowice

0 kilometres   2

0 miles   1

Wieliczka 🚉 **Wieliczka**

966

Siercza

Key

 Central Krakow

Motorway

Main road

Main road under construction

Minor road

Railway line

964

Podstolica

Pawlikowice

For keys to symbols *see back flap*

Central Krakow

Central Krakow embraces Wawel Hill and the historic Old Quarter surrounded by the Planty green belt, and the adjoining quarters. Major sights outside the centre of town are also included, and walks and one-day excursions suggested. Each area receives separate coverage in the Krakow Area by Area section, listing places of unique character and great importance in the history of the city.

Church of St Mary
With its asymmetrical silhouette, this church is Krakow's best-known landmark (see pp94–7).

Zygmunt Chapel
This 16th-century chapel is regarded as the greatest example of Renaissance architecture north of the Alps (see pp67–8).

Old Synagogue
This Renaissance synagogue in the Kazimierz quarter is the most outstanding building of the Jewish district (see p124).

Grunwald Monument
Surrounded by the sumptuous architecture of the Kleparz quarter, an imposing monument commemorates the victory over the Teutonic Knights in 1410 *(see p140)*.

Key

- Star sight
- Railway station
- Railway line
- City wall

0 metres 300
0 yards 300

Church of Saints Peter and Paul
The oldest Baroque church in Krakow is situated on Grodzka Street, which runs along the former royal route *(see pp82–3)*.

For keys to symbols *see back flap*

THE HISTORY OF KRAKOW

For many centuries Krakow was the capital of Poland and the country's largest city. Polish rulers resided at Wawel Castle. The royal court moved to Warsaw in 1609, after parliamentary sessions and the election of kings began to take place there. Until the collapse of the First Republic, however, Krakow continued to be regarded as the official capital. Deprived of its former status Krakow suffered a deep crisis in the 18th and 19th centuries.

Despite all the past upheavals, Krakow has retained its magnificence. It is more than 400 years since Krakow ceased to be the seat of national government, and yet the city maintains its leading role in preserving Polish national identity. Wawel, the seat of Polish kings, the Cathedral that bore witness to their coronations and houses their tombs, as well as the Paulite Church "On the Rock" in whose crypt prominent Poles are buried, belong to the most treasured national heritage. The 600-year-old Jagiellonian University, formerly known as the Academy of Krakow, is the oldest and one of the most important universities in the country and a pillar of Polish culture. Bearing in mind the small population of Krakow (approximately 760,000), visitors may be surprised by the great number of theatres, cabarets, concert halls and art galleries, which are always popular with regular audiences.

Polish historic cities suffered badly during World War II. Luckily, Krakow's losses were minimal. For those interested in old Polish art, Krakow, with its rich heritage, is certainly the place to go. For many years Krakow's architectural treasures were in a state of neglect, hidden beneath peeling plaster, cracking paint and layers of dirt caused by pollution, although many buildings have now been renovated and returned to their former splendour.

Krakow is different from some other large European towns in which historic inner cities have been transformed into open-air museums. The medieval Market Square remains at the heart of today's city. It is the venue for some of the most important events and the traditional meeting place for locals and visitors alike, all of whom enjoy Krakow's unique atmosphere and heritage.

View of Krakow with the Kościuszko Mound (in the foreground), a 19th-century lithograph, Museum of Krakow

◀ *Kościuszko's Defeat against the Russian-Prussian Force at Maciejowice in October 1794 by R. Weibezahl*

Krakow's Origins

Krakow is one of the oldest cities in Poland. The archaeological findings provide evidence of a Palaeolithic settlement, as well as those from the Neolithic period, and the Bronze and Iron Ages. The Celtic people and invaders from the east, namely the Scythians and Huns, also left important artifacts. In the early centuries AD Krakow and Lesser Poland bordered and traded with the Roman Empire. Written accounts date only from the 9th century and pertain to the Vistulan settlers who, by the end of the same century, came under the rule of the Great Moravian Empire. The Polish rulers from the House of Piast regained power only at the end of the rule of Mieszko I (around 992).

Extent of the City
■ AD 1000 □ Today

An imaginary view
of Wawel Castle

The cave in
Wawel Hill

King Krak
The legendary founder
of Krakow is believed
to have lived in the
early 8th century.

The Dragon of Wawel
*This woodcut comes from Sebastian
Münster's* Cosmographia universalis
*of 1544 and shows the legendary
dragon and his slayer, the cobbler
Skuba, below Wawel Castle.*

Earthenware with String Ornaments
These earthenware containers were among the
1st-century artifacts excavated at Nowa Huta
while constructing the new town.

c. 200,000 BC Earliest evidence of
settlements in the Krakow area

c. 1300 BC Lusatian
culture flourishes in
Lesser Poland

*Palaeolithic
stone tool*

| 200, 000 BC | 20000 | 0 | AD 200 |

c. 50,000 BC Evidence of a settlement
on Wawel Hill

1st – 4th century AD Krakow settlers
trade with the Roman Empire

Saints Cyril and Methodius
Methodius and his brother Cyril are two of the three Patrons of Europe. The former failed in his attempt to convert the prince of the Vistulans from paganism to Christianity. Soon after, their land was conquered by the Great Moravian Empire.

Where to See Prehistoric Krakow

Very little has survived from prehistoric times in Krakow. There are, however, two mounds worth a visit: the Krak Mound dominating the southern quarters, and the Wanda Mound near Mogiła village. The Archaeological Museum *(see p85)* houses many interesting artifacts from southern Poland, and the Krakow region in particular. The figure of the four-faced pagan idol Światowid is of special interest.

The Krak Mound contains, according to legend, a tomb of Krak, the ancient ruler of Krakow. In reality it was more likely to have been used as a religious site of the Celts.

Wawel means a hill surrounded by marshes

Iron Treasures
Iron objects in the form of elongated axes found at Wawel Hill were used as a form of payment in the 11th century.

Światowid
This statue represents a four-faced idol holding a cornucopia. Evidence of ancient pagan cults has been found at the Wawel and other sites.

600–1000 Vistulans establish their state, possibly with Krakow as the capital

965 Ibrahim Ibn Yaqub, an Arab traveller, comments on Krakow as a Czech city

400	600	800	1000

Early medieval earthenware vase

before 885 The Vistulans' state loses its independence. Krakow becomes part of the Great Moravian Empire

before 992 Mieszko I adds the former state of the Vistulans to his other territories

Krakow in the Early Middle Ages

Following the establishment of the bishopric in 1000 and the construction of the cathedral, Krakow became one of the most important centres of the Polish state. After the destruction of other centres in Lesser Poland (Małopolska) by the Czechs in the first half of the 11th century, Kazimierz the Restorer and his successors made Krakow their main seat. Following the death of Bolesław the Wrymouthed Poland was divided into duchies, and the Dukes of Krakow gained suzerain position. From 1138 to 1320 the dukes aimed to unite the remaining provinces. Despite the Tatar invasion in 1241, this period saw Krakow flourish.

Extent of the City
1253 ☐ Today

Bishop Stanisław in prayer

Szczerbiec
According to legend this is the sword of Bolesław the Brave with which he struck the Golden Gate of Kiev on entering the city in 1018. The sword was actually made in the 13th century. Today it is housed in the Crown Treasury as one of the most treasured regalia.

Denarius of Bolesław the Brave
Following the establishment of Krakow's bishopric in 1000, Bolesław made this city one of his seats.

c. **1038** Kazimierz the Restorer makes Krakow the capital of Poland

1000 Bishopric of Krakow established

1079–98 Construction of St Andrew's Church

c. **1044** Benedictine Abbey at Tyniec is established

1090–1142 Construction of second Cathedral at Wawel

| 1000 | 1025 | 1050 | 1075 | 1100 | 1125 |

1020 Construction of first Cathedral in Krakow begins

1079 Martyrdom of St Stanisław

Coat of arms of the Chapter of Krakow

ed Mitre of St Stanisław
e 13th-century mitre decorated
rls, sapphires and rubies
s to the riches of metropolitan
ow, one of the most important
hoprics in medieval Poland.

*Kazimierz the Restorer
after Jan Matejko*
It can be said that Krakow
owes its capital status to
this ruler, who settled here
around 1038 and established
a central administration.

The Death of Bishop Stanisław

*The conflict between Bishop
Stanisław of Szczepanów
(later canonized) and Bolesław
the Bold ended with the murder
of the bishop in 1079 and the
exile of the king. Both events
contributed to the weakening of
Poland. The cult of St Stanisław
began in the 15th century. This
scene decorates a 16th-century
chasuble (priest's vestment)
commissioned by Piotr Kmita.*

Where to See Romanesque Krakow

Krakow is rich in Romanesque
architecture. Most buildings
have survived in their original
form, though they have often
been enlarged and refurbished.
The Church of St Andrew
(see pp80–81) dates from this
period, as does St Adalbert's
(see p99) and the remains of the
earliest buildings at Wawel,
including the Rotunda of the
Virgin Mary *(see p65)* and the
little Church of the Holy
Redeemer *(see p170)*.

The Church of St Adalbert
was, according to legend,
consecrated by Adalbert
before his missionary journey
to Prussia in 997.

The Crypt of St Leonard
is a remnant of Krakow's
second cathedral. It was built
by Władysław Herman between
1090 and 1142.

Cloister at the Dominican Church

emy founded
ierz the Great
n of Corpus
gins

Bolesław the Curly is the first
to be buried at Wawel

1241 Tatars led by Batuhan destroy Krakow

1175 — 1200 — 1225 — 1250

er
barz (Florencja)
ts Charter

Benedictine Abbey at Tyniec

1250 Consecration of the Dominican Church

Gothic Krakow

The Charter granted to Krakow in 1257 facilitated urban development and allowed for a new and more structured plan. A Gothic defence wall surrounded the city, and Krakow began to flourish anew following the coronation of Władysław the Short in 1320. The new satellite towns of Kazimierz and Kleparz both received municipal charters. The architectural panorama of Krakow was substantially transformed by the building of many new churches and the Cathedral in the 14th and 15th centuries. The foundation of the Krakow Academy, and its subsequent renewal, contributed greatly to the development of culture and intellectual activities. The ideas of Italian humanism were known in Krakow early on.

Extent of the

☐ 1370

The coat of arms
of the Piasts

The Diptych Reliquary
A double leaf Gothic reliquary containing the relics of saints is decorated with the image of the Virgin Mary and that of Christ.

Saints Stanisław and Wacław shown standing on the battlement walls are patron saints of Krakow's Cathedral and the Kingdom of Poland.

A View of Late Gothic Krakow, 1493
This townscape from the 15th-century *World Chronicle* by Hartmann Schedel is the earliest known view of Krakow.

1285 Construction of Krakow's defence walls begins

Coat of arms of Kazimierz

1312 Revolt of German burghers, led by Albert

1364 Krakow Aca by Kazi

1340 Construc Christi Church

1250	1275	1300	1325	135

1257 Duke Bolesław the Chaste grants Krakow her Charter on 5 June

Crown of Kazimierz the Great (replica)

1335 Kazimierz the Gre grants Kazimierz its Cha

1366 Kl receive

The Supposed Mitre of St Stanisław
This ornate 13th-century mitre decorated with pearls, sapphires and rubies testifies to the riches of metropolitan Krakow, one of the most important bishoprics in medieval Poland.

King Bolesław the Bold

Where to See Romanesque Krakow

Krakow is rich in Romanesque architecture. Most buildings have survived in their original form, though they have often been enlarged and refurbished. The Church of St Andrew *(see pp80–81)* dates from this period, as does St Adalbert's *(see p99)* and the remains of the earliest buildings at Wawel, including the Rotunda of the Virgin Mary *(see p65)* and the little Church of the Holy Redeemer *(see p170).*

The Church of St Adalbert was, according to legend, consecrated by Adalbert before his missionary journey to Prussia in 997.

Kazimierz the Restorer after Jan Matejko
It can be said that Krakow owes its capital status to this ruler, who settled here around 1038 and established a central administration.

The Crypt of St Leonard is a remnant of Krakow's second cathedral. It was built by Władysław Herman between 1090 and 1142.

The Death of Bishop Stanisław

The conflict between Bishop Stanisław of Szczepanów (later canonized) and Bolesław the Bold ended with the murder of the bishop in 1079 and the exile of the king. Both events contributed to the weakening of Poland. The cult of St Stanisław began in the 15th century. This scene decorates a 16th-century chasuble (priest's vestment) commissioned by Piotr Kmita.

1138 Bolesław the Wrymouthed grants Krakow the status of a capital of the suzerain province

1173 Bolesław the Curly is the first Piast to be buried at Wawel

Cloister at the Dominican Church

1241 Tatars led by Batuhan destroy Krakow

| 1150 | 1175 | 1200 | 1225 | 1250 |

1141–1320 Polish dukes fight for Krakow

Benedictine Abbey at Tyniec

1250 Consecration of the Dominican Church

Gothic Krakow

The Charter granted to Krakow in 1257 facilitated urban development and allowed for a new and more structured plan. A Gothic defence wall surrounded the city, and Krakow began to flourish anew following the coronation of Władyslaw the Short in 1320. The new satellite towns of Kazimierz and Kleparz both received municipal charters. The architectural panorama of Krakow was substantially transformed by the building of many new churches and the Cathedral in the 14th and 15th centuries. The foundation of the Krakow Academy, and its subsequent renewal, contributed greatly to the development of culture and intellectual activities. The ideas of Italian humanism were known in Krakow early on.

Extent of the City
1370   Today

The coat of arms of the Piasts

The Diptych Reliquary
A double leaf Gothic reliquary containing the relics of saints is decorated with the image of the Virgin Mary and that of Christ.

Saints Stanisław and Wacław shown standing on the battlement walls are patron saints of Krakow's Cathedral and the Kingdom of Poland.

A View of Late Gothic Krakow, 1493
This townscape from the 15th-century *World Chronicle* by Hartmann Schedel is the earliest known view of Krakow.

1285 Construction of Krakow's defence walls begins

Coat of arms of Kazimierz

1364 Krakow Academy founded by Kazimierz the Great

1312 Revolt of German burghers, led by Albert

1340 Construction of Corpus Christi Church begins

| 1250 | 1275 | 1300 | 1325 | 1350 | 1 |

1257 Duke Bolesław the Chaste grants Krakow her Charter on 5 June

Crown of Kazimierz the Great (replica)

1335 Kazimierz the Great grants Kazimierz its Charter

1366 Kleparz (Florencja) receives its Charter

Krakow's Charter
The municipal status granted to Krakow was modelled on the Magdeburg law and contributed to uniform urban development.

Where to See Gothic Krakow

Some of the biggest attractions in Krakow are the Gothic buildings, such as the Barbican (*see p116*), St Florian's Gate (*see p113*), the Collegium Maius (*see pp108–9*), and large churches such as St Mary's (*see pp94–5*), the Dominican Church (*see pp118–19*), St Catherine's (*see p128*) and Corpus Christi (*see p125*). Some smaller churches, such as the Holy Cross (*see p117*), are equally interesting. The works by Veit Stoss are gems of Gothic art.

The coats of arms shown on both sides of the gate are those of Bolesław the Chaste who granted Krakow her Charter.

Krużlowa Madonna
This beautiful Madonna with Child is an interesting example of the influence of International Gothic on wood sculpture of Lesser Poland in the 15th century.

Seal of the Royal City of Krakow
The 14th-century Great Seal of Krakow (shown here with the image reversed) features the emblem of Poland, thus stressing the role of Krakow as its capital.

The Cathedral (*see pp66–71*) is the burial place of kings and the seat of the local archbishop.

The Church of the Holy Cross has a single nave whose interior is covered with palm vaulting.

1386 Grand Duke Jogaila of Lithuania becomes King Władysław II Jagiełło of Poland

Mace of the rector of the Academy of Krakow

1473 First Polish printing house of Łukasz Straube issues a calendar

| 1400 | 1425 | 1450 | 1475 | 1500 |

Before 1400 Collegium Maius is established

1400 Władysław Jagiełło reestablishes the Krakow Academy

1477–89 Veit Stoss works on the high altar at St Mary's

Coat of arms of the Jagiellonians

1492 Kazimierz Jagiellończyk dies

Renaissance Krakow

Krakow, the capital city, rapidly developed economically and began to change in appearance. The Cloth Hall, the city landmark, was remodelled in the Renaissance style, and the rich merchants of Krakow also began to modernize their houses. The art and culture of the Italian Renaissance was assimilated by the royal courts of King Aleksander and King Zygmunt the Old and his second wife Bona Sforza. Bartolomeo Berrecci, Giovanni Maria Padovano and other outstanding Italian masters established their workshops in Krakow during this time.

Extent of the City
1572　　Today

"The Sword Makers" from the Baltazar Behem Codex
This Codex of 1505 contains laws and privileges of the town guilds and is illustrated with 27 illuminations showing craftsmen at work.

Shield with the Polish eagle

Royal sceptre

Royal orb

A Tapestry with Satyrs
This is one of 160 tapestries commissioned in the 16th century by Zygmunt August for the Wawel Collection.

1502–5 Erection of King Jan Olbracht's monument, the first work of Renaissance art in Poland

1505 Baltazar Behem Codex made

Head in the Hall of Deputies

1525 Homage paid by the Prussians to the Polish King in the Market Square on 10 April

1543 The treatise *De revolutionibus* by Copernicus is published

1500　　**1510**　　**1520**　　**1530**　　**1540**

1504 Rebuilding of the Wawel Castle starts

1521 Zygmunt's Bell is hung

1513 First Polish book in print from the Ungler House

1519 Bartolomeo Berrecci begins work on Zygmunt's Chapel in the Cathedral

NICOLAI CO
PERNICI TORINENSIS
DE REVOLVTIONIBVS ORB-
um cœleftium, Libri VI.

Detail of the title page from Copernicus's treatise

A Renaissance Portal
The first post office in 16th-century Poland, serving the Krakow-Venice route, was situated in the house of Prospero Provana. Today the building houses the Hotel Pod Róża.

Cock of the Marksmen's Brotherhood
This gilt masterpiece, made in 1565, belonged to the members of the Brotherhood whose aim was to support soldiers responsible for the defence of the town.

Oval recess with Renaissance decoration

Monument of Zygmunt August
King Zygmunt August was a patron of the arts. It was through his commissions that the Royal Castle at Wawel was enriched with an outstanding collection of tapestries. The king's monument was made by Santi Gucci between 1574 and 1575, in Hungarian red marble.

Where to See Renaissance Krakow

Renaissance architecture was introduced by Italian masters during the rebuilding of the Royal Castle at Wawel in the early 16th century. The Zygmunt Chapel (*see pp66–71*), the Montelupis Monument at St Mary's Church (*see pp94–5*) and a number of houses at Kanonicza Street (*see p81*) are among the finest examples of Renaissance art and architecture in the city.

The arcaded courtyard at the Royal Castle at Wawel is one of the most beautiful in Europe (*see pp72–3*).

The Renaissance Cloth Hall (*see pp104–5*), topped with a characteristic parapet, displayed the prosperity of Jagiellonian Krakow.

After 1550 Santi Gucci comes to Poland

Tomb of Stefan Batory

1595 Santi Gucci works on the tomb of King Stefan Batory

1550	1560	1570	1580	1590

1569 Polish-Lithuanian commonwealth established

1586 First secular secondary school is opened

1595 Archconfraternity of The Passion established

1556–1559 Giovanni Maria Padovano rebuilds the Cloth Hall

1574 Coronation of the first elected king, Henri de Valois

1596 Royal court moves from Krakow to Warsaw

Baroque Krakow

The 17th and 18th centuries saw the decline of Krakow. After the king had moved his residence to Warsaw, he was followed by the noblemen who held high office. Foreign incursions and occupations, wars and the First Partition of Poland in 1772 all added to the city's woes. Despite a number of attempts at reform towards the end of the rule of Stanisław August Poniatowski, Krakow became a provincial, underdeveloped frontier town, though the atmosphere was enlivened by royal coronations and funerals. The failure of the Kościuszko Insurrection of 1794 and the subsequent Third Partition of Poland in 1795 brought an end to Krakow's prominence.

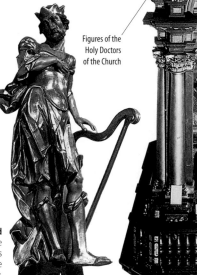

Extent of the City

1700   Today

The Evangelists with their symbols: eagle, angel, lion and ox.

Hood of the 1669 Coronation Cape

The eagle (the emblem of the Commonwealth) on the *cappa magna* of Bishop Tomicki, made for the coronation of Michał Wiśniowiecki, was embroidered with pearls and sapphires.

Figures of the Holy Doctors of the Church

Epitaph of King Władysław IV

The monumental and sombre interior of the Vaza Chapel in the Cathedral is decorated with black marble and features splendid memorial plaques of the Vaza dynasty.

King David

This late Baroque dancing figure in the Corpus Christi Church was made by Anton Gegenbaur in the second half of the 18th century

---

1626–9 Canopy of St Stanisław is erected in the Cathedral

1619 Church of Saints Peter and Paul is completed

1661 First Polish newspaper "Merkuriusz Polski" published by Jan Alexander Gorczyn's Press

Title page of "Merkuriusz Polski"

1600	1620	1640	1660	1680

1609 Zygmunt III Vaza finally abandons his Krakow residence in favour of Warsaw on 25 May

Zygmunt III Vaza

1655–7 Swedish, then Transylvanian, armies occupy Krakow

1676 University Press is established after the Academy buys Piotrowczyks' Press

1664–76 Vaza Chapel in the Cathedral is completed

Memorial Plaque of Bishop Denhoff
Memorial plaques of bishops in the cloister adjoining the Franciscan Church date from different periods. This plaque was made in the early 18th century, probably to a design by Baldassare Fontana.

A silver sarcophagus with the Bishop's mitre and crozier is a reliquary of St Stanisław.

Kołłątaj's Panoramic Map of Krakow
Hugo Kołłątaj led the reform of the University. In 1785 he also created this precise map of Krakow, which shows all the land owned by the city.

Canopy of St Stanisław
This canopy in the Wawel Cathedral was inspired by a number of unexecuted designs for the great baldachin in St Peter's in the Vatican.

Where to See Baroque Krakow

The earliest Baroque church, that was dedicated to Saints Peter and Paul *(see pp82–3)*, as well as much later churches including St Anne's *(see pp110–11)* and the Church of the Order of St John of God *(see p128)*, represent the best of Baroque architecture from Tylman von Gameren and Kacper Bażanka, among others.

The Church of Saints Peter and Paul is one of the finest early Baroque churches in Central Europe.

The façade of the Church of the Missionaries *(see p87)* was inspired by Roman Baroque architecture, in particular by the work of Bernini and Borromini.

Medal of Virtuti Militari

Hugo Kołłątaj

1734 Coronation of August III Wettin, the last to take place in Krakow, on 17 January

1791 Kazimierz and Kleparz are incorporated into Krakow

1794 Tadeusz Kościuszko takes his oath in the Market Square on 24 March

1768–72 Confederates of Bar fight for Krakow

| 1700 | 1720 | 1740 | 1760 | 1780 | 1800 |

1705 St Anne's Church is consecrated

1702–05 Krakow is invaded several times by the Swedes

1777–8 Hugo Kołłątaj reforms the Krakow Academy

1788 Astronomical Observatory established

1798 First permanent theatre building established in Krakow

Krakow in Galicia

In 1772 Austria occupied the southern part of Poland, called Galicia. After a period of Austrian occupation, Krakow was briefly incorporated into the Duchy of Warsaw. The Russian occupation followed. In 1815 the Republic of Krakow, which included the area round the city, was established, but by 1846 Krakow was under Austrian rule again. After a period of suppression, Galicia received extensive autonomy from the 1860s onwards. During the 19th century Krakow was the only Polish territory to enjoy relative freedom. It embarked upon a mission of safeguarding traditions and past historic successes, thus becoming the spiritual capital of Poland.

Extent of the City
☐ 1818   ☐ Today

Sarcophagus of Prince Józef Poniatowski
Of all the famous Poles who died abroad, Józef Poniatowski was the first to have his body brought back to receive a solemn funeral, which transformed itself into a patriotic demonstration.

A beggar woman receiving alms

Emperor Franz Joseph

The Opening of the Sarcophagus of Kazimierz the Great by Jan Matejko
An accidental discovery of the remains of the king prompted his second funeral in 1869, which became an event on a national scale, reminiscent of the glorious past.

The Entry of Emperor Franz Joseph in 1880

Franz Joseph was a popular ruler with the people of Krakow. He was believed to be behind the development of the city and its autonomy. A series of watercolours by Juliusz Kossak (1824–99), such as this one, depicts his stay in Krakow.

1800 Royal Castle at Wawel made into army barracks

1813–15 Krakow occupied by the Austrians

Ruins of the fire-damaged Dominican Church

1846 Krakow Uprising. Krakow becomes part of Austria

1800	1810	1820	1830	1840

1809 Krakow incorporated into the Duchy of Warsaw

1810–14 City walls demolished

1815 "Free, independent and strictly neutral city of Krakow" and her region established as the Republic of Krakow

1820–3 Kościuszko Mound constructed

Coat of arms of Galicia

House of Jan Matejko
Jan Matejko, whose particular genre of history painting imprinted in the nation's mind an image of its past, lived in this house *(see p116)*.

Inhabitants of Krakow greeting the Emperor

Design for the Mickiewicz Monument
This model by Antoni Kurzawa was never fully executed. It is held at the National Museum in Krakow.

Where to See 19th-Century Krakow

The architecture of Krakow in the 19th century was eclectic. The Renaissance Revival style predominated (for example the Academy of Fine Arts, *see p138*), and was often influenced by the monumental architecture of Vienna, the place where many of Krakow's architects trained. The University buildings are a good example of Gothic Revival in which the historic style is blended with vernacular features.

The Church of the Felician Nuns is one of the few buildings in the Romanesque Revival style *(see p146)*.

The Collegium Novum is a prestigious Gothic Revival building designed by Feliks Księżarski *(see p106)*.

The Krakow Uprising
The uprising of 1846 was intended to spark a revolt in all parts of partitioned Poland, but was suppressed by the Austrians.

1866 Local government established in Krakow with Józef Dietl as Mayor

1872 Academy of Skills established

1876 Czartoryski Collection opens to the public

1854 Society of Friends of Fine Arts established

1883–7 Collegium Novum built

1850	1860	1870	1880	1890

1850 Great fire of Krakow

Apparatus for condensing oxygen

1883 Two Krakow scientists, Z. Wróblewski and K. Olszewski, condense oxygen

1893 Słowacki Theatre opens

Modernist Krakow

At the end of the 19th century Greater Krakow was established and became a place of mass excursions from other parts of occupied Poland. People came to see the newly re-established University and the repossessed Wawel, which was then undergoing restoration. It was the period of "art for art's sake", and Krakow became a mecca for Polish artists. Modern life concentrated around artistic cafés, such as the Paon and the Jama Michalika, which were also venues for cabarets. The latter café housed the Zielony Balonik Cabaret. The ambience in Krakow was one of melancholy and decadence but life, permeated by patriotic Neo-Romantic symbolism, was lived here to the full. The outbreak of World War I put an end to this unique bohemian era.

Extent of the City

1900   Today

The Cathedral

House of Deputies of the new Parliament

Academies and museums

An amphitheatre modelled on the Barbican in Krakow

Stańczyk
This painting by Leon Wyczółkowski portrays the court jester, Stańczyk, in pensive mood, playing with marionettes of historic Polish characters.

"Życie"
This is the masthead of the magazine of the Polish Modernist movement. The contributors were the leading authors of the time.

1897 "Życie" weekly is established

1898 Stanisław Przybyszewski arrives in Krakow

1901 Palace of Art, the seat of the Society of Friends of the Fine Arts, is built

1903–5 Old Theatre (Teatr Stary) rebuilt in the Art Nouveau style

1895	1897	1899	1901	1903	1905

1895 Adam Mickiewicz's statue is unveiled

1898–1900 Stanisław Wyspiański decorates the Franciscan Church with murals and stained glass

1901 Premiere of *The Wedding* by Stanisław Wyspiański

Wyspiański's Art Nouveau murals in the Franciscan Church

Poster by Stanisław Wyspiański
This poster announces a lecture by S. Przybyszewski followed by a play by M. Maeterlinck.

Marionettes from the Zielony Balonik Cabaret
This cabaret and New Year's satirical show, staged by Karol Frycz, ridiculed the narrow-mindedness and hypocrisy of the Krakovians.

Reconstructed churches of St George and St Michael

Stadium modelled on Roman architecture

Polish Acropolis **by Stanisław Wyspiański**
The idea behind this design for the rebuilding of the entire Wawel Hill was to transform the Royal Castle into a political, social, academic and cultural centre of the liberated Poland. Its architecture was intended to reflect a synthesis of Polish history.

Where to See Modernist Krakow

Modernist Krakow was, above all, a city of literature and painting. Architecture from this period is scarce. There are, however, some magnificent buildings, such as the spider House "Pod pająkiem" *(see p153)* and the Palace of Art *(see p107)*. Art Nouveau interiors of exceptional beauty can be found at the Franciscan Church with its stained glass and murals, designed by Wyspiański *(see pp88–9)*, the Society of Physicians building *(see p134)* and the prestigious former Museum of Industry and Technology *(see p145)*.

During the rebuilding of the Old Theatre (Teatr Stary) in the Art Nouveau style its façade was decorated with a stucco floral frieze *(see p107)*.

The façade of the Church of the Discalced Carmelite Nuns, with its elaborate decoration, is in sharp contrast to its austere interior.

1906 Krakow sports clubs, Wisła and Cracovia, established

1907 Stanisław Wyspiański dies

1910 Riflemen's Union formed by Józef Piłsudski

1912 First cinema opens in Krakow

A late 19th-century armchair

1907 | **1909** | **1911** | **1913** | **1915**

1906 Building of the Chamber of Commerce and Industry completed

1910 Grunwald Monument unveiled

The sphere at the top of the Chamber of Commerce and Industry Building

1914 First Cadre Brigade of the Polish Legions marches out of Krakow on 6 August

Krakow in the Years 1918–1945

When World War I ended in 1918, Poland regained its independence after 123 years of foreign occupation. In the period between the two World Wars Krakow became a source for political, administrative and army staff for the whole of the Republic of Poland. Above all the city was a cultural and academic centre. The Modernist traditions were still present in the arts but soon gave way to a new generation of artists, such as the Formists, Capists (the Polish variant of Post-Impressionists), the avant-garde Krakow Group and the Cricot Theatre. During World War II the German Governor General had his headquarters in Krakow, and this was reason enough for the city to be spared destruction.

Extent of the City
◼ 1938   ☐ Today

Józef Piłsudski
The Commander by Konrad Krzyżanowski portrays well the personality and character of this uncompromising Polish soldier and politician.

Portrait of Nena Stachurska
This portrait is by S. I. Witkiewicz, who was one of the most unconventional artists of the 20th century. He called for the utopian ideal of "pure art".

Kościuszko Mound

Marshal Józef Piłsudski

Tribune

Figures decorating the Academy of Mines and Metallurgy Building
The first school of its type in liberated Poland was established to educate specialists for the industry in Silesia.

1918 Austrian Army disarmed in Krakow. Polish Liquidation Commission created on 31 October

1925 Tomb of the Unknown Soldier blessed

1923 Workers' unrest in Krakow

Jagiellonian Library

1918	1921	1924	1927	1930

1919 Academy of Mines and Metallurgy established

1921 Jesuit Church at Wesoła consecrated

Banner which was raised in liberated Krakow

1927 Juliusz Słowacki's remains brought to Krakow and buried at Wawel

1930–9 Jagiellonian Library completed

Funeral of Marshal Piłsudski
The funeral of the Commander, who was buried at Wawel in 1935, was the biggest state event in interwar Poland.

Demolition of Mickiewicz's Statue
During the German occupation all monuments of importance were demolished, including those of Mickiewicz, Kościuszko and Grunwald.

A military band gallops at the head of the troops.

The Cavalry Parade
The parade of the cavalry of the Second Republic took place at Błonie on 6 October 1933. Wojciech Kossak, member of a distinguished Krakow family of artists, painted this grand event.

Auschwitz (Oświęcim)

The name Oświęcim may have little meaning for most foreigners but the German name, Auschwitz, raises the spectre of death. During World War II the Nazis established Auschwitz *(see pp162–3)* and the nearby Birkenau (Brzezinka) *(see pp164–5)* concentration camps. Nearly 1.5 million people were put to death in these camps. The Auschwitz camp was set up in 1940 to subject Poles to terror and extermination. Before long the Nazis rounded up and transported people from the whole of Europe, and from 1942 Auschwitz and Birkenau became the largest extermination camps for Jews. A cynical inscription over the gate leading into the Auschwitz camp reads *"Arbeit macht frei"* ("Work makes you free").

It was in the Auschwitz Death Block that Maksymilian Kolbe, a Franciscan priest, gave up his life for another inmate. Kolbe (who was later canonized) was sentenced to death by starvation.

In the old barracks of Auschwitz there is an exhibition telling the history of the camp *(see pp162–3)*. Temporary displays are also organized. In Brzezinka, 3 km (1.8 miles) away, only some of the original 300 barracks remain, along with the loading platform. New prisoners were unloaded from railway wagons and segregated here.

1933 Cricot, the Artists'Theatre, is established	**1935** Piłsudski is given a state funeral at Wawel	**1939** Outbreak of World War II on 1 September	**1945** Soviet troops enter Krakow on 18 January
	1938 Dietl's statue erected		**1943** Jewish ghetto liquidated
1933	**1936**	**1939**	**1942**	**1945**

Statue of Józef Dietl

1937 Teaching commences at the Academy of Mines and Metallurgy

1941 Jewish ghetto established

1939 Krakow occupied by the Nazis on 6 September

Krakow after 1945

After World War II ended Krakow did not willingly accept the new Soviet-imposed regime. In 1946 the celebrations of the 3 May Constitution turned into clashes with tragic consequences. Many Krakovians claim that the industrial suburb of Nowa Huta, with its immense steelworks *(see p156)*, was built to "punish" the city for rejecting the 1946 Communist referendum. In fact, the site was chosen because of good rail links, proximity to the river, and Krakow's engineering and scientific heritage. It is also false to claim that pollution from Nowa Huta was meant to damage Krakow's ancient monuments. Krakow's problem with air quality is largely the result of domestic heating furnaces and vehicle fumes.

Tadeusz Sendzimir Steelworks
Formerly known as the Lenin Steelworks, the mills were expected to become a bastion of the Communist proletariat. Paradoxically, they became one of the main centres of opposition.

Banner of the Vatican

Papal high altar

Holy Mass during the Pope's Visit

The political transformation of Poland which took place after 1989 was welcomed in Krakow. The Mass celebrated in 1991 by Pope John Paul II in Market Square attracted unprecedented numbers of worshippers.

Mistrzejowice Church
Built between 1976 and 1983, the church was decorated with sculptures by Gustaw Zemła.

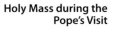

1946 Bloody suppression of 3 May celebrations

Builders' Brigade by H. Krajewska

1956 Piwnica pod Baranami Cabaret established

1967 Construction of the Ark of God Church in Nowa Huta begins

1978 Krakow included in the UNESCO World Heritage List

1980 Solidarity established

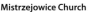

1945   **1950**   **1955**   **1960**   **1965**   **1970**   **1975**   **1980**

1949 Construction of Nowa Huta begins

1950 Nowa Huta becomes a borough of Krakow

1956 Cricot 2 Theatre established

1957 Celebrations of the city of Krakow's 700th anniversary

1964 600th anniversary of the Academy of Krakow

John Paul II

1978 Karol Wojtyła, the Metropolitan of Krakow, elected as Pope John Paul II

Demonstrations in Nowa Huta
During the period of martial law, street demonstrations in the workers' suburb of Nowa Huta often ended in riots.

Extent of the City

[ ] 1945   [ ] Today

Nobel Prize for Wisława Szymborska
The Krakow poet was awarded the 1996 Nobel Prize for Literature.

St Mary's Church

Polish banner

Sculpture Decorating the Tomb of Tadeusz Kantor
The theatre of Tadeusz Kantor (1915–90) had a Polish, as well as a European, dimension. This sculpture on his tomb was originally designed for his play *Wielopole, Wielopole*.

Where to see Modern Krakow

Very few postwar buildings in Krakow deserve notice. However, some examples of ecclesiastical architecture, namely the Abbey of the Fathers of the Resurrection designed by Dariusz Kozłowski, and two churches in Nowa Huta – the Ark of God and Mistrzejowice Church, are exceptional. An extensive programme of building renovation in old Krakow has been undertaken. Completed projects include the Krakow Arena and the Krakow Congress Centre, the latter opposite Wawel Hill.

The Ark of God Church in Nowa Huta *(see p156) is an example of modern ecclesiastical architecture, rich in impressive forms and symbolic content.*

1981 Martial law declared in Poland on 13 December (lifted on 22 July 1983)

1991 International Cultural Centre established

1992 European Month of Culture celebrations take place in Krakow in June

1996 Wisława Szymborska is awarded the Nobel Prize for Literature

2005 Pope John Paul II dies in Rome

2010 A plane crash kills President Lech Kaczyński and his wife; Bronisław Komorowski elected president of Poland

| 1985 | 1990 | 1995 | 2000 | 2005 | 2010 | 2015 | 2020 |

1981 Citizens Committee for the Rescue of Krakow established

1993 Czesław Miłosz, the winner of the Nobel Prize for Literature, becomes an honorary citizen of Krakow

A book by Czesław Miłosz

2004 Poland joins the European Union

2014 Canonization of Pope John Paul II

KRAKOW AT A GLANCE

Krakow was one of the few Polish cities to be saved from major destruction during many wars which devastated the country. The city has preserved not only its monuments but also a specific "antiquarian" atmosphere. Already in the 19th century Krakow was a destination for tourists from other countries as well as different parts of Poland. Krakow and Wieliczka were included on the very

first UNESCO World Heritage List. The section *Krakow Area by Area* describes many places of interest. To help make the most of your stay, the following 12 pages are a guide to the best Krakow has to offer. Each sight has a cross-reference to its own full entry. Below are the top ten tourist attractions to start you off. Take a journey back in time and enjoy sites of historic interest and beauty.

Krakow's Top Ten Tourist Attractions

Royal Castle Wawel
See pp72–5.

Krakow Cathedral
See pp66–71.

Kościuszko Mound
See p171.

Church of St Mary
See pp94–7.

Market Square
See pp100–3.

Church of St Anne
See pp110–11.

Planty
See pp168–9.

Collegium Maius
See pp108–9.

Remu'h Cemetery
See pp124–5.

Cloth Hall
See pp104–5.

◀ The splendid Art Nouveau ceiling designed by Stanisław Wyspiański in the Franciscan Church

Krakow's Best: Museums and Galleries

Krakow has dozens of museums, which are very varied in character. The Royal Castle at Wawel is the best known, offering visitors the chance to see collections housed in the royal chambers which date from the time when the Polish kings resided here. The Czartoryski Museum is the best place for Western art. The National Museum has rich collections of Polish art housed in a number of branches in the city centre.

National Museum in Krakow, Main Building

One of the best collections of 20th-century Polish art is housed here. The collection of Modernist art is particularly rich, and includes excellent sculptures by Konstanty Laszczka.

Museum of Krakow

This museum in Christopher Palace is devoted to the history of the city. Krakow is famous for her portable Christmas cribs, and the collection housed here is of great beauty.

Japanese Centre of Art and Technology

This modern building houses a collection of works from the Far East, much of which was donated by Feliks Manggha Jasieński. The *netsuke* (a kind of button) shown takes the form of a tiger.

0 metres	500
0 yards	500

Archaeological Museum

Many archaeological finds from the Lesser Poland area, as well as Egyptian mummies, are displayed here.

PLASEK AND NOWY ŚWIAT

KARMELICKA

KRUPNICZA

SMOLEŃSK

ZWIERZYNIECKA

F. STRASZEWSKIEGO

Vistula

WAWEL HILL

Czartoryski Museum
This fine bas-relief by the 17th-century Roman sculptor Alessandro Algardi depicts the Polish Jesuit Stanisław Kostka being admitted to the congregation of Jesuit saints.

House of Matejko
In the family house of Jan Matejko, some of his works, including this study for Joan of Arc, as well as his extraordinary collection of "antiquities", are brought together.

Gallery of 19th-Century Polish Art in the Cloth Hall
In 1879 Henryk Siemiradzki presented the National Museum with its first gift, his painting *The Torches of Nero.*

Galicia Jewish Museum
A collection of Judaica, one of the best in Central Europe, is housed in this Renaissance synagogue.

Royal Castle in Wawel
This royal residence houses an outstanding art collection which includes paintings, sculptures, gold work, arms and Oriental art. The tapestries are of particular interest.

Exploring Krakow's Museums and Galleries

Krakow's museum collections tell the history of the city and Polish culture in great detail. There are also a few specialized foreign collections. A visit to all the many museums would require several weeks but it is possible to concentrate on just the most important collections and still get to know the city well. For contemporary art, head to the Museum of Contemporary Art in Krakow (MOCAK) and the "Bunker of Art".

St Stanisław's Reliquary, Cathedral Museum *(see p64)*

The History of Poland and Krakow

The former residence of Polish rulers, the **Royal Castle** at Wawel is the best known of Krakow's museums. Outstanding tapestries and paintings are among the exhibits. The Armoury and Treasury are also open for visits. The latter houses the coronation sword *Szczerbiec*. Worth a visit is the archaeological display "Lost Wawel", which shows the Rotunda of the Virgin Mary (Krakow's first church). A computer-generated model of Wawel gives visitors an overview of the early 10th-century construction. The Gregorian chants sung by the Dominican Friars can be heard while viewing the programme.

The history of the former capital of Poland is told at the **Museum of Krakow**. The collections here include the insignia of municipal governments and those of guilds, seals featuring Krakow's coat of arms and many townscapes showing Krakow in the past.

The Jagiellonian University Museum is housed in the **Collegium Maius**, the oldest of the university's buildings. The museum brings together scientific equipment, of which some items are unique, as well as memorabilia left by former professors. Many rooms have retained their original furnishings.

The borough of Kazimierz was inhabited in the past mostly by Jews. This part of the city became a centre for their culture. The **Galicia Jewish Museum**, with its rich collection of Judaica, including liturgical objects, is dedicated to the Jewish heritage.

The election of the Archbishop of Krakow, Karol Wojtyła, to the pontificate was an important event in the history of the city. A room, recreated in the **Archdiocesan Museum**, commemorates the years spent by Karol Wojtyła in Krakow.

The altar by Jerzy Nowosielski, St Vladimir's Foundation, devoted to the Orthodox Church

Polish Art

In 1879 Henryk Siemiradzki presented Krakow with his painting *The Torches of Nero*. He thus initiated the establishment of the **National Museum in Krakow**. Poland was then still an occupied country and the intention was to raise patriotic awareness and the morale of the Poles. Only Polish art and works relating to the history of Poland were included. As a result, the museum has only a limited selection of Western art. Its collection of historical Polish art, on the other hand, is unparalleled. The museum has a dozen branches throughout the city. A large and outstanding collection of medieval and

Deputies' Hall in the Royal Castle at Wawel

Italian Landscape by Adam Chmielowski, National Museum in Krakow

Renaissance painting and sculpture used to take pride of place in the museum, but it has been moved to the Palace of Bishop Erazm Ciołek *(see p84)* where Polish art up to 1794 is now housed. Nineteenth-century Polish art, housed at the **Cloth Hall Gallery**, is also of great interest. Twentieth-century painting and sculpture can be admired in the Main Building. The museum has a programme of temporary monographic exhibitions concerned with the life and work of great Krakow artists such as Jan Matejko, Stanisław Wyspiański and Józef Mehoffer. The **Europeum** branch houses the museum's collection of Western European art, featuring important works by Brueghel the Younger and Lorenzo Lotto.

The **Cricoteka** displays the works of 20th-century painter and designer Tadeusz Kantor. The museum is housed in a striking modern building on the river bank.

The collection at **St Vladimir's Foundation** is devoted to the culture of the Orthodox Church among whose faithful were the Ruthenians who lived in the eastern borderlands of Poland. The collection features parts of iconostases and single icons from the 16th to 20th centuries.

Contemporary Polish and non-Polish art can be seen at the popular **Museum of Contemporary Art in Krakow (MOCAK)**, as well as at the **"Bunker of Art"**.

The **Archdiocesan Museum** has a magnificent collection of

Polish sacred art. The museum also organizes exhibitions of works on loan from leading church treasuries throughout the country as well as other countries.

Foreign Art

Those interested in Western art should visit the **Czartoryski Museum**. There are many fine works here, including *Landscape with the Good Samaritan* by Rembrandt, Romanesque gold work from the Maas region, Italian Renaissance majolica, and Meissen porcelain. The museum is closed for renovation until 2016. During this time, its most celebrated masterpiece, *The Lady with an Ermine* by Leonardo da Vinci, will be on display at Wawel Royal Castle.

The Manggha **Japanese Centre of Art and Technology** covers Japanese art. A bequest of objects from the Far East presented by Feliks Manggha Jasieński constitutes the core of the collection, which also includes works by contemporary artists.

Tin-glazed majolica plate (c. 1545) from the collection of the Czartoryski Museum

Local Culture and Natural History

The **Archaeological Museum** displays important objects found in the 19th century in Galicia *(see p32)*, which was then under Austrian occupation. One of them is the statue of Światowid fished out from the Zbrucz River. Other objects found during the construction of Nowa Huta and renovation works at Kanonicza Street were also added. There is also a notable collection of Egyptian mummies.

The **Ethnographic Museum** houses a large collection of folk art from the Lesser Poland region. Temporary exhibitions, which take place at the Krakowska Street branch, are always of interest.

An extremely well pre-served rhinoceros *(coelodonta antiquitatis)* from the Ice Age is a highlight of the **Natural History Museum**.

Skull of *coelodonta antiquitatis*, Natural History Museum

Museums and Galleries

Krakow's Best: Churches

The skyline of Krakow is dominated by churches. There are some 40 churches within the historic centre alone. There would be even more, however, as many churches were destroyed or dismantled in the 19th century. The surviving churches bear witness to the splendour of Krakow. The interiors are surprisingly rich in furnishings and house a variety of works of art in different artistic styles.

PLASEK AND NOWY ŚWIAT

KARMELICKA

ŁOBZOWSKA

KRUPNICZA

SMOLEŃSK

WAWEL HILL

Vistula

Church of St Anne
This church was created by two outstanding artists at the end of the 17th century – the architect Tylman van Gameren and the sculptor Baldassare Fontana.

Franciscan Church
Magnificent murals and stained glass by Stanisław Wyspiański decorate the Gothic interior of this church.

Cathedral
This Cathedral is a place where the history of the Polish state meets that of the Church and where national memorabilia are treasured.

| 0 metres | | 500 |
| 0 yards | | 500 |

Piarist Church
The Rococo façade of this church is flat, though it is richly decorated.

Church of St Mary
The most important church in the centre of historic Krakow, St Mary's is famous for its retable, made between 1477 and 1489, and its interior decoration, which dates from later years.

LUBICZ

OLD QUARTER

WESOŁA, KLEPARZ AND BISKUPIE

MIKOŁAJA KOPERNIKA

OKÓŁ AND STRADOM QUARTERS

STAROWIŚLNA

JÓZEFA DIETLA

KAZIMIERZ QUARTER

KRAKOWSKA

ŚW. WAWRZYNCA

Vistula

Dominican Church
This memorial plaque of Callimachus (Italian humanist, secretary to the Royal court), made after 1496 to the design of Veit Stoss, is to be found here. The remaining furnishings are mostly Neo-Gothic.

Church of Saints Peter and Paul
This is the finest early Baroque church in Poland from the leading architects of the late 16th century. It is decorated with exquisite carved statues and stuccowork.

St Catherine's Church
While visiting this church one should not miss the south porch decorated with stonework and tracery.

Exploring Krakow's Churches

Krakow's churches represent many different styles, from the Romanesque and Gothic through Baroque and later eclecticism to the modern. Fortunately the majority of churches were saved from wartime destruction and have not been damaged. Today their splendid interiors impress visitors to the city. However, Krakow's churches are not only tourist attractions but also places of pilgrimage. The relics of a number of saints and blessed, as well as many pious figures who enjoy a local cult, are laid to rest in the city's variety of churches.

St Andrew's Church

Pre-Romanesque and Romanesque

The earliest stone churches in Krakow date from the second half of the 10th century. They were built on the site of today's **St Adalbert's Church** and at Wawel, where the remnants of a number of rotundas have been found. Today the reconstructed Rotunda of the Virgin Mary *(see p65)*, originally from the late 10th century, can be visited. Built around 1079, **St Andrew's** is exceptional among the Romanesque churches. The **Church of the Holy Redeemer** dates from around the same period. The Crypt of St Leonard beneath the Cathedral is a remnant of the second cathedral built between 1090 and 1142. The remnants of the Church of St Gereon and the Chapel of St Mary of Egypt are also at Wawel.

Gothic

Slender silhouettes of Gothic churches enhance the city. Some buildings were, however, demolished in the 19th century during the programme of "tidying up" the old architecture. The **Franciscan Church** is the oldest to have survived. Its irregular plan of a Greek cross with an asymmetric nave is unusual. The **Church of the Holy Cross**, begun

Gothic vault in the nave of the Corpus Christi Church

around 1300, is worth visiting for its palm vaulting supported by a single pillar. **Krakow Cathedral** is certainly a major attraction. This three-aisled basilica with a transept and ambulatory, surrounded by chapels, was constructed between 1320 and 1364. The Monastery, **Church of St Catherine** and the **Corpus Christi** were both founded by Kazimierz the Great, while the **Dominican Church** was rebuilt during his reign. All three churches share the same structural and stylistic characteristics and were probably constructed by the same stonemasons, who moved from one site to another. **St Mary's** the city's main civic church, is also Gothic. It was under construction from the end of the 13th century until the late 15th century.

Towers, Domes and Spires in Krakow

The outlines of many church domes and spires dominate the skyline of old Krakow. They also bear witness to the historic and artistic changes that the city has undergone. The Gothic spires of St Mary's and Corpus Christi are among the tallest and most picturesque. Baroque styles are more common and include the Church of Saints Peter and Paul, St Anne's and the Cathedral Clock Tower.

Towers of the Church of St Andrew

Slender Gothic spire of St Mary's Church

Baroque dome of St Anne's Church

Renaissance and Mannerist

There is no complete church in Krakow in either the pure Renaissance or Mannerist styles, but the Zygmunt Chapel, built from 1519 to 1533, is regarded as the greatest example of Italian Renaissance north of the Alps. The chapel, with its spatial design and decoration, provided a model which was followed faithfully throughout Poland for many years.

Renaissance monuments by Jan Michałowicz of Urzędów and Giovanni Maria Mosca ("Il Padovano") can be seen in a number of churches. The career of the Italian Mannerist Santi Gucci, an equally fine artist, spans the last decades of the 16th century.

Baroque

Although in the 17th century Polish kings no longer resided in Krakow, many new ecclesiastical foundations were undertaken. The Jesuit **Church of Saints Peter and Paul** was the most magnificent. The church was completed by the royal architect

Baroque façade detail of the Church of the Missionaries

Giovanni Battista Trevano in 1609–19. The imposing Zbaraski Chapel in the **Dominican Church**, built between 1629 and 1631, is another fine example of early Baroque. The Canopy of St Stanisław and the Vaza Chapel, both in the Wawel **Cathedral**, exemplify the best of the High Baroque style. In the first half of the 17th century the interiors of a number of Gothic churches, such as St Mark's (see p112) were remodelled in the Baroque style. The century that followed brought about further architectural masterpieces, including **St Anne's Church**. A mention must also be made of the **Church of the Missionaries** whose exterior and interior were both modelled on Roman architecture, the **Piarist Church** with its airy façade, and the **Church of the Order of St John of God** whose façade displays dynamic articulation.

Neo-Classical and Eclectic

The late 18th-century choir and the high altar in the Church of the Norbertine Nuns are the only examples of ecclesiastical Neo-Classicism in Krakow. No building activity was undertaken until Galicia became autonomous, and new churches were only constructed in the second half of the 19th and first half of the 20th centuries. The **Church of the Felician Nuns** was built between 1882 and 1884 to designs by Feliks Księżarski, and the **St Joseph's Church** (1905–09) was designed by Jan Sas Zubrzycki. The **Jesuit Church** designed by Franciszek

Decoration of the porch of the Jesuit Church

Mączyński and decorated with sculptures by Xawery Dunikowski and Karol Hukan, is an outstanding example of 20th-century architecture.

Modern

A variety of designs were applied to modern churches of the second half of the 20th century. Amongst the most interesting are the **Ark of God** in Nowa Huta (architect Wojciech Pietrzyk, 1967–77), the Church of St Maksymilian Kolbe in Mistrzejowice (architect Józef Dutkiewicz, 1976–83) and the Church of St Jan Kanty at Bronowice Nowe.

Finding Krakow's Churches

Late Baroque Clock Tower of the Cathedral

Neo-Gothic spire of St Joseph's Church at Podgórze

Modern spire of the Ark of God Church in Nowa Huta

Exploring Krakow's Cemeteries

All over Europe the cult of commemorating the dead resulted in the establishment of many large cemeteries, with beautiful sculptures often decorating the tombs. Krakow is no different in this respect. Numerous cemeteries and mausolea in church crypts have been established here over the years. They were already regarded as tourist attractions in the 19th century and continue to be visited by tourists to the city.

The Jerzmanowski Mausoleum, Rakowicki Cemetery

Christian Cemeteries

At the end of the 18th century a Krakovian noted that "Every time one looks through the window one cannot but see graves and crosses in the centre of the city". At that time cemeteries used to be located near churches. The one at St Mary's was the largest. It was relocated at the end of the 18th century and the original burial site transformed into Mariacki Square. Many tombstones and epitaphs, often medieval, which commemorate those who died centuries ago, have survived on the exterior walls of the churches of St Mary and St Barbara. A number of mausolea, built as chapels by the patrician families of Krakow, also survive on the former site of St Mary's Cemetery.

The **Rakowicki Cemetery** was established outside the city in 1803 and is the oldest cemetery in use. It occupies a vast plot and its layout is transparent. Many old trees give the place a park-like appearance. Some tombstones, especially those made around 1900 by the best Polish sculptors of the time, are true works of art.

In 1920 a **Military Cemetery** was set up by the Rakowicki Cemetery (they have since merged). Polish soldiers who fell in the years 1914–20 and in September 1939, as well as British and Commonwealth airmen who lost their lives in World War II, all rest here.

The **Salwator Cemetery** is a far more modest place with no great monuments, but rather smaller tombstones decorated with small-scale but nevertheless interesting bas-reliefs. It is, however, a lovely place, picturesquely situated on a high hill and rich in varied fauna. One of the best times of year to visit Krakow's cemeteries is a few days either side of 1 November, when they glow under candlelight at night.

Jewish Cemeteries

For many centuries Jews constituted a substantial part of the population of Kazimierz, the so-called Jewish city. They were interred at the **Remu'h Cemetery**, established in 1533. This small plot, squeezed between buildings, has many layers of tombs which have been

The graves of British airmen, Military Cemetery

Monuments and Tombs

The monuments in Krakow's cemeteries show different ways in which people wished to commemorate the deceased. The medieval monuments show a stiff figure lying on a death bed placed under a canopy. The canopy symbolizes Heaven awaiting the soul. Elements glorifying the deceased were introduced into Baroque monuments. Female figures with attributes personified the virtues. Neo-Classical monuments were influenced by ancient sculpture. Fine sculptures and symbolic content are characteristic of the monuments in the Art Nouveau style.

Monument of Kazimierz the Great (died 1370) in the Cathedral

Sarcophagus of Kościuszko in the Cathedral crypt (1818)

Sarcophagus of Jan III Sobieski in the Cathedral (1760)

placed here over hundreds of years. The tombstones are engraved with Hebrew inscriptions and symbolic images that identify the religion and social rank of the deceased. The dense accumulation of tombstones within a tiny and bare space contributes to the unique character of this Jewish cemetery.

The **New Jewish Cemetery** is different. It was established in the 19th century and given, like other cemeteries, a park-like appearance. Tombstones are scattered randomly and surrounded by luxuriant vegetation. This is one of a few Jewish cemeteries in Poland which is still in use.

The Vaza Crypt in the Cathedral

View of Remu'h Cemetery

Crypts with Tombs of Great Poles

During the Partitions period (1795–1918) a number of celebrated Poles received state funerals. These events were intended to raise the patriotic feelings of the Polish people.

The Angel of Vengeance on the Monument to Victims of the 1848 Bombardment of Krakow (1913)

Church crypts were open to the public and transformed into pantheons of Poland's greatest citizens. The **Cathedral's Crypt** contains the most solemn royal tombs of all. The crypt is divided into galleries in which Polish rulers, leading poets and national heroes rest. Tadeusz Kościuszko and Prince Józef Poniatowski were interred here during the occupation of Poland; President Lech Kaczyński and his wife, who were killed in a plane crash in 2010, are also buried here.

The **Crypt in the Paulite Church "On the Rock"** is a resting place for those who made great contributions to the arts and sciences. The eminent historian Jan Długosz was buried here in the 15th century.

Monastic Cemeteries

The crypts beneath monastic churches are unique to Krakow. Their character reflects the unusual burial practices of particular religious orders.

The corpses in the **Crypt in the Church of the Reformed Franciscans** have been mummified naturally owing to the crypt's construction and ventilation. One can see here the corpses of poor friars lying on sand with their heads resting on a stone, as well as lay people in rich clothes resting in elaborate coffins. Over 700 laymen and around 250 Franciscan friars were buried here. The **Camaldolese**

Catacombs beneath the church in Bielany are different. Here, the corpses are laid at first in niches cut out in a wall and then bricked up. Some years later the bones are removed and placed in an ossuary with the exception of the skull, which is taken by one of the monks for the purposes of contemplation. The Camaldolese crypt strikingly shows that in the face of death all are equal.

Mummified monks in the Crypt of the Church of the Reformed Franciscans

Finding Krakow's Cemeteries

Camaldolese Catacombs *p172*
Cathedral's Crypt *pp68–71*
Crypt in the Church of the Reformed Franciscans *p112*
Crypt in the Paulite Church "On the Rock" *p129*
New Jewish Cemetery *p125*
Rakowicki Cemetery *Map 2 E1, 2*
Remu'h Cemetery *pp124–5*
Salwator Cemetery *p171*

Krakow's Famous Residents

Many leading personalities of Polish academic, cultural and public life were born in Krakow. Eminent scholars were educated at or drawn to the Jagiellonian University, which was sometimes called "a gem of all knowledge". Famous artists and writers chose to live here, attracted by the unique atmosphere of the city, which was enlivened by old traditions. The cult of such great figures as writer and artist Stanisław Wyspiánski, theatre director Tadeusz Kantor and painter Jan Matejko is still alive.

Helena Modrzejewska (1840–1909)
This famous actress began her career at the Old Theatre (Teatr Stary) She is buried in Krakow.

Stanisław Wyspiánski (1869–1907)
Best known for his play *The Wedding*, Wyspiánski was a dramatist, painter and designer. His great artistic visions are embedded in the Polish perception of national identity. He was born at Krupnicza 26.

PLASEK AND NOWY ŚWIAT

Wisława Szymborska (1923–2012)
This prominent poet was awarded the 1996 Nobel Prize for Literature. Szymborska's links with Krakow span more than 50 years. She lived at Krupnicza 22 in her youth.

Stanisław Lem (1921–2006)
One of the most widely read science-fiction authors in the world, Lem was also an essayist and critic. He studied medicine in Krakow.

Andrzej Wajda (born 1926)
A leading film and theatre director, Wajda was educated in Krakow. He was the main instigator of the Japanese Centre of Art and Technology, one of the city's best museums. Wajda won an Oscar for Lifetime Achievement in 2000.

John Paul II (1920–2005)
Before his elevation to the papacy, Karol Wojtyła was Suffragan Bishop, then Archbishop of Krakow from 1963 to 1978. He lived in the Archbishop's Palace on Franciszkańska 3.

Jan Matejko (1838–93)
The most renowned Polish painter of the 19th century, Matejko's vision of Polish history has influenced many generations. Krakow's Academy of Fine Arts and the large square next to it are named in his honour.

Krzysztof Penderecki (born 1933)
World-renowned composer and conductor, Penderecki was educated in Krakow. He was a Professor and Rector of the Music Academy.

Sławomir Mrożek (1930–2013)
An outstanding playwright and satirist, Mrożek began his career in Krakow as a journalist. After many years abroad, he returned and settled here in 1996. He is buried in the Church of Saints Peter and Paul.

Czesław Miłosz (1911–2004)
A poet, translator, Nobel Prize winner and honorary doctor of the Jagiellonian University, Miłosz was made an honorary citizen of Krakow in 1993. In his final years he lived at W. Bogusławskiego 6.

Tadeusz Kantor (1915–90)
A leading European artist and theatre director, Kantor established the world-famous Cricot 2 Theatre. For many years he worked at Kanonicza 5.

BASZTOWA

LUBICZ

SW. MARKA

SW. TOMASZA

WESOŁA, KLEPARZ AND BISKUPIE

RKET IARE

OLD QUARTER

GRODZKA

OKÓŁ AND STRADOM QUARTERS

STAROWIŚLNA

JÓZEFA DIETLA

KAZIMIERZ QUARTER

KRAKOWSKA

SW. WAWRZYŃCA

0 metres   500
0 yards   500

KRAKOW THROUGH THE YEAR

Beautiful and magical, Krakow is a city where old traditions are maintained. The bugle call that echoes at hourly intervals from the tower of St Mary's Church sets the rhythm of life. And life is lived here slowly, for one should not hurry when surrounded by stones a thousand years old. Embraced by the Planty, which had replaced the medieval walls, the old quarter remains at the heart of the city. It is not an open-air museum that visitors vacate at night. Although no longer the capital of Poland, Krakow is a cultural centre and one of the oldest university cities in Europe. There is something for everyone here. Press listings and other local media, as well as tourist agencies, are good sources of information.

The Emmaus Fair in Zwierzyniec on Easter Monday

Spring

In Podhale, the region at the foothills of the Tatra Mountains, vast fields of crocuses announce the arrival of spring. In Krakow, the opening of street cafés and people spilling onto the pavements heralds the new season.

March

International Festival of Alternative Theatre, Rotunda Club. The oldest event of its kind in which alternative theatres and fans of theatre are brought together.
Jazz Juniors, Rotunda Club. This is an international jazz festival for young musicians.
Festival of Organ Music, various venues. *(Mar–Apr).*

Easter

Palm Sunday *(Sun before Easter).* The blessing of palms in churches. A competition for the largest and best decorated palm takes place in Lipnica Murowana village, 41 km (25 miles) east of Krakow.
Holy Saturday is a day when baskets with food are taken to the church for a blessing, and symbolic tombs of Christ are venerated.
Easter Sunday is the most important Catholic feast.
Easter Monday. The Emmaus Fair takes place in Zwierzyniec and people are splashed with water *(Śmigus-dyngus)* throughout the city.

April

Paka Cabaret Festival. Amateur and professional satirical performers, Polish and foreign, all take part.

May

3 May Constitution Day celebrates the first Polish Constitution of 1791 with a Mass said in the Cathedral followed by the laying of wreaths at the Tomb of the Unknown Soldier. Afterwards, there are fairs and picnics.
Procession from Wawel to the Paulite Church "On the Rock" *(first Sun after 8 May, Feast of St Stanisław).* The Primate and bishops lead the procession and carry the relics of the patron saints of Poland, joined by the faithful in regional costumes.
Juvenalia. Krakow is ruled by students for a couple of days.
Krakow Film Festival *(May-Jun).* The oldest film festival in the country.
Krakow Spring Ballet Festival Słowacki Theatre, *(May–Jun).* Leading ballet companies of the world take part.

Archconfraternity of the Passion

Since 1595 the Good Friday processions of the Archconfraternity of The Passion have taken place in the Franciscan Church. The Brothers wear black habits with hoods covering the face. The ritual has remained unchanged for centuries. The Archconfraternity had the right to pardon those condemned to death.

Brothers in Procession

Average Daily Hours of Sunshine

Hours

[Bar chart showing average daily hours of sunshine by month from Jan to Dec, with values rising to a peak around May-Jun]

Sunshine Chart
May is the sunniest month of the year in Krakow, but June, July and August are usually also sunny. December is the gloomiest month.

Summer

Summer heat may be difficult to bear in Krakow. This is because of the city's location in a valley and its humid microclimate. Many bars, cafés and restaurants in the Old Quarter are open and busy till the early hours of the morning. Crowds of tourists are attracted not only by the heritage but also the nightlife and cultural events. Organ Recitals at the Benedictine Abbey at Tyniec are among the most famous events.

June

Corpus Christi (Boże Ciało)
(Thu in May or June). A great procession proceeds from Wawel to the Market Square. On Thursday a week after Corpus Christi *Lajkonik* canters around the town *(see p98)*.
Enthronement of the "king" Marksman, Market Square. The Marksmen's Brotherhood has existed since the Middle Ages. Its members are burghers who are members of craftsmen guilds. Their leader is the winner of the annual shooting competition. The outgoing leader passes the silver cock to the new "king" during a colourful ceremony.
Midsummer's Eve (Wianki) Sat preceding the eve of St John's Feast *(24 Jun)*. Candle wreaths are set adrift on the Vistula by Wawel and there are fireworks displays.
International Music Festival of Military Bands features gala shows of drill, parades in period uniforms and many concerts.

July

Summer Early Music Festival. Concerts are held in historic houses.
Summer Opera and Operetta Festival. Krakow Jazz Festival (Stary Jazz w Krakowie) *(Jul–Aug)*. A real treat for fans of traditional jazz.
Jewish Culture Festival *(early Jul)*, Kazimierz.

Poster announcing events during the Jewish Culture Festival

Outstanding Jewish performers from all over the world take part in this festival.

August

The Assumption of the Virgin Mary (Święto Wniebowzięcia Matki Boskiej) *(15 Aug)*. A Solemn Mass is said in the Cathedral. This is also the national holiday of the Polish Soldier, marking the 1920 victory over the Bolshevik Army.
International Festival of Music in Old Krakow *(15–31 Aug)*. One of the most prestigious events in Krakow, with recitals and concerts of orchestral and chamber music in the magnificent historic buildings of the Old Quarter.
International Folk Art Fair (Targi Sztuki Ludowj), *(12 days in Aug)*, Market Square. Folk artists and craftsmen from Poland and other countries demonstrate their handicrafts and folklore. One day is dedicated to concerts of folk music by the Polish Highlanders.

Enthronement of the "king" Marksman in the Market Square

Average Monthly Rainfall

Rainfall Chart
September is the wettest month in Krakow. Storms and cloudbursts may occur in summer. February and April are the driest months.

Autumn

On dry and sunny autumn days Krakow is beautifully shrouded in colours; the Planty chestnut trees turn golden and market stalls display baskets full of wild mushrooms from the woodlands of the mountain foothills.

Students return to Krakow by the end of September to take part in the inaugural celebrations of the new academic year. The hymn *Gaudeamus Igitur* can be heard sung at many colleges, and in particular at the Jagiellonian University, Poland's oldest university, established in 1364.

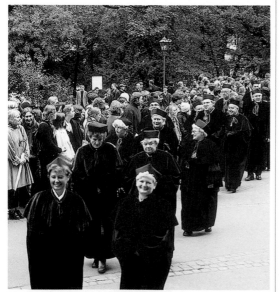

Inauguration of the academic year at the Jagiellonian University

September
Sacrum Profanum Festival
(early to mid-Sep). This annual festival is devoted to 20th-century music of all sorts, whether classical, pop or avant-garde. It has previously included appearances by the likes of Kraftwerk, Aphex Twin and Sigur Rós. Important buildings in the city are adapted and tailored to suit the festival's needs.

October
"Etude" International Film Festival (Międzynarodowy Festiwal Filmowy Etiuda). This festival sees the screening of short films by students from art schools and film schools from all over the world.

All Saints' Day

Early Music Festival (Festiwal Muzyki Polskiej) *(Oct–Nov)*. Organized simultaneously in a number of cities, the festival presents mainly the music of the Renaissance and Baroque performed on old instruments.

November
All Saints' Day (Dzień Wszystkich Świętych) *(1 Nov)*. Many Krakovians visit cemeteries to lay flowers and light candles on the graves. The views of the old Rakowicki Cemetery or of the beautifully located cemetery on the Hill of the Holy Redeemer (św. Salwator) are unforgettable. It is an old custom of Krakow to be able to buy, on this day only, so-called Turkish honey (caramelized sugar with walnuts or pistachios) at the entrance to cemeteries. Children, especially, look forward to this event.
Independence Day (Święto Niepodległości) *(11 Nov)*. After a Mass at the Wawel Cathedral, wreaths are laid at the Tomb of the Unknown Soldier by the Grunwald Monument in Matejko Square.
All Souls Jazz Festival (Krakowskie Zaduszki Jazzowe). Oldest jazz festival in post-

Average Monthly Temperature

Temperature Chart
Average maximum and minimum temperatures are show here. July and August are the hottest months with the temperature often exceeding 20°C, sometimes even reaching 30°C. Winter is cold and damp. The average temperature in January is -5°C.

communist Europe, with concerts in the Philharmonic hall and jazz clubs.

Nativity play being staged at the Franciscan Church

Winter

Krakow under a blanket of snow is a wonderful sight, but winter also brings misty and bitingly cold days.

Every year on the first Thursday of December a competition for the best Christmas crib (szopka) takes place by the Mickiewicz Monument in Market Square. The winning cribs are later displayed at the Museum of Krakow. The tradition of making Christmas cribs, unique to Krakow, goes back to medieval Christmas plays.

Nativity scenes at churches are also worth visiting. The one outside the Franciscan Church, with real people and animals, is best known. It can be seen only on Christmas Eve and Christmas Day.

Stalls selling handmade Christmas decorations and traditional delicacies fill the Market Square during the Christmas Fair.

Carol singers in traditional costume in Floriańska Street at Christmas time

December
Christmas Eve (Wigilia) (24 Dec). The evening begins with a meat-free meal. Midnight Masses are said and the Zygmunt Bell rings at Wawel.
Christmas (Święto Bożego Narodzenia) (25 and 26 Dec). Christmas Day and the day after are public holidays. Masses are celebrated in all churches.
New Year's Eve (Sylwester) (31 Dec). A crowd, several thousand strong, gathers in Market Square to see in the New Year. The Wielopolski Palace, the seat of local government, is the venue for one of the grandest balls in Poland. Distinguished guests arrive from all over the world, and the proceeds go to charity.

January
New Year's Day (Nowy Rok) (1 Jan). Public holiday. A month of balls and parties begins on this day.

Christmas decoration

February
"Fat Thursday" (Tłusty czwartek) (last Thu before Lent). Everybody eats doughnuts. The Gazeta w Krakowie, the local supplement to the Gazeta Wyborcza, rates the bakeries to help people choose the best doughnuts in Krakow.
Shrovetide (Ostatki), (last Sat and Tue of the Carnival season, before Ash Wednesday). This is a time of parties before Lent.

Public Holidays
New Year's Day (1 Jan)
Epiphany (6 Jan)
Easter Monday (Mar/Apr)
Labour Day (1 May)
Constitution Day (3 May)
Corpus Christi (Thu 8 weeks after Easter)
Assumption (15 Aug)
All Saints' Day (1 Nov)
Independence Day (11 Nov)
Christmas (25 & 26 Dec)

The Gothic cloister at the Collegium Maius ▶

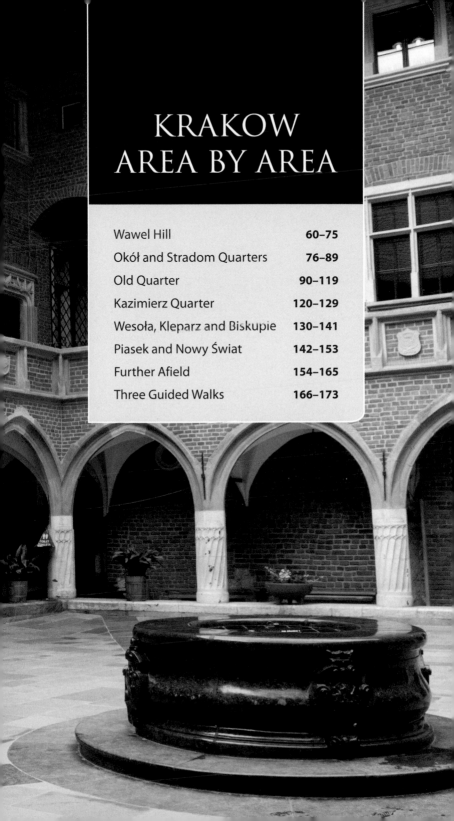

KRAKOW
AREA BY AREA

WAWEL HILL

Wawel Hill was inhabited by the Vistulan (Wiślanie) people in ancient times. The settlement came to prominence during the reigns of Bolesław the Brave and Kazimierz the Restorer. The latter made Wawel the seat of his political power. In the late medieval period, from the 14th century onwards, the royal residence and a new cathedral were built. The Cathedral houses the relics of St Stanisław, patron saint of Poland. The last rulers of the Jagiellonian dynasty transformed the Gothic castle into one of the most magnificent Renaissance royal residences in Central Europe. They also endowed the Cathedral with important works of art and architecture. Although the capital of Poland was moved from Krakow to Warsaw at the end of the 16th century, royal coronations and funeral ceremonies continued to take place in Krakow. A series of events in the 17th and 18th centuries led to the dilapidation of the Castle. The Austrian army was garrisoned here from 1795 until the early 20th century. The Castle and Cathedral have both regained their former magnificence through an intensive restoration programme. Fortunately, Wawel was saved from destruction in both World Wars.

Sights at a Glance

Churches

❸ *Krakow Cathedral pp66–71*

Historic Sights, Buildings and Monuments

❶ Fortifications and Towers
❷ Statue of Tadeusz Kościuszko
❼ Archaeological Site
❽ Dragon's Lair

Museums

❹ Cathedral Museum
❺ *Wawel Royal Castle pp72–3*
❻ "Lost Wawel" Exhibition

☐ **Restaurant** *see p190*
1 Pod Basztą

0 metres 100
0 yards 100

See also Street Finder maps 3, 5 & 6

◀ The grounds of Krakow Cathedral, on Wawel Hill

For keys to symbols *see back flap*

Street-by-Street: Wawel Hill

The Wawel is exceptional because of its first-class collections and its unique atmosphere. To savour it unhindered by large crowds you should plan an early-morning visit when the Cathedral and Castle courtyard are nearly deserted. Groups of tourists from every corner of the world gather here before noon, thereby enlivening the place. A trip to the Cathedral, where a variety of styles intermingle, as well as to the Royal Castle, is a must for visitors to Krakow.

❷ Statue of Tadeusz Kościuszko
The statue of Kościuszko stands at the entrance to Wawel Castle. Kościuszko was the general who led the Insurrection of 1794 against the Russian army. His ashes rest in the Cathedral crypt.

The Coat of Arms Gate

❹ Cathedral Museum
The museum houses a collection of sacred art, as well as a selection of insignia and memorabilia of the Polish kings, including the coronation robe of Stanisław August Poniatowski.

❽ Dragon's Lair
This cave, consisting of a number of interconnecting chambers, and a sculpture of a fire-belching dragon is a much loved attraction. It is particularly popular with children.

Key

— Suggested route

❶ Fortifications and Towers
The compact but varied defence system on Wawel Hill was constructed from the 15th to the 19th centuries.

⑤ ★ Wawel Royal Castle
A visit to the Castle includes the interior with its display of 16th-century tapestries, regalia, gold treasures and lavish Oriental objects.

Locator Map
See Street Finder maps 3, 5 & 6

The "Hen's Claw" Wing (Kurza Stopka) is the most prominent remnant of the medieval castle. It was erected during the reign of Jadwiga and Władysław II Jagiełło.

❸ ★ Krakow Cathedral
The 19th-century sarcophagus of St Jadwiga, the Queen of Poland, is among many monuments associated with the history of the Church and Nation.

❻ "Lost Wawel" Exhibition
Arranged in the former royal kitchen in the cellars, this special exhibition includes among its most interesting exhibits a reconstruction of the Rotunda of the Virgin Mary.

0 metres   50
0 yards   50

❼ Archaeological Site
The foundations of medieval buildings are exposed on this site.

❶ Fortifications and Towers

Wawel Hill. **Map** 3 C1 (5 C5). 🚌 304, 522. 🚊 3, 6, 8, 10, 18, 40.

The fortifications surrounding Wawel Hill date from different periods. Three massive towers – the Thief's Tower (Złodziejska), Sandomierz and Senator's Towers (the latter also called Lubranka) are dominant features of the architectural silhouette of the Wawel. They date from the second half of the 15th and early 16th centuries, when the royal residence was rebuilt by the Jagiellonians. New, mainly earth fortifications designed by Jan Pleitner were erected under Władysław IV between 1644 and 1646 on the Castle's northern terrace. The southeast bastion and redan (fortification of two parapets) were constructed in the early 18th century for King August II. Later in the century star-shaped fortifications designed by Bakałowicz and Mehler were built on the side of the Vistula River. The Austrians expanded the system between 1849 and 1852. Two round towers, forming part of the Austrian additions, have survived. The Wawel Castle was thus transformed into a citadel surrounded by a complex defence system.

The Coat of Arms Gate and part of the fortifications surrounding Wawel Hill

❷ Statue of Tadeusz Kościuszko

Wawel Hill. **Map** 3 C1 (5 C5). 🚌 304, 522. 🚊 3, 6, 8, 10, 18, 40.

The statue of Tadeusz Kościuszko, general and main leader of the 1794 Uprising in Poland *(see p31)* and a participant in the American Revolution, was erected in 1921. It was designed by Leonard Marconi and completed by Antoni Popiel. The statue was destroyed by the Germans in 1940. The present reconstruction was donated in 1960. When approaching the Władysław bastion, where the statue stands, you can see a number of plaques mounted in the brick wall. These commemorate the donors who contributed to the restoration works carried out within the Castle during the inter-war years. Also of interest is the Coat of Arms Gate by Adolf Szyszko-Bohusz.

Stirrup that belonged to the Grand Vizier Kara Mustafa, Cathedral Museum

❸ Krakow Cathedral

See pp66–71.

❹ Cathedral Museum

Wawel 3. **Map** 3 C1 (5 C5). **Tel** 12 429 33 21. 🚌 304, 522. 🚊 3, 6, 8, 10, 18, 40. **Open** 9am–5pm Mon–Sat (Nov–Mar: to 4pm). 🚭

The Cathedral Museum was established in September 1978 by the then Archbishop Karol Wojtyła, the Metropolitan of Krakow. The display consists of objects from the Cathedral treasury. Among the exhibits are a sword, which was purposely broken in two places at the funeral of the last Jagiellonian king, Zygmunt August; the coronation robe of Stanisław August Poniatowski; the replica of the royal insignia found inside the royal coffins buried beneath the cathedral, and the stirrup of the Grand Vizier Kara Mustafa which was presented to the Cathedral by King Jan III Sobieski following his victory at the Battle of Vienna (1683). The outstanding collection of reliquaries, church vessels and vestments includes objects found in the tomb of Bishop Maur, as well as memorabilia of John Paul II.

❺ Wawel Royal Castle

See pp72–3.

❻ "Lost Wawel" Exhibition

Wawel Hill 5. **Map** 3 C1 (5 D5). **Tel** 12 422 51 55. 🚌 304, 522. 🚊 3, 6, 8, 10, 18, 40. **Open** Apr–Oct: 9:30am–1pm Mon, 9:30am–5pm Tue–Fri, 10am–5pm Sat & Sun; Nov–Mar: 9:30am–4pm Tue–Fri, 10am–4pm Sat & Sun. **Closed** public hols. 🚭 Free Mon (Apr–Oct), Sun (Nov–Mar). 🔳 **wawel.krakow.pl**

This special exhibition, arranged in the basement of the former royal kitchen (now occupied

The Sandomierz Tower, one of the three Wawel defence towers

by the administration office), will appeal to those interested in the medieval history of Wawel. There were possibly ten churches on Wawel Hill in the past. The Rotunda of the Virgin Mary (Sts Felix and Adauctus), unearthed in 1917 during excavations carried out by Adolf Szyszko-Bohusz, is of great interest. The excavations also brought to light the remnants of a man's body as well as some articles of jewellery nearby. It is believed that the circular rotunda formed part of the first palatium (the seat of the first ruler of Wawel), and was built sometime in the late 10th or early 11th century. Its plan resembles a quatrefoil, with strong evidence of Czech influences in the design of the structure. The rotunda was almost completely destroyed in the 19th century.

The exhibition also includes a virtual computer model of the Wawel architecture, which enables visitors to travel into the past to the early 10th century. The computer reconstruction of the medieval buildings shows the state of current research into the early history of Wawel. The models of the so-called Rotunda B, the Rotunda of the Virgin Mary and other buildings, including the palatium, the Church of

The Archaeological Site

St Gereon and the Cathedral, give a clear picture of the overall layout.

❼ Archaeological Site

Wawel Hill. **Map** 3 C1 (5 C5). 🚌 304, 522. 🚋 3, 6, 8, 10, 18, 40.

The archaeological site is an open area where foundations of medieval buildings can be seen. The buildings were numerous and once formed a small town. A vicarage in the Renaissance style was among them. All the buildings were demolished by the Austrians in 1803–04 and replaced by a drill ground. The lower parts of the walls of St Nicholas, the small Romanesque church rebuilt in the Gothic style during the reign of Kazimierz the Great, are of particular note. This church was an interesting example of

a single nave church, supported on one central column. The plan of the small church of St George is also easy to discern.

❽ Dragon's Lair

Wawel Hill. **Map** 3 C1 (5 C5). **Tel** 12 422 51 55. 🚌 304, 522. 🚋 3, 6, 8, 10, 18, 40. **Open** daily. Apr, Sep & Oct: 10am–5pm; May & Jun: 10am–6pm; Jul & Aug: 10am–7pm.

Within Wawel Hill there are a number of rock caves. The earliest records of these caves date from the 16th century and are thought to be associated with criminality. A pub and a brothel were here in the 18th century. In the 19th century the Austrians sealed the entrance when constructing the fortification walls.

The Lair is open only during the summer months. Some 135 spiral steps lead down into the den, and there are 145 m (476 ft) of tunnels in total, of which only a part can be visited. The bronze statue of the Dragon, designed by Bronisław Chromy, which stands at the exit, was made in 1972.

According to legend, the inhabitants of ancient Krakow were terrorized by a dragon until one day a brave shoemaker, named Skuba, cheated the monster with a sheep stuffed with sulphur. The dragon swallowed the bait. When the sulphur heated its gut, the dragon drank so much water from the Vistula that its body burst. To reward the shoemaker King Krak gave him the hand of his daughter in marriage.

The metal monster belches fire and is seen as a major attraction by younger visitors.

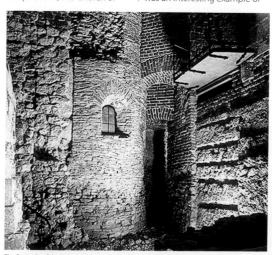

The Rotunda of the Virgin Mary at the "Lost Wawel" Exhibition

❸ Krakow Cathedral

No other building is as strongly associated with the history of Krakow, and the whole nation, as the Cathedral. The existing building is the third to have been built on this site. The Cathedral was built by Władysław the Short to house the relics of St Stanisław, who was much venerated by the Poles. The basilica consists of a nave with single aisles, non-projecting transept, and a choir with an ambulatory. There are also three towers. Many chapels adjoin the aisles. The chapels date from different periods and have been remodelled many times. The internal structure of the Gothic cathedral is now obscure because of later additions. Today the interior displays a variety of styles. Despite this eclecticism the layout of the interior is straightforward.

Exterior of the Cathedral
Although dating from different periods, all the distinct parts of the Cathedral make a unique and picturesque ensemble.

Clock Tower
The top of the tallest tower is decorated with four statues of the patron saints of the Kingdom of Poland and the Cathedral: Wacław, Adalbert, Stanisław and Kazimierz (Casimir).

Entrance
The bones of an "ancient creature" hang above the entrance. According to legend the end of the world will come when they fall. The letter K on the door is the initial of Kazimierz the Great, during whose reign the Cathedral was completed.

KEY

① Bell tower

② Baroque spire from the first half of the 18th century

③ Załuski Chapel

★ Zygmunt Tower
The Zygmunt bell in the tower, cast in 1520, is the largest in Poland. It weighs nearly 11 tons and is more than 2 m (6.5 ft) in diameter.

VISITORS' CHECKLIST

Practical Information
Wawel Hill 3. **Map** 3 C1 (5 C5).
Tel 12 429 33 21. Cathedral,
Zygmunt Tower, Royal Tombs:
Open Apr–Oct: 9am–5pm
Mon–Sat, 12:30–5pm Sun;
Nov–Mar: 9am–4pm Mon–Sat,
12:30–4pm Sun. **Closed** Easter,
Sun in Advent, Christmas Day,
1 Jan, 1 Nov.

Transport
128, 522. 3, 6, 8, 10, 18, 40.

High Altar
The high altar was commissioned in 1649 by Piotr Gembicki, one of the most powerful bishops in 17th-century Krakow.

★ Zygmunt Chapel
This chapel is a mausoleum of the rulers of the Jagiellonian dynasty. Surmounted by a gilt dome, it is a Renaissance masterpiece.

Potocki Chapel
Remodelled in the 19th century, this chapel features *The Crucifixion* by the 17th-century Bolognese artist Giovanni Francesco Barbieri, "Il Guercino".

1020 Laying of the foundation stone of the Cathedral

1320–64 Third Cathedral built

1521 The Zygmunt bell hung

1626–9 St Stanisław's Canopy erected

1664–76 Vaza Chapel built

1000　　**1250**　　**1500**　　**1750**

1090–1142 Second (so-called Herman) Cathedral built

Clock on the Clock Tower

1519–33 Zygmunt Chapel built by Bartolomeo Berrecci

1758–66 Bishop Załuski's Chapel built

Interior of the Cathedral

The Cathedral of Krakow is exceptional not only for the works of art which are housed here, but also because it has borne witness to many historical events such as coronations, royal weddings and funerals, as well as thanksgiving ceremonies. The Cathedral enjoys not only high sacred status but it also acquired symbolic importance during the occupation of Poland when it became a treasury of objects commemorating national glory. The great Polish playwright Stanisław Wyspiański chose the cathedral as a dramatic setting for his play *Deliverance*. The Cathedral reflects the past but also continues to exert much influence.

❷ Poets' Crypt
Adam Mickiewicz and Juliusz Słowacki, the two foremost Polish poets, are buried here. The remains of Mickiewicz were laid here in 1890 and those of Słowacki in 1929.

❼ Zygmunt Chapel
The splendid double Monument of King Zygmunt the Old (top; by Santi Gucci, 1574–75) and his son, King Zygmunt August (below; by Bartolomeo Berrecci, 1530s) is the outstanding artistic feature of the Cathedral.

Entrance to the Crypt

Czartoryski Chapel

The Cathedral Crypt houses the tombs of kings and distinguished Poles.

Chapel of the Holy Trinity

❽ Sarcophagus of King Kazimierz Jagiellończyk
One of the most affecting works of Veit Stoss, this was made in 1492, the year of the king's death.

❶ Canopy of St Stanisław
This altar, the largest in the Cathedral, is dedicated to Poland. It was probably designed by Giovanni Battista Trevano. The silver reliquary in the form of a coffin, containing the relics of St Stanisław, was made by Peter von der Rennen from 1669 to 1671.

Treasury

Sacristy

Chapel of the Virgin (Batory Chapel)

❹ Tomb of King Stefan Batory
The work of an outstanding sculptor, Santi Gucci, this tomb was created in 1595. It is a fine example of Mannerist decoration.

❺ Tomb of King Jan III Sobieski
Overloaded with Baroque decoration, the tomb of King Jan III (died 1696) and his wife was made in 1760 to the designs of Francesco Placidi.

❻ Tomb of King Jan Olbracht
Created from 1502 to 1505, the decoration of the recess around the tomb is the earliest example of Renaissance art in Poland. The design is modelled on a Roman triumphal arch. The sarcophagus retains late Gothic forms.

❸ Crucifix of Queen Jadwiga
According to legend the Queen prayed in front of this expressive crucifix (c.1380), which has become a place of mass pilgrimage. The relics of the Queen, who became a saint, rest in the altar.

Key

— Suggested route

Exploring Krakow Cathedral

Krakow Cathedral requires more than one visit to do justice to the magnificent building. Its interior with its variety of styles, from medieval to modern, is simply overwhelming. It is worth returning here for a careful visit to all the chapels in the aisles, and to the monuments and tombs of the kings and prominent people in the crypt. It is also possible to look at works in chronological order. The artistic backdrop adds to the spirituality of the Cathedral, which is above all else used for worship. To avoid the crowds, the best time to visit is in the early morning or just before closing time.

Chapels

The chapel of the Holy Cross, erected on the initiative of King Kazimierz Jagiellończyk and his wife Elisabeth von Habsburg, has retained much of its medieval character. The cycle of old Russian wall paintings is one of the largest ensembles to have survived. It is of the Pskov School. Two triptychs of the Holy Trinity and the Virgin Mary of Sorrows both date from the second half of the 15th century. The most interesting furnishing is the tomb of Kazimierz made by Veit Stoss with Huber of Passau. The king is shown in majestic resplendence. It is also a dignified image of death. The stained-glass windows were designed by Józef Mehoffer in the Art Nouveau style.

The Zygmunt Chapel (1519–33), designed by Bartolomeo Berrecci, is of exceptional beauty. The chapel is considered one of the purest examples of the Italian Renaissance outside Italy. It was modelled on the best Italian architectural and decorative works. The silver altar was made between 1531 and 1538 in Nuremberg by Melchior Baier to the designs of Peter Flötner. The royal tombs are equally interesting. The interior is peaceful and majestic and conveys the spirit of 16th-century humanism. Bishop Tomicki's Chapel is also Renaissance in style.

Remodelled by Bartolomeo Berrecci from 1526 to 1535, the chapel played an important role as a model for mausolea for the nobility and gentry. The Chapel of the Virgin Mary (King Stefan Batory's Chapel) houses a 17th-century Baroque tabernacle with the Holy Eucharist. The tomb of Batory and the royal stalls were designed by Santi Gucci. The Vaza Chapel, probably also designed by the same architect, exemplifies a 17th-century interior: monumental,

heavy forms executed in black marble with large epitaphs. It acts as a reminder of the fragility and transcience of earthly life.

Among the chapels constructed in the 18th century, two are of particular interest. The Lipski Chapel (1743–7), designed by Francesco Placidi, catches the light and plays with shadows. The decoration of Bishop Załuski's Chapel (1758–66) employs the allegory of the passage through the gate (note the enlarged entrance).

The *Crucifixion* by Guercino and the statue of the Risen Christ by Bertel Thorvaldsen are to be seen in the Chapel of Bishop Filip Padniewski. This Renaissance chapel was remodelled in the 19th century for the Potocki family. The statue of Włodzimierz Potocki in the Holy Trinity Chapel is also by Thorvaldsen.

The altar in the Zygmunt Chapel

Intricately carved stalls in the choir of the Cathedral

Furnishings

As well as the canopy of St Stanisław, particularly noteworthy are the epitaphs of the bishops of Krakow placed on the pillars, and decorated with busts of the deceased. Marcin Szyszkowski, Piotr Gembicki, Jan Małachowski and Kazimierz Łubieński all rest here, providing eternal company for the relics of St Stanisław. The Baroque stalls in the choir were made around 1620; additions were made in the 19th century. The bas-relief epitaph of Cardinal Fryderyk Jagiellończyk shows superb craftsmanship. It was made after 1503 in the Vischer workshop in Nuremberg. The throne of Bishop Piotr Gembicki has splendid Baroque decoration. The organ loft, made around 1758 to the design of Francesco Placidi, is also of much interest.

Sarcophagi and Tombs

The cathedral is a resting place for Polish rulers, and all its medieval tombs follow a particular model. They show a figure laying in state on a massive sarcophagus, decorated with allegorical figures of the king's subjects lamenting the death of their sovereign. A dog, symbolizing fidelity, is usually placed at the king's feet, and the head of the ruler rests on a lion, the symbol of power. A stone canopy is suspended over the tomb. The tomb of Władysław the Short,

dating from the mid-14th century is the earliest sarcophagus of this type. Kazimierz Jagiellończyk was the last to have such a monument erected. Two tombs of a much later date were inspired by this early type of sepulchre. The beautiful and majestic tomb of Queen Jadwiga is one of them. It was executed with great delicacy in white Carrara marble by Antoni Madeyski in 1902. The tomb is one of the most visited places of pilgrimage in the Cathedral. The other sarcophagus, also by Madeyski, was erected in 1906. It is a cenotaph (tomb without a corpse) commemorating King Władysław III Warneńczyk, who was killed in 1444 at the Battle of Varna against the Turks. His

The tomb of Władysław Jagiełło

body was never found, giving rise to stories about his miraculous salvation.

Royal Tombs

The Royal Tombs were placed in the crypt following the construction of the Zygmunt Chapel, which is a mausoleum. Zygmunt the Old and his sons are buried in the crypt under the chapel. Earlier rulers were buried in the Cathedral, except Bolesław the Brave, Bolesław the Bold, Przemysław II, Louis of Anjou, Władysław III Warneńczyk and Aleksander Jagiellończyk. A crypt was also constructed for the Vaza dynasty. Later rulers were buried beneath the Chapel of the Holy Cross and in St Leonard's crypt. In 1783 the last Polish king, Stanisław August Poniatowski, commissioned a grandiose sarcophagus for Jan III Sobieski. The elected kings Henri de Valois, August II of Saxony and Stanisław August Poniatowski do not rest in the Wawel. Two national heroes, Kościuszko and Prince Józef Poniatowski, were laid here during the Partitions of Poland. State funerals of Piłsudski and General Sikorski took place in the Cathedral in the 20th century.

The sarcophagi of the Vaza kings

⑤ Wawel Royal Castle

Little is known about the earliest Wawel residence. The Romanesque palatium was probably built by Kazimierz the Restorer; later Władysław the Short started to construct a new building but it was only completed by Kazimierz the Great. The present Renaissance castle was constructed in the first half of the 16th century. At the start of the 17th century the apartments in the north wing were remodelled in the early Baroque style. After the royal court moved from Krakow to Warsaw, the castle fell into ruin. Further devastation was caused by the occupying foreign powers. Early in the 20th century the castle was given back to Krakow, and restoration was begun.

Castle Guide

The Crown Treasury and Armoury, each with a separate entrance, are situated on the ground floor together with a number of state rooms. The remaining state rooms and other apartments are on the first and second floors. After leaving the Senators' Hall a visit to the "Orient in the Wavel Collections" exhibition on the first and second floors in the west wing is recommended.

Senators' Hall

Senators' Staircase

First floor

Crown Treasury and Armoury

This 11th-century chalice belonged to the Abbots of Tyniec and is now in the Treasury. Adjacent to the Treasury is the Armoury with its rich collection.

The Castle Courtyard

A mix of architectural styles can be found at the castle. One of the highlights is the beautiful Renaissance-style court yard, built in the 16th century.

Access to the Courtyard

Entrance to the Crown Treasury and Armoury

Key

- ☐ Royal Apartments
- ☐ Treasury
- ☐ Armoury
- ☐ "Orient in the Wawel Collections" Exhibition
- ☐ Non-exhibition area

★ **Birds Hall**
This Baroque hall with a marble fireplace is the first of a suite of rooms decorated in the Vaza style.

Deputies' Staircase

Second floor

Leonardo da Vinci's *Lady with an Ermine*

Ground floor

Entrance to the Royal Apartments

★ **Hall of Deputies**
This hall, used for debates by the lower house of Parliament *(Sejm)*, is decorated with a coffered ceiling containing realistically carved heads, as well as tapestries and a decorative frieze.

King's Bedroom
In the first half of the 16th century, the king's bedroom, the dining room and the apartments of the ladies-in-waiting were all situated on the first floor.

Study in the "Hen's Claw" Wing
An allegory of music and putti, surrounded by musical instruments, can be admired on the ceiling here.

Statues decorating the exterior of Krakow Cathedral, situated on Wawel Hill ▶

OKÓŁ AND STRADOM QUARTERS

Okół was probably the earliest settlement at the foot of Wawel. Timber-built houses and a palisade enclosure were already here in the 10th century. The settlement developed along the so-called Salt Route which led from Hungary to Greater Poland. The quarter became elitist as a result of its proximity to the Royal Castle and the Cathedral. High-

ranking clergy resided here and many churches were built.

The development of Stradom, situated between Okół and Krakow, was hindered by its location on peat marshes and the vicinity of the Wawel fortress. Splendid churches and palaces were constructed here from the mid-17th century. Stradom developed rapidly at the end of the 1800s.

Sights at a Glance

Churches and Monasteries
- ❸ Church of Saints Peter and Paul pp82–3
- ❹ Church of St Andrew
- ❺ Church of St Martin
- ❼ Church of St Giles
- ⓯ Franciscan Church pp88–9
- ⓲ Church of the Bernardine Nuns
- ⓳ Bernardine Church
- ㉑ Church of the Missionaries

Museums and Galleries
- ❿ Archdiocesan Museum
- ⓫ Palace of Bishop Erazm Ciołek
- ⓬ St Vladimir's Foundation
- ⓭ Cricoteka
- ⓮ Archaeological Museum
- ㉒ Natural History Museum

Historic Parks
- ㉓ Dietl Plantations

Historic Monuments and Buildings
- ❷ Collegium Iuridicum
- ❻ Royal Arsenal
- ❾ Deanery
- ⓰ Wielopolski Palace
- ⓱ Statue of Józef Dietl
- ⓴ Częstochowa Seminary

Historic Streets
- ❶ Grodzka Street
- ❽ Kanonicza Street

Restaurants *see p190*
1. Balaton
2. Il Calzone
3. Copernicus
4. Miód Malina
5. Pod Aniołami
6. Pod Baranem
7. Sakana Sushi Bar
8. Smak Ukrainski
9. Trattoria La Campana

0 metres 200
0 yards 200

See also Street Finder maps 1, 3 & 6

◀ Statues of the Apostles at the entrance to the Church of Saints Peter and Paul   **For keys to symbols** *see back flap*

Street-By-Street: Okół

The historic Okół district is more or less in line with the southern part of the medieval centre of Krakow. It is a picturesque area. Those who want a change from the regular plan of the Old Quarter will enjoy Okół's curving streets and dead-end mews, lined with some outstanding buildings. Fortunately the great fire of Krakow in 1850 did not damage the buildings in Okół, and much of the original architecture can still be seen here.

② Collegium Iuridicum
This sculpture, *Luca di Nara*, in the courtyard is by Polish-born Igor Mitoraj. It was presented to the Jagiellonian University by the artist, who now lives in Italy.

⑭ Archaeological Museum
The collections here tell the prehistory of the Polish lands.

⑬ Cricoteka
The Cricot 2 Theatre and Museum are located in this Gothic house.

⑫ St Vladimir's Foundation
This building houses artifacts explaining the life of the Ruthenas in the Polish-Lithuanian Commonwealth.

⑪ Palace of Bishop Erazm Ciołek
This beautiful building is now home to the National Museum's collection of Polish art from the Middle Ages to the beginning of the 19th century.

⑩ Archdiocesan Museum
The collection consists of objects from churches in the Krakow Archdiocese that are no longer used in the liturgy.

⑨ Deanery
The arcaded courtyard of this small house, formerly a canonry, gives the impression of a magnificent Renaissance residence.

⑧ Kanonicza Street
This quiet street has retained much of the old royal character of Krakow.

❸ ★ Church of Saints Peter and Paul
This early Baroque Jesuit church is a masterpiece of 17th-century Polish architecture. The façade, with its rich sculptural decoration, is remarkable.

Locator Map
See Street Finder maps 1, 3 & 6

❶ Grodzka Street
The town houses situated along one of the oldest streets in Krakow were once palaces.

❹ ★ Church of St Andrew
This is the best preserved example of Romanesque architecture in Krakow.

❺ Church of St Martin
This small early Baroque church was transformed into the Augsburg Protestant Church in the early 19th century.

❻ Royal Arsenal
This entrance to the Arsenal is one of the most beautiful 17th-century doorways in Krakow.

0 metres 50
0 yards 50

Key
— Suggested route

❼ Church of St Giles
This is a rather modest Gothic church dating from the first half of the 14th century.

Historic Grodzka Street, lined with picturesque buildings

❶ Grodzka Street
Ulica Grodzka

Map 1 C5 (6 D4). 🚊 1, 3, 6, 8, 18, 40.

Grodzka is one of the oldest streets in Krakow. In the past it formed part of the important Salt Route from Hungary to Greater Poland. As part of the Royal Route it bore witness to coronation and funeral processions of Polish kings.

Grodzka Street was once lined with many palaces and a few churches. These palaces were rebuilt and converted into town houses. Grodzka is a lovely street full of character, owing to its irregular plan, varying width and diverse architecture.

❷ Collegium Iuridicum

ul. Grodzka 53. **Map** 1 C5 (6 D4).
Tel 12 633 63 77. 🚊 1, 3, 6, 8, 18, 40.
Open 10am–1pm Tue & Thu, 11am–2pm Sun.

The Collegium Iuridicum of the Academy of Krakow was founded early in the 15th century through the bequest of Queen Jadwiga. The excavation work carried out at the site has confirmed that the building had replaced a large trade hall, probably built in

the 14th century on the orders of Władysław the Short. The remnants of the hall have survived in the basement. The Collegium Iuridicum was rebuilt several times. The works were funded by Bishop Jan Rzeszowski, among others. The elaborate doorway decorated with the University's emblem was made around 1680. The College was entirely rebuilt after a fire in 1719 and the two-tier arcaded courtyard

Two-tier arcaded courtyard of the Collegium Iuridicum

added. The Institute of the History of Art is housed here, as was, until recently, the Zoological Museum of the Jagiellonian University. The museum is due to reopen in 2016 in a campus on the outskirts of the city.

In the summer months concerts and theatrical performances take place in courtyard, which features a sculpture by Igor Mitoraj.

❸ Church of Saints Peter and Paul
Kościół św. św. Piotra i Pawła

See pp82–3.

❹ Church of St Andrew
Kościół św. Andrzeja

ul. Grodzka 56. **Map** 1 C5 (6 D4).
Tel 12 422 16 12. 🚊 1, 3, 6, 8, 18, 40.
Open 7:30am–5pm daily and during services.

The Church of St Andrew in Okół is regarded as one of the finest examples of Romanesque architecture in Poland. It was built between 1079 and 1098 as a foundation of Sieciech, the powerful Palatine to Duke Władysław Herman. It was rebuilt around 1200. The towers and aisles were extended and a transept added. According to the chronicler Jan Długosz this was the only church in Krakow to resist the Tatar invasion of 1241. Around 1702 it was remodelled in the Baroque style to the designs of Baldassare Fontana, who also covered the internal walls and vaulting with stuccowork. Mural paintings by Karl Dankwart complete the decoration. Among furnishings worth noting are the pulpit, in the form of a boat, and the high altar with an imposing ebony tabernacle decorated with silver ornaments.

The treasury in the convent adjoining the church houses some priceless objects, such as a portable mosaic depicting the Virgin Mary from the end of the 12th century, 14th-century

Church of St Andrew with its two spires

marionettes used in Christmas nativity plays, and early medieval reliquaries.

❺ Church of St Martin
Kościół św. Marcina

ul. Grodzka 58a. **Map** 6 D4. **Tel** 12 446 64 30. 🚊 8, 10, 18. **Open** 10am–1pm Mon–Sat and during services.

The first church was probably built on this site in the 12th century. In 1612 the Discalced Carmelite Nuns were brought here. The old church was demolished and in 1637–40 the nuns commisioned a new, rather small church in the early Baroque style. After the convent was closed down, the church was taken over by the Protestant community. The interior was converted according to the needs of the Lutheran liturgy. The high altar features a 14th-century crucifix and *Christ Calming the Storm,* painted by Henryk Siemiradzki in 1882.

❻ Royal Arsenal
Arsenał Królewski

ul. Grodzka 64. **Map** 6 D5. 🚊 8, 10, 18. **Closed** to the public.

In the first half of the 16th century Zygmunt the Old built an arsenal and a cannon foundry next to the city wall. They formed part of Krakow's fortifications. The present building was remodelled in 1927 by the architect Stanisław Filipkiewicz, who juxtaposed the Baroque structure of the arsenal with an austere extension thus achieving an interesting effect.

❼ Church of St Giles
Kościół św. Idziego

ul. Św. Idziego 1. **Map** 6 D5. 🚊 8, 10, 18. **Open** 10am–1pm Tue–Fri.

According to historic evidence made popular by a song by Ewa Demarczyk (of the Piwnica pod Baranami Cabaret), this church was "built in 1082 by Władysław Herman and his wife Judith, after they bore a child through the intervention of St Giles". The present church was built in the early 14th century. In 1595 the Dominicans took over and soon remodelled it.

Among the furnishings, the stone stalls are particularly interesting. They were made in 1629 by reusing fragments of the Renaissance tomb of St Jacek (otherwise known as St Hyacinth) from the Dominican Church.

❽ Kanonicza Street
Ulica Kanonicza

Map 1 C5 (6 D4). 🚊 3, 6, 8, 10, 18, 40.

Kanonicza Street formed the last stretch of the Royal Route leading towards Wawel. From the 14th century onwards it was lined with the houses of Krakow's canons, who were given the use of these houses for life when they took up office in the Chapter of Krakow. Each successive inhabitant tended to modernize their house. As a result, Gothic houses acquired arcaded Renaissance courtyards, Baroque doorways or Neo-Classical façades. The canons could afford to spend lavishly owing to their elite status within the church.

The great diversity of architectural styles which can be found within the narrow and winding little Kanonicza Street gives it a picturesque character.

Decorative bas-relief plaque of 1480 on the Długosz House, Kanonicza Street

❸ Church of Saints Peter and Paul

This church, modelled on the Jesuit Church of Il Gesù in Rome, is considered to be one of the most magnificent early Baroque churches in Central Europe. The history of its construction and the name of the architects involved are the subjects of an ongoing debate among architectural historians. The foundation stone was laid in 1596. The leading Jesuit architect, Giovanni de Rosis, contributed the design, and works were carried out by Giuseppe Brizio and Giovanni Maria Bernardoni. In 1605 the church neared its completion but, due to some structural problems, a number of walls had to be dismantled and rebuilt to an altered design. The court architect Giovanni Battista Trevano was put in charge of the second stage.

Cartouche with an Eagle
This exquisitely carved coat of arms belonged to the main founder of the church, King Zygmunt III Vaza.

Organ Gallery
The late Baroque organ gallery with a curved balustrade, designed by Kacper Bażanka, is in contrast with the austere and monumental architecture of the church. It is located inside, just above the main entrance.

Statues of the Apostles
This railing was designed by Kacper Bażanka and is decorated with copies of statues originally carved by David Heel from 1715 to 1722.

Statue of St Ignatius Loyola
The founder of the Society of Jesus is depicted in this late Baroque sculpture by David Heel. The adjoining statues are of Stanisław Kostka, Francis Xavier and Aloysius Gonzaga.

Main entrance

Stuccowork (1622–39)
The stuccowork above the high altar is by Giovanni Battista Falconi and includes scenes from the lives of Saints Peter and Paul, patrons of the church.

★ Tomb of Bishop Andrzej Trzebicki
The monumental decoration of this tomb, created in 1695–96, commemorates the bishop with true Baroque ostentation.

Entrance to the Skarga Crypt

Statue of Piotr Skarga
The author of *Parliamentary Sermons* died in 1612 and was buried in the crypt beneath the high altar. This statue of Father Skarga was made by Oskar Sosnowski in 1869 and placed in the church in the early 20th century.

★ High Altar
Made in 1726–28 to Kacper Bażanka's design, the high altar was conceived to convey a call for unity between the Roman Catholic and Orthodox Churches.

Massive portal of the medieval Deanery

❾ Deanery
Dom Dziekański

ul. Kanonicza 21. **Map** 1 C5 (6 D4).
🚋 1, 3, 6, 8, 10, 18, 40.

This house is considered to be the most beautiful of all the canons' houses in Krakow. The medieval house was completely rebuilt in the 1580s, probably by the architect and sculptor Santi Gucci. The arcaded courtyard with its magnificent decoration, carved in stone, the impressive portal and the *sgraffiti* on the façade all date from this period. The statue of St Stanisław in the courtyard was added in the 18th century. In the 1960s this was home to the future Pope and then Suffragan Bishop of Krakow, Karol Wojtyła.

❿ Archdiocesan Museum
Muzeum Archidiecezjalne

ul. Kanonicza 19. **Map** 1 C5 (6 D4).
Tel 12 421 89 63. 🚋 1, 3, 6, 8, 18, 40.
Open 10am–4pm Tue–Fri, 10am–3pm
Sat & Sun. 🚫 ☑

This house is traditionally associated with the residence of St Stanisław while he was a canon in Krakow, hence the name, St Stanisław's House.

It was actually built in the 14th century but entirely remodelled in the late 18th century. The Archdiocesan Museum is now housed here. It runs a programme of temporary exhibitions of sacred art based on loans from church treasuries in the Krakow Archdiocese. Interesting goldwork displays have taken place here.

Part of the Archdiocesan Museum is given over to the room of Karol Wojtyła, who became Pope John Paul II. The room has been faithfully reconstructed here as it stood originally in the adjoining Deanery, where he lived.

⓫ Palace of Bishop Erazm Ciołek
Pałac biskupa Erazma Ciołka

ul. Kanonicza 17. **Map** 1 C5 (6 D4).
Tel 12 433 59 20. 🚋 6, 8, 10, 18, 40.
Open 10am–4pm Tue–Sun. 🚫 free
on Sun (permanent collection).

This museum was once home to the great diplomat and patron of the arts Bishop Erazm Ciołek (1474–1522). A magnificently distinguished residence, it has been extensively renovated and now houses the National Museum's large and notable collection of Polish Art. The house was built in a mix of Gothic and Renaissance styles, while the collection within ranges from the 12th to the 18th centuries. The latter includes such gems as large 15th-century tryptichs from Krakow guilds, exquisite Orthodox icons and encolpions, which reveal the ever-increasing influence and power of Western Europe in the 17th and 18th centuries.

⓬ St Vladimir's Foundation
Fundacja św. Włodzimierza

ul. Kanonicza 15. **Map** 1 C5 (6 D4).
Tel 12 421 92 94. 🚋 1, 3, 6, 8, 10,
18, 40. **Open** call in advance. 🚫

St Vladimir's Foundation is based in a 14th-century house which displays fine Renaissance decoration. Icons from disused Orthodox churches in the Beskidy, Bieszczady and Tomaszów

Karol Wojtyła's room in the Archdiocesan Museum

Lubelski regions, dating mainly from the 17th and 18th centuries, are kept here.

The Greek Catholic Chapel is dedicated to the martyr saints Boris and Gleb and is decorated with paintings by Jerzy Nowosielski. This contemporary Krakow artist is influenced by Byzantine art but uses modern forms of expression.

The sanctuary features the miraculous icon of the Korczmin Madonna.

⑬ Cricoteka

ul. Kanonicza 5. **Map** 1 C5 (6 D4). **Tel** 12 422 83 32. 🚋 1, 6, 8, 18. **Open** 10am–2pm Mon & Wed–Fri; 2–6pm Tue. 🐾

The former canon's house at 5 Kanonicza Street has retained much of its Gothic form. In 1980 it became the home of the renowned avant-garde theatre Cricot 2. This theatre was founded in 1956 on the initiative of Tadeusz Kantor, the outstanding painter and stage designer. It became famous for performances which were permeated by a symbolic representation of man's existence. Performances relied on traditional theatrical forms while also borrowing from the "happenings" fashionable at the time. The most unusual sets added a surreal flavour. *The Dead Class*, *Wielopole, Wielopole* and *Let Artists Drop Dead* were among Cricot 2's most successful productions. After the death of Kantor in 1990 his actors continued his work.

The house in Kanonicza Street is too small to have a stage, so performances take place in other venues. The Cricoteka housed here is a small museum and archive documenting the work of the theatre since its inception. Costumes, stage designs and props, photographs of the performances, as well as drawings and paintings by Kantor, are all here.

⑭ Archaeological Museum
Muzeum Archeologiczne

ul. Poselska 3. **Map** 1 C5 (6 D4). **Tel** 12 422 71 00. 🚌 304, 522. 🚋 1, 3, 6, 8, 10, 18. **Open** 9am–3pm Mon, Wed & Fri; 9am–6pm Tue & Thu; 11am–4pm Sun (Jul & Aug: 11am–6pm Mon-Fri, 10am–3pm Sun). 🐾 free on Sun.

The museum is housed in the former Friary of the Discalced Carmelites, founded in 1606. At the end of the 18th century the Austrian authorities took the building over and converted it into a prison. Mostly political prisoners were held here. In 1945 a group of imprisoned soldiers was rescued following heroic action by the Home Army (AK). After the prison closed down a museum was established here.

The Archeological Museum has its beginings in 1850, it was initially called the Museum of Antiquities.

The collection includes artifacts that tell the earliest history of the Lesser Poland region, but also Egyptian mummies. The statue of the idol Światowid, salvaged from the Zbrucz River, jewellery found in the tomb of a Scythian princess in Ryżanówka, gold objects from the tomb of a Hun from Jakuszowice and iron objects used as a form of payment *(see p23)* are the highlights of the collection.

⑮ Franciscan Church
Kościół Franciszkanów

See pp88–9.

Elaborate porch at the entrance to the Wielopolski Palace

⑯ Wielopolski Palace
Pałac Wielopolskich

Plac Wszystkich Świętych. **Map** 1 C5 (6 D3). **Tel** 12 616 12 07. 🚋 1, 3, 6, 8, 18. **Open** by prior telephone arrangement only.

This palace was sold in the second half of the 19th century and transformed into a seat of municipal administration. Following remodelling work carried out in 1907–12 by architect Jan Rzymkowski, the building acquired a simplified modern form. A porch supported by pseudo-Romanesque columns was added to the wall facing Poselska Street. An Art Nouveau frieze with coats of arms of various cities can also be seen here. Inside the palace, the Debate Room and Portrait Hall are worth visiting.

Archaeological Museum and garden

⓱ Statue of Józef Dietl
Pomnik Józefa Dietla

Pl. Wszystkich Świętych.
Map 1 C5 (6 D3). 🚊 1, 3, 6, 8, 18.

Józef Dietl (1804–78) was a medical professor who advocated treating the sick in spas. He was Rector of the Jagiellonian University, and became the first President (Mayor) of Krakow to be elected, in 1866, in the autonomous Galicia. He reformed the education system in Krakow, set up a project for the renovation of the city's heritage and was responsible for the restoration of the Cloth Hall.

The statue of Dietl was made between 1936 and 1938 by Xawery Dunikowski. The artist not only created the monumental figure but also took a great deal of trouble to find it a prominent location. Using a model, he travelled all over Krakow and tried it out in various places before deciding on the present location in All Saints Square. The result is stunning. The Statue of Dietl is regarded as one of the grandest and best located monuments in Poland.

⓲ Church of the Bernardine Nuns
Kościół Bernardynek

ul. Poselska 21. **Map** 1 C5 (6 D4).
Tel 12 422 22 46. 🚊 1, 3, 6, 8, 18.
Open 9am–6:30pm daily and during services.

A small convent of the Bernardine Nuns was established in Poselska Street in 1646. The Church of St Joseph was built here between 1694 and 1703 for the nuns. Though small and modest the church interior displays splendid furnishings which include altars and a pulpit from the workshop of Jerzy Hankis. The miraculous image of St Joseph and Child in the high altar was a gift from Jakub Zadzik, Bishop of Krakow, who possibly received it from Pope Urban VIII.

Interior of the small Church of the Bernardine Nuns

A small 17th-century statue of the child Jesus in the side altar is much venerated. It originally came from the Church of the Nuns of St Colette in Stradom and is therefore called the Koletański Christ.

⓳ Bernardine Church
Kościół Bernardynów

ul. Bernardyńska 2. **Map** 3 C1 (6 D5).
Tel 12 422 16 50. 🚊 3, 6, 8, 10, 18.
Open during services only.

Giovanni da Capistrano, the reformer of the Franciscan Order, later canonized, arrived in Krakow in 1453. For the next year he preached repentance and the renouncement of wealth and the immoral way of life. He also incited the people against the Jews. Influenced by his sermons, a few Krakovians took up the habit of the Reformed Franciscans, then called the Observants but known as the Bernardines in Poland. In 1453 Cardinal Zbigniew Oleśnicki built in Stradom a small timber church for this new monastic community, and soon after began building a large brick church. It was completed by Jan Długosz after Oleśnicki's death.

In 1655, while preparing to defend Krakow against the Swedes, Stefan Czarniecki gave orders to set fire to the Bernardine Church, which was located at the foot of Wawel Hill, so that the invaders could not use the church for their own protection. The beautiful statue of the Virgin and Child with St Anne, from Veit Stoss's workshop, and remnants of Mannerist tombs (now on the porch wall) are the only furnishings to have survived.

The new Baroque Church of the Bernardines was built between 1659 and 1680. Krzysztof Mieroszewski is believed to have been the architect. The marble shrine of Blessed Simon of Lipnica was erected in 1662 and the high altar between 1758 and 1766.

The 17th-century Baroque Bernardine Church

⑳ Częstochowa Seminary
Seminarium Częstochowskie

ul. Bernardyńska 3. **Map** 3 C1 (6 D5).
🚊 3, 6, 8, 10, 18.

In 1925 the Bishop of Częstochowa, Teodor Kubina, founded a seminary affiliated with the Faculty of Theology at the Jagiellonian University, for seminarists from his diocese. The monumental Modernist building was constructed between 1928 and 1930 to the designs of Zygmunt Gawlik and Franciszek Mączyński. The seminary is no longer in operation.

The façade is decorated with sculptures which were carved under the supervision of Xawery Dunikowski, one of the foremost Polish sculptors of the 20th century. The bas-relief at the top is particularly interesting. It shows Christ blessing the allegorical figure of Poland and the representatives of all social ranks, as well as the Virgin Mary accompanied by clergymen. The scene depicting a seminarist tempted by the devil, also on the façade, is worth noting.

Relief of a seminarist tempted by the devil, Częstochowa Seminary

Baroque façade of the Church of the Missionaries

al Quirinale designed by Gianlorenzo Bernini. Some of the methods applied by Bażanka, such as the use of mirrors in the nave to direct reflected light onto the chapels, are characteristic of High Baroque. The church is regarded as one of the finest examples of 18th-century Baroque Polish architecture.

The same applies to the interior. Most altarpieces were painted by Tadeusz Kuntze and decorated with sculptures by Antoni Frączkiewicz.

㉑ Church of the Missionaries
Kościół Misjonarzy

ul. Stradomska 4. **Map** 3 C1 (6 E5). **Tel** 12 422 88 77. 🚊 103, 124.
🚊 3, 6, 8, 10, 18. **Open** 2–7pm daily and during services.

The Missionaries were brought to Stradom in 1682 but built the Church of the Conversion of St Paul only in the years 1719 to 1728. The architect, Kacper Bażanka, was influenced in his design by two outstanding examples of Roman Baroque architecture. The interior of the Krakow church resembles that of Francesco Borromini's Church of the Magi at the Collegio di Propaganda Fide, and the exterior is close to Sant'Andrea

㉒ Natural History Museum
Muzeum Przyrodnicze

ul. Św. Sebastiana 9/11. **Map** 3 D1 (6 E5). **Tel** 12 429 10 49. 🚊 3, 6, 8, 10, 18. **Open** 9am–3pm Mon–Fri, 11am–7pm Sat & Sun. 🖼

The core of the Natural History Museum was the collection of the Physiographic Commission of Krakow's Learned Society, established in 1865. It consisted mainly of stuffed birds and invertebrates. Today, the museum keeps live fish, reptiles and mammals; it also boasts a tropical rainforest display. A rhinoceros dating from the Pleistocene era, found in 1920 in Starunia, is a highlight of the collection.

㉓ Dietl Plantations
Planty Dietlowskie

Map 4 D1 (6 E5, F4). 🚊 128, 184.
🚊 12, 22.

The old river bed of the Vistula, from Stradom to Kazimierz, was filled in during the years 1878 to 1880 and transformed into a modern thoroughfare designed by Bolesław Malecki. It was a dual carriageway 1 km (0.6 mile) in length and 100 m (328 ft) wide, with a garden in the middle. The new scheme was named Planty Dietlowskie after Józef Dietl *(see p87)*. This President of Krakow was the first to advocate the filling in of the old Vistula bed which hindered the integration of Krakow with Kazimierz. Both sides of the avenue are lined with high tenement blocks and elegant public buildings, one of which is the PKO Bank built between 1922 and 1924.

Tree-lined avenue separating Dietl's dual carriageway

⓯ Franciscan Church

The Franciscans arrived in Krakow in 1237. The construction of the church was undertaken in 1255 as a foundation of Duke Bolesław the Chaste and his wife the Blessed Salomea. After the Swedish invasion, which caused much damage, the church was rebuilt in the Baroque style. The great fire of Krakow in 1850 damaged the church again. It was rebuilt partly in the Neo-Romanesque and partly in the Neo-Gothic style. The work of Stanisław Wyspiański on the interior decoration is of prime importance. Around 1900 this artist executed the Art Nouveau murals and designed a series of unusual stained-glass windows in expressive colours.

A 13th-century wall of the first church

Blessed Salomea
Stanisław Wyspiański's stained glass in the north window of the choir shows the foundress of the church who rejected the ducal coronet before taking the habit of a Poor Clare nun.

★ **Mater Dolorosa**
This late Gothic image by Master Jerzy, of Mary surrounded by angels holding instruments of Christ's Passion, is much venerated.

★ **Murals**
The polychrome decoration features flowers and conveys the Franciscan love of nature. This work illustrates the novel means of artistic expression employed by Wyspiański in sacred art.

Chapel of The Passion
The brothers of the Confraternity of The Passion have met in this chapel since the end of the 16th century to conduct their rituals (see p54). Their liturgy is theatrical and evokes the spirit of Baroque devotion.

Cloister
Portraits of Krakow's bishops were hung in the cloister of the Franciscan Friary from the 15th to the mid-20th centuries.

Portrait of Bishop Piotr Tomicki
This beautiful Renaissance portrait of Bishop Tomicki, painted before 1535 by Stanisław Samostrzelnik, is worth seeing in the cloister gallery.

Tomb of Giovanni Gemma (died 1608)
The monument to the Venetian physician to King Zygmunt III Vaza is one of the most interesting sepulchral sculptures of late Mannerism in Poland.

★ **Wyspiański's Stained-Glass** *Let It Be*
This expressive image of God the Father emerging from the cosmic chaos was rendered using bold colours and sinuous, flowing Art Nouveau forms.

Restaurants lining colourful Market Square

Sights at a Glance

Churches

Historic Streets and Squares

Historic Monuments and Buildings

Museums and Galleries

OLD QUARTER

In 1257 Duke Bolesław the Chaste gave Krakow her charter. This law was of key importance to the city as it determined local government and trade privileges, thus stimulating the city's future development. The charter stipulated strict rules for this development: a large, centrally located square surrounded by a regular grid of streets was to become the city centre. The size of each plot determined the size of the houses. Although the architecture became ever more opulent, this urban scheme has survived almost intact. To this day the Old Quarter remains the heart of modern, fast-developing Krakow. It is an area with a great concentration of important historic sights for visitors to enjoy.

See also Street Finder maps 1, 5 & 6

0 metres   200
0 yards   200

Street-by-Street: Market Square

The Market Square (Rynek Główny) is located in the centre of Krakow's Old Quarter. Public, cultural and commercial activities have always concentrated around the Market Square. Museums and galleries of both old and modern art can be found here. Antiquarian shops selling works of art, bookshops and the best restaurants, cafés and bars are located in the houses around the square. Each summer nearly 30 street cafés open until the early hours. Flower stalls, street musicians, artists selling their works by the Cloth Hall and the general hustle and bustle made by the vendors of souvenirs and their clients all contribute to the lively atmosphere of this area.

❹ Market Square
This is the largest town square anywhere in Europe. The life of medieval Krakow was centred around the square.

❺ ★ Christopher Palace
A branch of the Historical Museum of the City of Krakow is housed in this palace.

❼ ★ Cloth Hall (Sukiennice)
Originally a market hall, the Sukiennice houses shops, cafés and a renowned gallery of 19th-century Polish art.

❻ Town Hall Tower
The only remaining fragment of the Old Town Hall, the tower was remodelled after World War II.

SŁAWKOWSKA
ŚW. JANA
SZCZEPANSKA
MARKET SQUARE
SZEWSKA
ŚW. ANNY
WIŚLNA

0 metres 50
0 yards 50

❶ ★ Church of St Mary
The main parish church in Krakow is renowned for its Gothic high altar, one of the largest in the world, carved by Veit Stoss.

Locator Map
See Street Finder maps 1 & 6

❷ St Mary's Square
The parish cemetery was originally located on this site.

❸ St Barbara's Church
The architecture of the church is medieval. Its furnishings are mainly Rococo but also include this 15th-century Pietà.

"The Magical Cab", the poem by K. I. Gałczyński, was inspired by a horse-drawn cab similar to one that you can hire here for a sightseeing trip.

Statue of Adam Mickiewicz
This is a popular meeting point for Krakovians.

❾ St Adalbert's Church
This is one of the oldest churches in Krakow. The picturesque structure is at the end of the vista formed by Grodzka Street.

Key

— Suggested route

❶ Church of St Mary
Kościół Mariacki

St Mary's, or the Church of the Assumption of the Virgin, was the main parish church of Krakow's burghers. It is a Gothic basilica composed of nave, aisles and side chapels. There are two towers. The north tower was extended in the early 15th century and in 1478 topped with a spire by Matthias Heringk. It was the city's watch-tower. Inside the church there are many outstanding works of art, among which the magnificent high altar by Veit Stoss *(see pp96–7)* should be mentioned. Other furnishings include the Baroque pulpit, marble altars decorated with paintings by the Italian artist Giovanni Battista Pittoni, and Renaissance tombs in the chapels.

Bugle-Call Tower
The spire is decorated with turrets and topped by a gilt crown. The famous bugle-call *(hejnał)* is played here at hourly intervals and broadcast at noon by the Polish radio.

The Porch (1750–52)
The late-Baroque porch was designed by Francesco Placidi. Carved busts of the Apostles and saints by Karol Hukan were added to the door panels in 1929.

Main entrance

1221–2 Building of the Romanesque church		**1392–7** Nave and aisles built	**1477–89** High altar completed		**1585** Choir stalls completed
1200	**1300**	**1400**		**1500**	**1600**
End of the 13th century Construction of the Gothic church begins	**1355–65** New choir built	**1478** North tower receives a spire	*Detail of the main door*		

Choir Stalls
The stalls were made in 1585 but the biblical scenes in low relief which decorate the backs of the seats date from 1635.

The Montelupi Tomb
This Mannerist tomb of one of the richest Krakow families was made around 1600 in the workshop of Santi Gucci.

Visitors' entrance

★ **The Ciborium**
This Renaissance ciborium (receptacle for containing the Eucharist) at the entrance to the choir was made around 1552 to the design by Giovanni Maria Mosca.

KEY

① **The tracery of the Great West Window** was designed by Jan Matejko and the stained glass is by Józef Mehoffer and Stanisław Wyspiański.

② **South Bell Tower**

③ **High Altar** *(see pp96–7)*

④ **The murals** on the walls and vault were designed and executed by Jan Matejko between 1890 and 1892.

★ **The Slacker Crucifix** (1496)
The figure of the suffering Christ, carved in stone by Veit Stoss, is the most expressive sculpture ever made by the artist.

Exploring St Mary's: The High Altar

The high altar by Veit Stoss was made between 1477 and
1489. It is dedicated, like the church itself, to the Assumption
of the Virgin Mary. The altar is a polyptych, some 11 m (36 ft)
long and 12 m (39 ft) high. It was even higher originally. The
iconography determined its composition. The shutters were
closed throughout the liturgical year but opened during
important church feasts. The treatment of the human figure
is naturalistic, dynamic and dramatically expressive. The low
reliefs and figures of saints are masterpieces of late-Gothic art.

The Lamentation
The design of this particular
panel was influenced by
Netherlandish painting.

The Meeting of
St Anne and
St Joachim

The middle shutters
are opened every day
at 11:50am.

The Capture
of Christ

The Crucifixion

The Three Maries
at the Sepulchre

The Descent into Hell

The Birth of
the Virgin

The Presentation of the
Virgin in the Temple

The Risen Christ
appearing to Mary
Magdalene

The Entombment

**The Presentation of
Christ in the Temple**
In this scene the artist tries
to recreate the interior
of the temple.

Christ among the Doctors
This scene testifies to Stoss'
masterly depiction of the
diverse physiognomies.

Veit Stoss (Wit Stwosz)

Veit Stoss (1447–1533), one of the greatest wood-carvers of the late Gothic age, was born in Horb am Neckar in Germany. He lived in Krakow from 1477 to 1496, where he was exempted from paying taxes by the City Council. He created a number of sculptural works here.

The Coronation of the Virgin

St Adalbert

St Stanisław

The Annunciation

The Nativity

The Assumption
Mary and Christ are raised to Heaven by eight angels.

The Ascension

The Resurrection

The Adoration of the Magi

Pentecost

Predella with the Tree of Jesse

The Death of the Virgin
The figure of the youthful Mary is one of the greatest sculptures ever made in Poland.

St John
Slightly hesitant, the saint is about to put a cape on the fainting Mary.

❷ St Mary's Square
Plac Mariacki

Map 1 C4 (6 D2).

St Mary's Square was once a parish graveyard. It was relocated between 1796 and 1804. The statue of the Virgin Mary which was here originally is now in the Planty by Jagiellońska Street. The bas-relief attributed to Veit Stoss, which once decorated the Calvary Porch, has survived and is now in the National Museum. A copy can be seen on the wall at No. 8 on the square. The prelate House and a Vicarage are among the houses in which original beamed ceilings and plasterwork have survived. St Barbara's Church is on the east side of the square, which also features a small water pump decorated with a figure of a student of medieval Krakow. It is a copy of a figure from the high altar in St Mary's *(see pp96–7)*.

❸ St Barbara's Church
Kościół św. Barbary

Mały Rynek 8. **Map** 1 C4 (6 D2). **Tel** 12 428 15 00. **Open** during services.

According to a legend St Barbara's Church was built using the bricks that were left over from the construction of the Church of St Mary. St Barbara's actually dates from 1394 to 1399, which coincides

The Gothic porch with Christ in Gethsemane at St Barbara's

with one of the stages in the construction of St Mary's. Between 1415 and 1536 sermons were delivered in Polish in the former church, and in German in the latter. During this period the patricians of Krakow were mostly German and it was only much later that they became a minority among the Polish population. In 1586 the church was taken over by the Jesuits. Piotr Skarga preached here and Jakub Wujek, the translator of the Bible, is buried here. Added on the outside from 1488 to 1518 is a late Gothic chapel with a porch decorated with sculptures made by Veit Stoss' workshop. Furnishings date mostly from the 18th century but there is also an interesting early 15th-century Pietà in stone and a 15th-century crucifix on the high altar.

A student of medieval Krakow, St Mary's Square

❹ Market Square
Rynek Główny

See pp100–103.

❺ Christopher Palace
Pałac Krzysztofory

Rynek Główny 35. **Map** 1 C4 (6 D2). Museum of Krakow: **Tel** 12 619 23 03. Cellars: **Open** 10am–5pm Wed–Sun for temporary exhibitions. Main building: **Closed** for restoration until 2018. ♿ Ⓦ mhk.pl

This is one of the oldest and most beautiful palaces in Krakow, with a magnificent arcaded courtyard. It was remodelled between 1682 and 1685 by Jacopo Solari for Kazimierz Wodzicki, one of the richest noblemen in Lesser Poland.

The Palace is named after St Christopher, whose 14th-century statue decorates the building. It houses the Museum of Krakow, which is dedicated to the history and culture of the city (closed for renovation until 2018). Old documents, maces, gold artifacts from local workshops, memorabilia and paintings are all on display.

In the cellars there is a café and the art gallery of the Krakow Group (Grupa Krakowska), which was first established in 1930 and then revived in 1957.

The *Lajkonik*

Every year, on the Thursday ending the Corpus Christi octave, a parade led by a figure known as the *Lajkonik* proceeds from the Convent of the Premonstratensian Nuns in Zwierzyniec to the Market Square. The event commemorates the victory over the Tatars in 1287. On his way, the *Lajkonik* strikes some spectators with his mace, a sign which is thought to bring good luck, especially to girls. At the Market Square the *Lajkonik* receives a symbolic tribute. The original costume of the *Lajkonik*, designed in 1904 by Stanisław Wyspiański, is now in the Museum of Krakow.

The *Lajkonik*

❻ Town Hall Tower
Wieża Ratuszowa

Rynek Główny 1. **Map** 1 C4 (6 D2). Museum: **Tel** 12 426 43 34. **Open** Apr–Oct: 10:30am–5:30pm daily. 🏛

Until the early 19th century there were several public buildings on Market Square: the Town Hall, the Small Weigh-House, the Large Weigh-House and a pillory. The 70 m- (230 ft-) high Town Hall Tower is, unfortunately, the only structure to have survived. The Gothic Town Hall itself was remodelled many times and finally demolished in 1846. The present dome is Baroque. The tower houses a branch of the Museum of Krakow dedicated to the history of local government and is a venue for the Ludowy Theatre.

❼ Cloth Hall
Sukiennice

See pp104–105.

❽ Rynek Underground
Podziemia Rynku

Rynek Główny 1. **Map** 1 C4 (6 D2). **Tel** 12 426 50 60. **Open** Apr–Oct: 10am–10pm daily (to 8pm Mon, to 4pm Tue); Nov–Mar: 10am–8pm daily (to 4pm Tue). Book in advance via the website or by phone. **Closed** 1st Tue of month. 🏛 free Tue. 🌐 **podziemiarynku.com**

This high-tech museum, tracing the story of the city, opened in September 2010 and is located under Market Square. The underground vaults contain displays on transport and trade as well as archaeo- logical finds such as the remains of an 11th-

Church of St Adalbert on Market Square

century cemetery and ancient coins and clothing. The museum cleverly blends modern technology with interactive exhibits and more traditional museum displays.

❾ St Adalbert's Church
Kościół św. Wojciecha

Rynek Główny 3. **Map** 1 C4 (6 D3). **Open** May–Sep: 9am–6pm daily (from 1:30pm Sun); Oct–Apr: 9am–5pm daily. 🏛

The small church of St Adalbert is one of the oldest in Krakow. A legend tells that St Adalbert preached here before leaving on his missionary journey to try to convert the Prussians in 997. The architecture of the church

amalgamates several styles, from Romanesque and Gothic, through Renaissance and Baroque, to the modern interior design. This mixture reflects various stages in the development of the Market Square, an exhibition on which is located in Rynek Underground. The display includes a cross-section of the ground beneath the square, as well as medieval water pipes and other objects found during the excavations carried out after World War II, which have also revealed the remnants of the building dating from the time of St Adalbert.

Rynek Underground is 4 m (13 ft) below Market Square

❹ Market Square: North and West Sides

The charter given to Krakow in 1257 determined the plan of the city. The square located in the middle of the medieval city has remained the centre of Krakow ever since. This square, some 200 m (656 ft) by 200 m (656 ft), is surrounded by a regular grid of streets, with three streets on each side. Only the off-the-grid location of the Church of St Mary, which pre-dates the charter, and Grodzka Street, with its funnel-like shape, vary the rigidity of the urban planning in this area. There were formerly many buildings in the square, but of those the Cloth Hall and the Town Hall Tower are the only ones to have survived. The square was a venue for many important events, including coronation ceremonies.

Deer House
This was once an inn. Johann Wolfgang von Goethe and Tsar Nicholas I both stayed here.

Horse House

Phoenix House

Kenc House

North Side

**Palace of the Rams
(Pałac Pod Baranami)**
One of the most magnificent palaces owned by the Potocki family now houses a famous cabaret.

"Piwnica Pod Baranami" Cabaret

The cabaret which is housed in the Palace of the Rams was established in 1956. Although it was originally intended to exist no longer than "five years, possibly even less", the cabaret has been active for more than 50 years and is one of Krakow's top attractions. Piotr Skrzynecki (1930–97) was the founder and heart and soul of the cabaret. Wiesław Dymny, Ewa Demarczyk, Marek Grechuta, Krystyna Zachwatowicz, Zygmunt Konieczny, Leszek Wójtowicz, Anna Szałapak, Grzegorz Turnau and Zbigniew Preisner were among the best-known contributors and performers. The cabaret is a lively place full of poetry and music, joy and laughter.

Piotr Skrzynecki

West Side

Lamb House

House with a Tin Roof

Małachowski Palace

Betman House
This is also known as "Under the Beheaded" after a bas-relief which depicts the martyrdom of St John the Baptist.

Locator Map
Market Square: North and West sides

42 Market Square
belonged to the Boner family and in the 19th century to the renowned collector Feliks Manggha Jasieński.

Margrave's House
A former mint and presently a bank, the façade of this house features a splendid Rococo portal.

Red House

Eagle House (Dom Pod Orłem)
The basement of this fine Renaissance house formerly contained the Starmach Gallery of contemporary art.

House under Three Stars

Christopher Palace (Pałac Krzysztofory)
This palace *(see p98)* houses the Museum of Krakow, among whose highlights is a gilded plaque, made in 1609, depicting St Eligius.

Spiš Palace (Pałac Spiski)
is home to the exclusive Hawełka Restaurant *(see p191)*.

❹ Market Square: South and East Sides

There are many stories about the Market Square. According to one of the legends Krakow's pigeons are the enchanted knights of Duke Henryk Probus, who agreed to their metamorphosis in exchange for gold that he needed to secure papal acceptance for his coronation. The knights were supposed to regain their human form after the coronation. But the duke lost the gold and his knights are still awaiting the promised transformation. The legend about the two brothers who built the St Mary's towers is more popular. When the older mason completed the taller tower he stabbed his younger brother to death in order to prevent him from surpassing his work but then, remorseful, killed himself.

Madonna House (Dom Pod Obrazem)
Formerly the palace of a wealthy burgher family called Cellari, its façade is decorated with the Madonna painted in 1718.

South Side

Wierzynek Restaurant

Hetman's House (Kamienica Hetmańska)
The Baroque portal leads to shops on the ground floor, in which Gothic vaults with carved keystones have survived.

Potocki Palace (Pałac Potockich)
Behind the Neo-Classical façade the original interiors and a small arcaded courtyard have survived.

East Side

Grey House (Kamienica Szara)

4 Market Square
This is one of a few houses with Art Nouveau decoration. It was added during the remodelling carried out in 1907–8 by Ludwik Wojtyczka.

Prince's House (Kamienica Książęca)
The famous sorcerer Master Twardowski is reputed to have lived here in the 16th century. The house is decorated with a statue of St Giovanni da Capistrano.

Locator Map

⬜ Market Square: South and East sides

Lanckoroński House, also known as "Under the Evangelists," features the remnants of an 18th-century chapel on the first floor.

The pharmacy "Under the Gold Crown" was once housed here. Its emblem has survived above the entrance.

Kromer House (Kamienica Kromerowska)

The Raven House (Kamienica Pod Krukiem) is a seat of the International Centre of Culture and Krakow's Cultural Club.

Canary House (Kamienica Pod Kanarkiem)

Lizards House (Kamienica Pod Jaszczurami)
Gothic vaults have survived in this house, in which a student club is located.

Italian House (Dom Włoski)
The first Polish post office was housed here and coaches passed through this arch.

Boner House (Kamienica Bonerowska)
This is topped by a beautiful Mannerist parapet decorated with herms.

❼ The Cloth Hall (Sukiennice)

The Cloth Hall originated from a covered market. A stone structure protecting the stalls, with an internal passage, was probably here at the time of Kazimierz the Great. It was rebuilt to the design of Giovanni Maria Mosca following a fire in 1555, and remodelled entirely in 1875 by Tomasz Pryliński. The Gallery of 19th-century Polish Art is housed here. The stalls sell a variety of souvenirs. The Noworolski Café, one of the best in Krakow, is a good place to relax after seeing the paintings.

Folly (1894) by Władysław Podkowiński
This Modernist painting aroused much controversy. It began a Symbolist phase in Podkowiński's career.

Four-in-hand (1881) by Józef Chełmoński
Paintings by Symbolists as well as Realists are exhibited alongside the *Four-in-hand*.

Entrance to stalls

Arcades
The side arcades and oriels were added during the rebuilding in 1875. The arcades echo the medieval architecture of Venice.

★ *Blue Hussars* by Piotr Michałowski
A separate room is dedicated to the work of Michałowski, the foremost Polish Romantic artist who lived between 1800 and 1855.

★ *Wernyhora* by Jan Matejko
Jan Matejko and Henryk Siemiradzki were both exponents of 19th-century history painting which is displayed in the room dominated by Matejko's *Prussian Homage.*

Entrance to Rynek Underground Museum

Entrance to Gallery of Polish Art

***The Death of Ellenai* by Jacek Malczewski**
Characteristic of the artist's early work, which was permeated by the memories of people who had been imprisoned in Siberia, this painting was inspired by a poem by Juliusz Słowacki.

***The Chocim Treaty* by Marcello Bacciarelli**
Late 18th- and early 19th-century Neo-Classical paintings are displayed in the same room.

KEY

① **The Renaissance parapet** is not only decorative but also offers protection from fire.

② **Roof with sunken rafters**

③ **Renaissance parapet**

John Paul II

Karol Wojtyła was born in 1920 in Wadowice *(see p160)*, but lived in Krakow for many years. He arrived here in 1938 to read Polish philology at the Jagiellonian University. The outbreak of World War II put a stop to his studies. During the war he worked for the Solvay Chemical Plant and was active in the underground Rhapsody Theatre. In 1942 he entered the underground theological Seminary. As a devout priest and artists' friend, he became very popular. Despite his election to the Apostolic See in 1978 his links with Krakow remained as close as ever. He continued to return here with his apostolic missions on many different occasions, until his death in 2005.

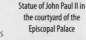

Statue of John Paul II in the courtyard of the Episcopal Palace

⓾ Episcopal Palace
Pałac Biskupi

ul. Franciszkańska 3. **Map** 1 C5 (5 C3). **Tel** 12 429 74 14. ⓰ 1, 3, 6, 8, 18. **Closed** to the public.

First recorded in the 13th century, this is one of the oldest buildings in Krakow. It was damaged by fire and remodelled several times. Giovanni Maria Mosca contributed to the decoration. The present palace dates from the times of Bishop Piotr Tomicki (16th century) and Bishop Piotr Gembicki (17th century). A fire in 1850 caused extensive damage but the splendid furnishings have partly survived.

John Paul II lived here between 1964 and 1978. He was then the Archbishop of Krakow. A statue of him, made in 1980 by Ione Sensi Croci, is in the courtyard.

⓫ Collegium Novum

ul. Gołębia 24. **Map** 1 B4 (5 C3). **Tel** 12 422 10 33. ⓰ 1, 8, 15, 18.

The Collegium Novum replaced the Jerusalem College after it was destroyed by fire in the 19th century. The ruins were demolished between 1883 and 1887 and the new building constructed. Its official opening turned into a patriotic demonstration attended symbolically by delegations from all three parts of the partitioned Poland. According to the contemporary records the architect of the new building, Feliks Księżarski, intended to emulate the vernacular architecture, especially the crystal vaults and decoration of the Collegium Maius, but in fact he imitated German and Austrian models. The magnificent staircase is similar to the one in the Town Hall in Vienna. The College is the seat of the Rector of the Jagiellonian University. It also houses departmental offices, the bursary and the Great Hall where inauguration and graduation ceremonies take place. The Hall has a beamed and coffered ceiling and is decorated with portraits by Jan Matejko.

⓬ Statue of Copernicus
Pomnik Mikołaja Kopernika

ul. Gołębia. **Map** 1 B4 (5 C3). ⓰ 1, 2, 8, 15, 18.

The statue of Nicolaus Copernicus was made in 1900 by Cyprian Godebski. The astronomer is represented as a young scholar holding an astrolabe. The statue was originally in the courtyard of the Collegium Maius, but was moved to the present location in front of the Witkowski College in 1953. The statue was intended to function as a fountain.

⓭ Collegium Maius

See pp108–109.

⓮ Collegium Nowodvorianum

ul. Św. Anny 12. **Map** 1 B4 (5 C2). **Tel** 12 422 04 11. ⓰ 4, 8, 14, 15, 18. ⓱ 124, 152, 502.

The Collegium Nowodvorianum was founded by Bartłomiej Nowodworski, a Knight Hospitaller of St John, Secretary to the King and a warrior in the Battle of Lepanto. This foundation was a result of his bequest of 1617 to the Classes, one of the university colleges and the first secular secondary school in Krakow, established in 1586. The Collegium was built between 1636 and 1643 by

The Neo-Gothic building of the Collegium Novum

Arcaded courtyard of the Collegium Nowodvorianum

Jan Leitner. A beautiful courtyard with arcades and a grand stairway is one of the best preserved Baroque buildings in Krakow. The offices of the Collegium Medicum are housed here.

⓯ Church of St Anne
Kościół św. Anny

See pp110–11.

⓰ Old Theatre
Teatr Stary

ul. Jagiellońska 1. **Map** 1 C4 (5 C2). **Tel** 12 422 80 20. 🚋 2, 4, 8, 13, 14, 15. 🚌 124, 152, 502. Museum: **Open** 11am–1pm Tue–Sat and one hour prior to performances.

The Old, or Modrzejewska Theatre is named after the great actress Helena Modrze-jewska. The oldest theatre building in Poland, it has been in use continuously since 1798. It was remodelled in the Neo-Renaissance style between 1830 and 1843 by Tomasz Majewski and Karol Kremer. The next major rebuilding was undertaken from 1903 to 1905 by Franciszek Mączyński and Tadeusz Stryjeński. The reinforced concrete construc-tion applied to the interior, and the exterior Art Nouveau decoration, both date from

this time. The stucco frieze was made in 1906 by Józef Gardecki. The plaques on the Jagiellońska Street side commemorate the composer Władysław Żeleński, the director Konrad Swinarski and the actor Wiktor Sadecki.

The Old Theatre is regarded as one of the best in Poland. Many outstanding directors have worked here, including Zygmunt Hübner, Konrad Swinarski and Andrzej Wajda. There is a small theatre museum on the ground floor.

⓱ Palace of Art
Pałac Sztuki

Plac Szczepański 4. **Map** 1 C4 (5 C1). **Tel** 12 422 66 16. 🚋 2, 4, 8, 13, 14, 15. 🚌 124, 152, 502. **Open** 8:15am–6pm Mon–Fri, 10am–6pm Sat & Sun. 🎨

In 1854 the Friends of the Fine Arts Society was established in Krakow for the

encouragement of Polish art. The Society embarked upon the organization of exhibitions by living artists, the acquisition of paintings and sculptures and the setting up of a comprehensive records office gathering documents of the history of Polish art in the 19th and early 20th centuries. The Art Nouveau building was designed by Franciszek Màczyński and modelled on the famous Secession Pavilion in Vienna. The finest Krakow artists worked on the decoration. Jacek Malczewski designed the frieze depicting the vicissitudes of fortune and the struggle of artistic genius. The sculptors Antoni Madeyski, Konstanty Laszczka and Teodor Rygier contributed busts of great Polish artists. A portico attached to the façade is topped with a statue of Apollo crowned with a sun halo. Exhibitions of 19th-century and contemporary art are held here.

⓲ "Bunker of Art"
"Bunkier Sztuki"

Plac Szczepański 3a. **Map** 1 C4 (5 C2). **Tel** 12 422 10 52. 🚋 2, 4, 8, 13, 14, 15. 🚌 124, 152, 502. **Open** noon–8pm Tue–Sun. 🎨 💻

This gloomy building in the Socialist Realist style of the 1960s is regarded as one of the ugliest in the city centre. However, it is the venue for some of the most interesting exhibitions of contemporary art, by both Polish and foreign artists. The "Bunker of Art" also features one of Krakow's most popular cafés.

Sculptural decoration on the Palace of Art

⑱ Collegium Maius

The Collegium Maius is the oldest building within the Academy of Krakow (now the Jagiellonian University). It was constructed in the 15th century by amalgamating a number of town houses. Lecture rooms and accommodation for professors were originally located here. In the 19th century the building housed the Jagiellonian Library. Between 1840 and 1870 the architects Karol Kremer, Feliks Księżarski and Hermann Bergman rebuilt the college in the Neo-Gothic style. After World War II the University Museum, established in 1867, was moved here.

★ Libraria
The Libraria was built in the 16th century as the College Library. Today it is a meeting place of the Senate and is decorated with portraits of rectors and professors of the University.

Oriel
This oriel window projecting from the Stuba Communis enlivens the austere exterior wall.

★ Stuba Communis
The Stuba Communis, or Common Room, served as the professors' refectory. The hall features a 14th-century statue of Kazimierz the Great and a 17th-century staircase made in Danzig.

University Treasury
The insignia of the rector, including a late 15th-century mace bequeathed by Bishop Zbigniew Oleśnicki and that of Queen Jadwiga from around 1405, are among the treasures.

Entrance

Copernicus Room
The Room is dedicated to the great astronomer, who studied here between 1491 and 1495, thus rendering the Academy famous. The display features the so-called Jagiellonian armillary sphere made in 1510.

Cloister
The Gothic cloister, whose columns have a cut crystal-like decoration, is reminiscent of those in medieval Italian universities.

Green Hall
A collection of national memorabilia, including the piano that Frédéric Chopin played, can be visited by prior arrangement.

★ Great Hall
The Great Hall features stalls used by the Senate during the ceremonies at which honorary degrees are conferred.

Chapel
The former apartment of John of Kęty, the professor of theology who became the patron saint of the Jagiellonian University, has been converted into a chapel, which is on the ground floor.

KEY

① Porta Aurea (Golden Gate)

② **A lavishly inlaid door** was originally in the Senior Room of the old Town Hall.

③ Rector's Stairs

⑮ Church of St Anne

A professor of the Krakow Academy, John of Kęty (Jan Kanty) was already considered a saint at the time of his death in 1473, when he was buried in the Gothic Church of St Anne. Following his beatification, the Senate of the Academy commissioned Tylman van Gameren to build a new church. The construction began in 1689 under the supervision of Father Sebastian Piskorski. The Italian architect and sculptor Baldassare Fontana contributed the decoration and most of the furnishings, including the altars, between 1695 and 1703. He was assisted by the painters Carlo and Innocente Monti and Karl Dankwart. St Anne's, with its sumptuous interior, is considered to be a leading example of Baroque ecclesiastical architecture in Poland.

Procession Commemorating St John of Kęty, 1767
To mark the canonization of John of Kęty, a procession with his holy relics was held in Krakow. The saint's relics were carried into the Church of St Anne with great pomp and ceremony.

Nave
The architecture, sculpture and painting all contribute to the decoration of the nave and vault, and exemplify particularly well the wholeness of the Baroque design.

West Portal
The "scenographic" effect of the main entrance to the Church is a result of the superimposition of three portals, one within another.

Main entrance

Gloria Domini
The dome fresco by Carlo and Innocente Monti is an allegory of triumphant Catholicism, represented as the true Christian faith.

★ **High Altar**
The high altar is decorated with sculptures by Baldassare Fontana. The altarpiece, depicting the Virgin and Child with Anne, is by Jerzy Eleuter Siemiginowski, painter to Jan III Sobieski.

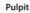

Pulpit
The angel supporting the pulpit was carved in 1727 by the Krakow artist Antoni Frączkiewicz, who was influenced by the art of Baldassare Fontana.

★ **Shrine of St John of Kęty**
The relics of the saint rest in a sarcophagus supported by four figures personifying the faculties of the Academy of Krakow: Theology, Philosophy, Law and Medicine.

Choir Stalls
The stalls are decorated with paintings by Szymon Czechowicz, a leading Polish painter of the 18th century.

⑲ Szołayski House
Kamienica Szołayskich

Plac Szczepański 9. **Map** 1 C4 (5 D2).
Tel 12 433 54 50. 🚌 124, 152, 304,
424, 502. 🚋 2, 4, 8, 13, 14, 18, 20, 24.
Open 10am–6pm Tue–Sat,
10am–4pm Sun. 🎫 free Sun.
W muzeum.krakow.pl

The oldest parts of this building,
which house a branch of the
National Museum in Krakow,
date from the 15th century.
Since then, Szołayski House has
served as a private residence,
part of a monastery and a
newspaper office. Since 1934, it
has been an exhibition space,
except for a period during
World War II when it was
occupied by the Nazis. In 2003,
it was dedicated to the life and
works of Stanisław Wyspiański
(1869–1907), Krakow's foremost
Art Nouveau artist. Its role has
now been expanded to display
the works of other Polish artists
of the same period, as well as
temporary exhibitions on
other notable Polish figures.

Helenka by Stanisław Wyspiański

⑳ Church of the Reformed Franciscans
Kościół Reformatów

ul. Reformacka 4. **Map** 1 C4 (6 D1).
Tel 12 422 06 23. 🚌 124, 152, 502.
🚋 2, 3, 4, 8, 13, 14, 15, 20.
Open during services only.

The Church of the Reformed
Franciscans was built
between 1666 and 1672. The
architecture and modest furnishings conform to the strict
rule of the order. The altarpiece

Crucifix on the altar in the Church of
St Mark

on the left that depicts
St Kazimierz (Casimir) is
an outstanding example
of 17th-century work.
    The specific microclimate
within the crypt beneath
the church causes the
reposing corpses to undergo
mummification. Those
visitors seeking a shocking
experience may request
access to the crypt.

㉑ Church of St Mark
Kościół św. Marka

ul. Św. Marka 10. **Map** 1 C4 (6 D1).
Tel 12 422 21 78. 🚌 124, 152, 502.
🚋 3, 4, 5, 13, 15, 20.
Open during services only.

The early Gothic
church of the Monks
of St Mark was
founded in 1263
by Duke Bolesław
the Chaste. It has
been remodelled
a number of times
throughout its
history and the
interior acquired
an early Baroque
appearance in the
first half of the 17th
century. The high
altar, with its lavish
Mannerist ornamenta-
tion, was made in 1618
in the workshop of
Baltazar Kuncz. On
the left is the 17th-
century tomb of
Blessed Michał Gie-
droyć (died 1485).

㉒ Polish Academy of Skills
Gmach Polskiej Akademii Umiejętności

ul. Sławkowska 17. **Map** 1 C4 (6 D1).
Tel 12 424 02 00. 🚌 124, 152, 502.
🚋 3, 4, 5, 13, 15, 20. **Open** 9am–4pm
Mon–Fri. **W** pau.krakow.pl

The building was constructed
between 1857 and 1866 as the
seat of the Academic Society of
Krakow, which in 1872 became
the Academy of Skills, the first
academic body to bring
together scholars from all three
parts of partitioned Poland. It
was designed by Filip Pokutyński
in the Neo-Renaissance style.
The exterior is decorated with
portrait medallions of people
in low relief who made
important contributions to
Polish academic and cultural life.
Inside, a small meeting room
features an impressive coffered
ceiling. The rich print collection
includes works by Albrecht
Dürer and Rembrandt.

㉓ St John Street
Ulica św. Jana

Map 1 C4 (6 D2). 🚌 124, 152, 502.
🚋 3, 4, 5, 13, 15, 20.

This quiet street leading away
from the Market Square,
and closed off at its

Portal to the House of the Cistercian Abbots of Jędrzejów,
20 St John Street

north end by the façade of the Piarist Church, is lined with a selection of fine secular and ecclesiastic Baroque and Neo-Classical buildings.

The House of the Cistercian Abbots of Jędrzejów at No.20 is of particular interest. Remodelled in 1744 by Francesco Placidi, the house is decorated with a magnificent late Baroque portal featuring atlantes.

The Wodzicki Palace at No.11 was given a Neo-Classical façade by Ferdinand Nax after 1781. Around 1818 the Bernardine Friary was converted after a great deal of rebuilding.

㉔ Church of St John
Kościół św. Jana

ul. Św. Jana 7. **Map** 1 C4 (6 D2). **Tel** 12 422 65 00. 124, 152, 502. 3, 4, 5, 15, 20. **Open** during services only.

The chronicler Jan Długosz records that this church was founded in the 12th century. The Romanesque architecture has been lost through much remodelling. The Gothic buttresses still project from the exterior side walls, but the façade and the interior are Baroque. The high altar of 1730 is decorated with sculptures by Antoni Frączkiewicz and the 16th-century miraculous Madonna, the Refuge of Prisoners.

㉕ Czartoryski Museum
Muzeum Czartoryskich

See pp114–15.

㉖ Piarist Church
Kościół Pijarów

ul. Pijarska 2. **Map** 1 C4 (6 D1). **Tel** 12 422 17 24. 124, 152, 502. 3, 4, 5, 13, 15, 20. **Open** during services only.

This Baroque church was built between 1718 and 1728 probably to designs by Kacper Bażanka. The Rococo façade designed by Francesco Placidi was added in 1759 to 1761. Inside, the church is decorated with frescoes by a master of

illusion, Franz Eckstein. The high altar painted on the wall is by the same artist, as is the fresco in the nave vault that glorifies the name of the Virgin Mary. The altars in the aisles feature 18th-century paintings by Szymon Czechowicz.

The crypt under the church is renowned for the decoration of Christ's Tomb, which usually alludes symbolically to patriotic themes, and is set up here every year during Holy Week. The crypt is also a venue for theatre performances and various exhibitions.

The Rococo interior of the 18th-century Piarist Church

St Florian's Gate at the end of Floriańska Street

㉗ St Florian's Gate and the City Wall Remnants
Brama Floriańska i Resztki Murów Miejskich

Map 2 D4 (6 E1). 124, 152, 502. 3, 4, 5, 13, 15, 19.

In 1285 Duke Leszek the Black gave Krakow the right to have the city surrounded by walls. These fortifications developed during the following centuries, finally consisting of inner and outer moated walls and 47 towers. Eight fortified gates lead into the city. With the introduction of artillery, the defence system became redundant. Disused, it fell into disrepair by the end of the 18th century. The walls were dismantled early in the 19th century and later replaced by the Planty gardens *(see pp168–9)*. St Florian's Gate, dating possibly from the end of the 13th century, and a small stretch of the adjoining walls have been saved, largely through the efforts of Professor Feliks Radwański. East of St Florian's Gate is the Haberdashers' Tower, and the towers of the Joiners and Carpenters are to the west.

㉕ Czartoryski Museum

At the core of the Czartoryski Museum is the collection assembled late in the 18th century by Princess Izabella Czartoryska. It was initially at Puławy, but partly moved to Paris following the 1830 November Uprising. In 1876 the collection was brought to Krakow, thanks to the efforts of Prince Władysław Czartoryski. It is located in three houses and the adjoining City Arsenal at St John Street, where works are displayed in period interiors but may be subject to changes of location during extensive renovation work.

Madonna and Child
By the Venetian Vincenzo Catena, this painting is a highlight of the Czartoryski's Italian collection.

Jesuit Saints
This fine bas-relief by the 17th-century Roman sculptor, Alessandro Algardi, depicts the Polish Jesuit, Stanisław Kostka, being admitted to the congregation of Jesuit saints.

Gallery Guide
There is no gallery space on the ground floor. The first-floor display is dedicated to Polish history of the 14th–18th centuries as well as Western European decorative arts. The picture gallery is on the second floor.

Porcelain Figures
These two figures of a Polish nobleman and noblewoman were made in Meissen.

Entrance

Nautilus Cup
The museum collection is rich in decorative arts and includes this 17th-century drinking vessel made in Danzig (now Gdańsk) from a large shell.

★ *Lady with an Ermine*
by Leonardo da Vinci
During renovations, this
late 15th-century portrait
is on display at Wawel
Royal Castle *(see pp72–3)*.

VISITORS' CHECKLIST

Practical Information
ul. Św. Jana 19. **Map** 1 C4 (6 E1).
Tel 12 422 55 66. **Closed** for
renovations until June 2016.
🖼 📷 🌐 **muzeum-czartoryskich.krakow.pl**

Transport
🚊 2, 3, 4, 5, 12, 13, 14, 15, 24.
🚌 124, 152, 424, 502, 512.

Second
floor

Portrait of a Boy **by
Caspar Netscher**
This sweet little
portrait is one of
several paintings in
the collection by
lesser Dutch artists
of the 17th century.

First floor

★ *Landscape with the Good Samaritan*
by Rembrandt
A masterpiece in the collection of Western painting,
this treatment of the natural world is breathtaking.

Landscape **by Alessandro
Magnasco**
This dramatic landscape is
characteristic of Italian painting
of the 18th century.

Ground
floor

Key

▢ Non-exhibition space

▢ History of Poland
   1300–1900

▢ Decorative Arts of Western Europe

▢ Picture Gallery

The impressive exterior of the Barbican

In 1910 Michalik extended and redecorated the premises to designs by Franciszek Mączyński. The main room received a glass ceiling. Karol Frycz designed the interior decoration, furniture and most of the stained glass in the Art Nouveau style.

The café is still an inviting place where customers can go back in time and enjoy the atmosphere of the fin de siècle, as well as see enduring folk shows.

㉘ Barbican
Barbakan

ul. Basztowa. **Map** 2 D3 (6 E1). 🚊 3, 4, 5, 13, 15. 🚌 124, 152, 502.

The Barbican, a round bastion, was constructed in 1498–99 after King Jan Olbracht was defeated by the Turks in Bukowina, and further Turkish incursions were feared. It shows the changes that had been introduced to military architecture as a result of the rapid development of artillery. This relatively low structure projecting from the city walls with a considerable overhang enabled the defenders to fire with precision at the enemy from the loop-holes, positioned at different levels. The Barbican was originally surrounded by a moat and linked to St Florian's Gate by a corridor. It is the best preserved barbican in Europe.

㉙ Jama Michalika Café
Jama Michalika

ul. Floriańska 45. **Map** 2 D4 (6 E1). **Tel** 12 422 15 61. 🚊 3, 4, 5, 13, 15. 🚌 124, 152, 502. **Open** noon–midnight daily. 🅿

In 1895 Jan Michalik opened a patisserie near the Market Square. It became very popular with students of the Fine Arts School who called the place *jama* (grotto) for its lack of windows. Poets, writers and artists soon joined them and in 1905 established the cabaret Zielony Balonik (The Green Balloon) here. The performances, based on texts by Tadeusz Boy-Żeleński, soon attracted a large audience. Satirical Christmas puppet shows, with marionettes by Ludwik Puget and Jan Szczepkowski, became particularly popular.

㉚ Matejko House
Dom Matejki

ul. Floriańska 41. **Map** 2 D4 (6 E1). **Tel** 12 433 59 60. 🚊 3, 4, 5, 13, 15. 🚌 124, 152, 502. **Open** 10am–6pm Tue–Sat, 10am–4pm Sun. 🅿 free on Sun. 🅲

The artist Jan Matejko was born here in 1838, and in 1873 returned to live with his family. He rebuilt the house and added a new façade designed by Tomasz Pryliński in the Neo-Baroque style. After Matejko died in 1893 the house was transformed into a museum and opened to the public five years later. The statue of a hussar on horseback, on the ground floor, was part of Leon Wyczółkowski's design for the Matejko Monument. The private rooms on the first floor have remained unchanged, while the second floor is used for a display of the artist's works, which include cartoons for the murals that are in the Church of St Mary. His studio on the third floor is full of the props and curiosities he collected. Pieces of old armour and instruments of torture excavated on the site of the old Town Hall are of particular interest.

㉛ Floriańska Street
Ulica Floriańska

Map 1 C4, 2 D4 (6 D2–E1, 2). 🚊 3, 5, 13, 15, 20. 🚌 124, 152, 502.

This street, leading from St Florian's Gate to the Market Square, formed part of the Royal Route which became fully established after the court moved from Krakow to Warsaw.

The interior of the Jama Michalika Café

Visitors in front of St Florian's Gate on Floriańska Street

The Royal Route was often used by a sovereign arriving for a coronation, and again when his body was taken in procession for the funeral at Wawel. In the 19th century Floriańska was the busiest street in Krakow, with trams introduced in 1881. Medieval walls have survived in most houses, but the original architecture has been lost through later remodelling. More storeys and new eclectic façades were added to most buildings early in the 20th century, when Floriańska gained its present appearance.

❷ Słowacki Theatre
Teatr im. Juliusza Słowackiego

Pl. Świętego Ducha 1. **Map** 2 D4 (6 E2). **Tel** 12 424 45 00. 🚊 2, 4, 5, 8, 13, 15, 20. 🚌 124, 152, 502.

The proposal for a new theatre in Krakow, one which would replace the small and dilapidated Old Theatre, was put forward in 1872. Jan Zawiejski submitted the design and was

put in charge of the works which were to be financed entirely through donations. The foundation stone was laid in 1891, and the theatre opened in 1893. Zawiejski designed an opulent building in which vernacular elements, such as the parapet inspired by the Cloth Hall, and foreign influences were blended into an eclectic whole. Allegorical sculptures decorate the exterior of the theatre.

The opulent interior features a grand staircase decorated with stuccowork by Alfred Putz. The four-tiered auditorium can seat up to 900 people. The stage curtain, one of the major attractions, was painted by Henryk Siemiradzki. It depicts Apollo striking an accord between Beauty and Love, surrounded by muses as well as other allegorical figures which represent Art drawing inspiration from man's fate.

❸ Church of the Holy Cross
Kościół św. Krzyża

ul. Świętego Krzyża 23. **Map** 2 D4 (6 E3). **Tel** 12 429 20 56. 🚊 2, 4, 5, 8, 15. 🚌 124, 152, 502. **Open** during services only.

The Gothic church of the Order of the Holy Cross was built in two stages. The construction of the choir began immediately after 1300. The main nave and tower date from the first half of the 14th century. The interior is extremely well preserved and the nave impresses with its

intricate pattern of vaulting ribs, supported on a single, round pillar. Among its furnishings, the Gothic font made in 1423 by Jan Freudenthal and the late Renaissance triptych in the Węgrzyn Chapel (next to the porch) are of particular interest. There are also various Baroque altars and stalls, as well as a number of memorial plaques of famous sculptors, active at the end of the 19th century, which are worth seeing.

The Church of the Holy Cross

❹ Church of the Dominican Nuns
Kościół Dominikanek

ul. Mikołajska 21. **Map** 2 D4 (6 E3). **Tel** 12 422 79 25. 🚊 2, 3, 8, 10, 13, 20. **Open** during services only.

The church, dedicated to the Virgin Mary, Queen of Snow, was founded in 1632–34 by Anna Lubomirska. Prior to the church, a fortified manor of Albert, Krakow's *wójt* (chief officer), was on this site in the 14th century. As a result of Albert's revolt against King Władysław the Short, a new building for the local government was erected. The latter was converted in the 1620s into a convent for the Dominican nuns. The church contains a miraculous 17th-century icon of the Virgin.

❺ Dominican Church
Kościół Dominikanów

See pp118–19.

The eclectic façade of the Słowacki Theatre

㉟ Dominican Church

The Dominicans began the construction of a new church in 1250. It contained the shrine of St Jacek, a place of mass pilgrimage. Opulent mausolea, modelled on the Zygmunt Chapel at Wawel, were added in the 17th century by noble families, and in the 18th century the church was furnished with late Baroque altars. The fire of Krakow in 1850 destroyed the church almost completely. It was rebuilt by 1872 and today is an important evangelical centre which attracts masses of the faithful.

Cloister
The Gothic cloister was a burial place of burghers whose memorial plaques and tombs can still be seen here.

★ Zbaraski Chapel
The fine decoration of the chapel, built in 1627 to 1633 by the Castelli artists, is in sharp contrast with the monumental forms of the altar and tombs in black marble.

Tomb of General Jan Skrzynecki (died 1860)
This beautiful monument carved by Władysław Oleszczyński commemorates the hero of the November Uprising of 1830.

★ **Shrine of St Jacek**
The Renaissance Chapel of St Jacek
was rebuilt around 1700 by Baldassare
Fontana, who also designed this
magnificent monument. The chapel
is decorated with paintings by
Tommaso Dolabella.

VISITORS' CHECKLIST

Practical Information
ul. Stolarska 12. **Map** 1 C5 (6 D3).
Tel 12 423 16 13.
Open 6:30am–8pm daily
W krakow.dominikanie.pl

Transport
🚋 1, 3, 6, 8, 18.

Chapel of the Virgin Mary of the Rosary
In 1621 the Virgin of the Rosary icon was
carried in a procession to secure, through
prayers, victory over the Turks at Chocim.

The Myszkowski Chapel
This was built between 1603
and 1614 by masters from Santi
Gucci's circle, using marble from
the Świętokrzyskie (Holy Cross)
Mountains. Portrait busts of the
Myszkowskis form part of the
splendid decoration of the dome.

KEY

① **The Lubomirski Chapel** displays
lovely paintings and sculptures.

② **Crowstep gable**

③ **The memorial plaque of Filippo
Buonacorsi (Callimachus)** (died
1496) honours the great humanist
at the Polish royal court *(see p47)*.

④ **Choir stalls**, pulpit and
confessionals, all in the Neo-Gothic
style, date from the second half of
the 19th century.

**Tomb of Prospero
Provano**
The monument of this
salt magnate (died
1584) is one of the
finest Polish sculptural
works of circa 1600. It
is located next to the
Myszkowski Chapel.

Street-by-Street: Szeroka Street Area

The Jewish quarter was located in the east part of Kazimierz and concentrated first around Szeroka Street, then Libusza Square, which was later known as New Square. As well as the Jews displaced here in the late 15th century from Krakow, Czech and German refugees also came to live in Kazimierz. The Jewish community had its own jurisdiction and culture, and was never totally assimilated with the Poles. Many synagogues, baths, schools and cemeteries were established in Kazimierz, which became an active centre of Judaic culture and learning. The Nazis annihilated this unique world. However, a number of art galleries and restaurants have been opened here which evoke the past.

❶ Tempel Synagogue
The decoration of this synagogue, built in the Neo-Renaissance style, was influenced by Moorish art.

Jewish Tombs

The signs carved on tombs convey symbolic meanings. The grave of a rabbi is indicated by hands joined in prayer. Basins and jugs for the ritual ablution of hands can be found on graves of the Levites. Three interlaced snakes feature on the grave of a physician, and a crown of knowledge on that of a learned man. A lion or a six-pointed star of David signifies a descendant of Judah.

| 0 metres | 50 |
| 0 yards | 50 |

Key

— Suggested route

The Kupa Synagogue
This was built in the 17th century and financed by the Kahal of Kazimierz. It was remodelled many times and was also used for non-religious purposes.

6 ★ Remu'h Cemetery
The Wailing Wall commemorates the tragic fate of the Jews from Krakow during World War II.

Locator Map
See Street Finder maps 4

Bath (mikvah)   Poper Synagogue

DAJWOR

SZEROKA

5 Remu'h Synagogue
This synagogue is dedicated to the rabbi Remu'h, who was reputed to be a miracle worker. His grave is still venerated by pious Jewish pilgrims.

Synagogue on the Hill

2 Isaak's Synagogue
The stuccowork in this Baroque synagogue is of great interest

3 High Synagogue
With its late Gothic architecture and Renaissance decoration, this is one of Krakow's most picturesque synagogues.

4 ★ Old Synagogue
This menorah is among the treasures in Poland's oldest synagogue. The building was destroyed by the Nazis, and later restored.

❶ Tempel Synagogue
Synagoga Tempel

ul. Miodowa 24. **Map** 4 D1 (6 F5).
🚋 1, 3, 6, 8, 9, 10, 11, 13, 18, 19, 22.
🚌 128, 184. **Open** Mon–Fri.

The most recent of the synagogues in Kazimierz, the Tempel, was built in the Neo-Renaissance style between 1860 and 1862. It is used by non-Orthodox Jews. Inside note the stained glass and period decoration.

Façade of Isaak's Synagogue

❷ Isaak's Synagogue
Bożnica Izaaka

ul. Kupa 18. **Map** 4 D1. **Tel** 12 430 55 77. 🚋 3, 8, 9, 11, 13. 🚌 128, 184. **Open** 9am–7pm Sun–Fri. **Closed** public hols.

This synagogue was built between 1638 and 1644 as a foundation of Izaak Jakubowicz, an elder of the Jewish community. Inside, the plaster work by Giovanni Battista Falconi has survived in a large nave with a barrel vault. The Jewish Education Centre is housed here.

❸ High Synagogue
Bożnica Wysoka

ul. Józefa 38. **Map** 4 D1.
🚋 3, 8, 9, 10, 11, 13.

This synagogue dates from 1556 to 1563. It is a picturesque structure supported by buttresses. A Renaissance portal is worth noting. Only a few furnishings have survived, including a money box and the remains of an altar. The Studio for the Restoration of Monuments is located here.

❹ Old Synagogue
Synagoga Stara

ul. Szeroka 24. **Map** 4 D1. 🚋 3, 9, 11, 13. Galicia Jewish Museum: **Tel** 12 422 09 62. **Open** Apr–Oct: 9am–5pm Tue–Sun, 10am–2pm Mon; Nov–Mar: 10am–2pm Mon, 9am–4pm Tue–Thu, Sat & Sun, 10am–5pm Fri. **Closed** first Sat & Sun of each month. 🎫 free Mon. 📷

The Old Synagogue was used in the past as a temple and was also a seat of the Kahal and other offices of the Jewish community. Religious and social life was concentrated here. The synagogue houses the Galicia Jewish Museum, which is dedicated to the history and culture of Krakow's Jews.

The brick building dates back to the mid-15th or beginning of the 16th century. Its present appearance is the result of a remodelling in 1557–70. The parapet, and Gothic interior with ribbed vaulting supported by slender columns, all date from then.

The hall used for prayer is almost bare, in accordance with the rule of the Jewish religion. The *bimah*, an elevated platform with an iron balustrade used for readings from the Torah, is the only piece of furnishing.

The east wall features the *aron hakodesh*, an ornamental shrine for the Torah Scrolls.

Entrance to the Remu'h Synagogue and Cemetery

❺ Remu'h Synagogue
Bożnica Remuh

ul. Szeroka 40. **Map** 4 D1. **Tel** 12 421 29 87. 🚋 3, 9, 11, 13. **Open** 9am–4pm Sun–Fri (May–Sep: to 6pm). **Closed** during services. 📷 ♿

One of the two still active synagogues, the Remu'h temple is used by Orthodox Jews. It was founded by Israel Isserles Auerbach around 1553 and named after his son, the great author and philosopher Rabbi Moses Remu'h.

Inside, the *bimah* and an ornamental *aron hakodesh* are worth noting.

❻ Remu'h Cemetery
Cmentarz Remuh

ul. Szeroka 40. **Map** 4 D1. 🚋 3, 9, 11, 13, 24. **Open** 9am–4pm Sun–Fri.

The Remu'h Cemetery, established in 1533, is one of the very few Jewish cemeteries

Hall of Prayers in the Old Synagogue

in the whole of Europe with so many tombs, both gravestones (matzeva) and sarcophagi. Their rich floral and animal decoration is of particular interest.

The cemetery was almost entirely destroyed during World War II. However, the tomb of Remu'h, which still attracts pilgrims from all over the world, was spared from Nazi destruction. Over 700 tombs have been excavated since World War II. They were probably buried during the Swedish invasion in the early 18th century. The Wailing Wall by the entrance was made using fragments of tombstones destroyed during the war.

Town Hall in Kazimierz, housing the Ethnographical Museum

❼ New Jewish Cemetery
Nowy Cmentarz Żydowski

ul. Miodowa 55. **Map** 4 E1. 🚋 3, 9, 11, 13, 24. **Open** 9am–5pm Sun–Fri.

Established in the early 19th century, this cemetery is a burial place of the great Jews of Krakow of the 19th and 20th centuries. All Kazimierz's rabbis and many of the great benefactors of Krakow rest here. They include Józef Oettinger and Józef Rosenblatt (professors of the Jagiellonian University), Józef Sare (the city President), and Maurycy Gotlieb (one of the foremost Polish artists of the 19th century).

❽ Corpus Christi Church
Kościół Bożego Ciała

ul. Bożego Ciała 26. **Map** 4 D2. 🚌 128, 184. 🚋 3, 6, 8, 10, 18, 20, 22. **Open** 9am–noon and 1:30–7pm Mon–Sat and during services.

Corpus Christi Church was built on marshland where, according to legend, a monstrance (religious container) with the Eucharist stolen from the Collegiate Church of All Saints had been found. A mysterious light shining in the darkness indicated the site where the profaned monstrance had been abandoned. The construction of

the church, founded by King Kazimierz the Great, began in 1340 and was completed in the early 15th century. As a parish church it was bestowed by local burghers with sumptuous furnishings, most of which have survived.

In 1634 to 1637 the high altar was decorated with a painting of The Nativity by Tommaso Dolabella, court artist to Zygmunt III Vaza. The large stalls for monks, matching the altar, were made in 1632. An opulent 17th-century stone altarpiece with the relics of Blessed Stanisław Kazimierczyk is located in the north aisle.

The altar of Christ the Redeemer, decorated with sculptures by Anton Gegenbaur, is also worth noting. A slab in the north aisle indicates the burial place of the architect Bartolomeo Berecci, who was assassinated in 1537.

Image of the Madonna in the Church of Corpus Christi

❾ Kazimierz Town Hall
Ratusz kazimierski

Pl. Wolnica 1. **Map** 4 D2. **Tel** 12 430 55 75. 🚌 128, 184, 502. 🚋 3, 8, 10, 40. Ethnographical Museum: **Open** 11am–7pm Tue, Wed, Fri, Sat; 11am–9pm Thu; 11am–3pm Sun. **Closed** public hols. 🚫 📷

The Town Hall was the seat of local government until 1791. The oldest parts of the building date back to 1414, the year of its foundation. After much remodelling, the north section of the Town Hall was finally completed in 1620. The south section was added in 1875 to 1877 by Filip Pokutyński.

The Ethnographic Museum was established here in 1947. Its rich collection includes costumes from Lesser Poland and Silesia, traditional Krakovian Christmas cribs, folk art and musical instruments.

❿ Hospital of the Order of St John of God
Szpital Bonifratrów

ul. Trynitarska 11. **Map** 4 D6. **Tel** 12 379 71 00. 🚌 128, 184, 522. 🚋 8, 10, 12, 18, 22, 40.

This monumental building was constructed between 1897 and 1906 to commemorate the 50th anniversary of Emperor Franz Joseph's reign. Designed by Teodor Talowski in the late Modernist style, the façade, with its central bay projection, is of particular interest.

Church of the Order of St John of God, detail of the façade

⓫ Church of the Order of St John of God
Kościół Bonifratrów

ul. Krakowska 48. **Map** 4 D2. **Tel** 12 430 61 22. 🚌 128, 184, 522. 🚊 8, 10, 19, 22, 40. **Open** during services only.

This interesting Baroque church was built between 1741 and 1758 to designs by Francesco Placidi. A rather small structure is hidden behind a monumental, wavy façade inspired by the best designs of the leading Roman Baroque architect, Francesco Borromini. The façade, intended to be viewed at an angle, closes the vista formed by Krakowska Street. Inside, the excellent *trompe-l'oeil* painting of the vault was made by Josef Piltz of Moravia in 1757–58. It depicts St John of Matha buying slaves from the heathens. The side altars, with their architectural forms painted directly on the walls, are unusual. They are decorated with Rococo paintings, among which the effigy of St Cajetan is worth noting.

⓬ Church of St Catherine
Kościół św. Katarzyny

ul. Augustiańska 7. **Map** 4 D2. **Tel** 12 430 62 42. 🚌 128, 184, 522. 🚊 8, 10, 18, 19, 22. **Open** during services only.

According to the chronicler Jan Długosz, the Church of St Catherine was built by King Kazimierz the Great as a penance for murdering Father Marcin Baryczka in 1349. Baryczka delivered a document issued by bishops excommunicating the king. The king repaid the messenger with the order to have Baryczka drowned in the Vistula. However, the construction of the church possibly began in 1343 and continued until the early 16th century. Regarded as one of the most beautiful Gothic churches in Krakow, its furnishings were lost in the 19th century when it

Fresco in the cloister in the Church of St Catherine

was briefly transformed into a warehouse. The Baroque high altar, decorated with the *Mystical Marriage of St Catherine* by Andrea Venesta, 1634, has survived. Worth visiting is the Gothic cloister which dates from the time of Kazimierz the Great. It features late Gothic murals and large 17th-century paintings. Two chapels adjoin the cloister: one houses the miraculous *Madonna of Consolation* and the other relics of Blessed Isaiah Boner.

⓭ Paulite Church "On the Rock"
Kościół Paulinów Na Skałce

ul. Skałeczna 15. **Map** 3 C2. **Tel** 12 423 09 48. 🚌 128, 184, 522. 🚊 8, 10, 18, 19, 22. **Open** 9am–4pm Mon–Sat and during services. The Crypt: **Open** Apr–Oct: 9am–5pm daily; Nov–Mar: on request. 🅿

A small church of St Michael "On the Rock" was recorded already in the 11th century. This was the site where Bishop Stanisław of Szczepanów, later canonized, was murdered *(see pp24–5)*.

In the 14th century this small Romanesque church was replaced by a large Gothic church founded by Kazimierz the Great. Four hundred years later it was in danger of collapsing. It was rebuilt in the late Baroque style, between 1733 and 1742. The design by Anton Gerhard Müntzer was modified by Antonio Solari. The uniform furnishings all date from the 1740s. A small font by the church is decorated with a statue of St Stanisław, made in 1731. The tormentors of the saint, who are said to have quartered his body, threw his cut-off finger into the font. The water is reputed to have had healing properties ever since.

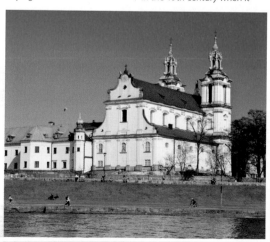

Paulite Church and Monastery "On the Rock"

The Crypt in the Church "On the Rock"

Jan Długosz, the great Polish historian of the Middle Ages, was buried in the crypt beneath the Church "On the Rock" in 1480. In 1876 it was decided to transform the crypt into a national pantheon for the burial of those who had made important contributions to Polish culture. The architect Teofil Żebrawski remodelled the crypt, transforming it into a gallery with a separate chapel housing the altar. Recesses were designed to house the sarcophagi. The stained-glass window above the altar depicts the Madonna of Częstochowa, the Queen of Poland. Coats of arms of provinces of the Polish-Lithuanian Commonwealth were painted on the vault.

Sarcophagus of Adam Asnyk
(1838–97)
This foremost Polish poet of 19th-century Positivism rests in a sarcophagus made by Karol Knaus and Jan Tombiński.

Altar

Sarcophagus of Karol Szymanowski

Sarcophagus of Henryk Siemiradzki

Sarcophagus of Wincenty Pol

Sarcophagus of Tadeusz Banachiewicz

Sarcophagus of Czesław Miłosz

Entrance

Sarcophagus of Jacek Malczewski

Sarcophagus of Teofil Lenartowicz

Sarcophagus of Józef I. Kraszewski

Sarcophagus of Jan Długosz

Sarcophagus of Ludwik Solski

Sarcophagus of Lucjan Siemieński (1807–77)
The sarcophagus of this popular writer and critic was designed by Karol Knaus. The portrait medallion is by Jan Tombiński.

Stanisław Wyspiański
(1869–1907)
The monumental sarcophagus of Wyspiański was designed by Jan Rzymkowski.

WESOŁA, KLEPARZ AND BISKUPIE

A number of settlements developed around Krakow over the centuries. They were linked culturally and economically with Krakow but were independently administered. As there were no specific boundaries between them and land ownership often changed, the settlements north and east of the city walls developed to constitute a complex urban mosaic, and included Przedmieście Mikołajskie, the royal town of Kleparz, and the privately owned Wesoła, Lubicz and Biskupie. They all looked like

small towns. Imposing churches and a few palaces were surrounded by irregularly scattered residential timber buildings. Merchants and craftsmen who were active here avoided paying taxes to the Town Hall, thus contributing to the economic decline of Krakow. As a result, in 1791 the City Council decided to incorporate these quarters into Krakow. This part of the city saw the greatest surge in building activity during the great development of Krakow in the second half of the 19th century.

Sights at a Glance

Historic Monuments and Buildings

2 Society of Physicians
6 Astronomical Observatory
8 Former Main Railway Station
10 Grunwald Monument
11 National Bank of Poland
12 Academy of Fine Arts
13 Polish State Railways Headquarters
15 Globe House

Churches and Monasteries

1 Church of St Nicholas
3 Jesuit Church pp136–7
4 Church of the Immaculate Conception of the Virgin Mary
5 Church of the Discalced Carmelite Nuns
9 St Florian's Church
14 Church of St Vincent de Paul
16 Church of the Nuns of the Visitation

Historic Parks

7 Jagiellonian University Botanical Gardens

☐ **Restaurants** see p193
1 Jarema
2 Trzy kroki w szaleństwo

| 0 metres | 300 |
| 0 yards | 300 |

See also Street Finder maps
1, 2 & 3

◄ The metal globe crowning the pyramidal tower of Globe House

For keys to symbols see back flap

Street-by-Street: Along Kopernika Street

Wesoła Quarter, originally a small settlement by the Romanesque Church of St Nicholas, developed along the old route to Mogiła, which is today Kopernika Street (ulica Mikołaja Kopernika). Its skyline was dominated by churches, monasteries and suburban residences of the nobility, set in well-kept gardens. In the 19th century a number of university buildings, mostly hospitals belonging to the Medical School, were built here. Some of these buildings display interesting architectural forms.

❸ ★ **Jesuit Church**
This is one of the most interesting examples of modern ecclesiastical architecture.

❷ ★ **Society of Physicians**
The metal balusters were designed by Stanisław Wyspiański in the Art Nouveau style, featuring sinuous floral ornaments.

A medieval stone pillar to the dead by the Church of St Nicholas is unique. It was originally located in the courtyard of St Valentine's Hospital in Kleparz.

❶ **Church of St Nicholas**
For centuries this church was a landmark of the settlement which developed along the Krakow-Mogiła route.

Kopernika Street
lined densely with trees, is one of the most beautiful streets in Krakow.

Locator Map
See Street Finder maps 1 & 3

❺ Church of the Discalced Carmelite Nuns
The Baroque façade, one of the most beautiful in Krakow, is worth seeing.

❻ Astronomical Observatory
Belonging to the Jagiellonian University, with its elegant architecture and location next to the Botanical Gardens, this observatory looks more like a Neo-Classical villa than a university building.

STRZELECKA

KOPERNIKA

ŚNIADECKICH

❼ Jagiellonian University Botanical Gardens
Exotic and local flora make the gardens a favourite place for days out.

Key

— Suggested route

❹ Church of the Immaculate Conception of the Virgin Mary
The entrance to the Baroque interior is through this monumental portal.

0 metres	50
0 yards	50

Madonna and Child with Saints Adalbert and Stanisław

❶ Church of St Nicholas
Kościół św. Mikołaja

ul. Kopernika 9. **Map** 2 D4 (6 F3). **Tel** 12 431 22 77. 🚋 1, 10, 11, 13, 14, 15, 19, 22, 40. **Open** during services only.

Recorded in the first half of the 13th century, this is one of the oldest churches in Krakow. The remnants of the Romanesque church and a Gothic portal have survived in the chancel. During Swedish occupation, in 1665, the church was plundered and burned and the present church is the result of a Baroque remodelling undertaken between 1677 and 1682. Furnishings were commissioned by the Academy of Krakow, whose patronage over this collegiate foundation goes back to 1465. A coat of arms of the Academy (a shield with crossed maces) decorates the backs of the stalls. The high altar was probably designed by Francesco Placidi. It features an effigy of St Nicholas and architectural decoration forming coulisses. The church also houses a late Gothic triptych, depicting the Coronation of the Virgin, and a Renaissance Madonna and Child with Saints Adalbert and Stanisław, patron saints of Poland. A bronze font, dating from 1536, is worth noting.

It is also of interest that Feliks Dzierżyński, who was to become the founder of the *Cheka* (Bolshevik secret police) and a Bolshevik revolutionary, was married in this church in 1910.

❷ Society of Physicians
Gmach Towarzystwa Lekarskiego

ul. Radziwiłłowska 4. **Map** 2 D4 (6 F2). **Tel** 12 422 75 47. 🚋 1, 10, 11, 13, 14, 15, 19, 22, 40. **Open** 10am–2pm Tue & Fri, 4–8pm Wed.

This building was constructed in 1904 to designs by the architects Władysław Kaczmarski and Józef Sowiński. A rather modest Neo-Classical exterior is in contrast to the sumptuous interior decoration designed by Stanisław Wyspiański. This multi-talented artist created complex decoration in which, typically for the Art Nouveau movement, the arts and crafts complement each other. Wyspiański chose colour schemes for the walls and designed the exquisite stained glass showing *Apollo, The Solar System*, as well as the metal balusters and furniture.

Apollo, The Solar System, a stained-glass window by Stanisław Wyspiański in the Society of Physicians building

❸ Jesuit Church
Kościół Jezuitów

See pp136–7.

The Baroque Church of the Immaculate Conception

❹ Church of the Immaculate Conception of the Virgin Mary
Kościół Niepokalanego Poczęcia NMP

ul. Kopernika 19. **Map** 2 E4. 🚋 2, 10, 11, 13, 14, 15, 19, 40. **Open** 8am–4pm daily and during services.

This church, also known as the Church of St Lazarus, was used in the past by novices of the order of the Discalced Carmelites. The rigidity of the Baroque architecture of this church, built between 1634 and 1680, reflects the strict building regulations of the Carmelite order. Large and complex, the high altar dominates the small interior. Modelled on the high altar in the Carmelite Church of Santa Maria della Scala in Rome, it was made in 1681 of black marble from the Dębnik quarry, which was owned by the Carmelites.

❺ Church of the Discalced Carmelite Nuns
Kościół Karmelitanek Bosych

ul. Kopernika 44. **Map** 2 E4. **Tel** 12 421 41 18. 🚋 124, 152, 522. 🚋 4, 5, 9, 10, 11, 14, 15, 40. **Open** during services only.

A large convent was built in the neighbourhood of the friary of the same order between 1720 and 1732.

The church is small and has a Greek cross groundplan. The interior with its many columns is impressive. The sumptuous façade has elegant decoration in the late Baroque style.

The architect of the church is unknown. Karol Antoni Bay of Warsaw and Kacper Bażanka are considered likely to have designed it. Due to the strict rule of the order, the church is open to the public only during services. The painting on the high altar depicts Saint Theresa of Avila, to whom the church is dedicated.

Portal in the Church of the Discalced Carmelite Nuns

❻ Astronomical Observatory
Obserwatorium Astronomiczne UJ

ul. Kopernika 27. **Map** 2 F4. **Tel** 12 425 14 57. 124, 128, 184, 522. 4, 5, 9, 10, 15, 20, 40. **Closed** to the public.

The establishment of the Observatory in Wesoła was directly linked to the reform of the Academy of Krakow carried out in the 1770s by Hugo Kołłątaj, a task he was given by the Commission for National Education. As a result, experimental sciences gained

a more prominent role in the curriculum. The suburban Jesuit residence, taken over by the Commission after the abolition of the order, was rebuilt to house the Observatory. Stanisław Zawadzki, the architect to King Stanisław Augustus, redesigned the building in an austere Neo-Classical style. He decorated the façade with astronomical signs.

The building is now occupied by the Jagiellonian Botanical Institute. A modern astronomical observatory is located in the former Skała fortress in Bielany.

❼ Jagiellonian University Botanical Gardens
Ogród botaniczny UJ

ul. Kopernika 27a. **Map** 2 F4. **Tel** 12 421 26 20. 124, 184, 502. 4, 5, 9, 10, 15, 19, 40. **Open** May–Aug: 9am– 7pm, Sep–Oct: 9am–5pm. Greenhouses: **Open** 10am–6pm Sat–Thu. Museum of Botanical Gardens: **Open** 10am–2pm Wed & Fri, 11am–3pm Sun.

Next to the Observatory, the Botanical Gardens of the Jagiellonian University are located on the former grounds and lodge of the Czartoryski family. The gardens were established in 1780 by Jan Jaśkiewicz and designed by the Viennese gardener Franz Kaiser. A 500-year-old oak tree in the depths of the garden, as well as exotic and native plants, are particularly worth seeing. Also of interest are late-Gothic pillars, originally from the Collegium Maius, used here as plinths supporting plant pots.

Two of the gardens' palm houses are interesting examples of 19th-century architectural structures. They are

Flowers in the Botanical Gardens

complemented by a third, 20th-century palm house designed by Stanisław Juszczyk and built in 1964 to mark the 6th centenary of the Jagiellonian University. Busts of celebrated botanists decorate the gardens.

❽ Former Main Railway Station
Budynek dawnego dworca głównego

Pl. Kolejowy 1. **Map** 2 D3 (6 F1). most bus and tram routes.

A railway link was established in 1847 between Krakow and Silesia, known as the Northern, or Franz Joseph Railway. Between 1844 and 1847 a new station was built north of the city. Designed by Piotr Rosenbaum, it was considered to be one of the most elegant stations in Europe. It was later rebuilt. In 1898 Teodor Talowski constructed a viaduct next to the station, in the Romanesque Revival style. The building is no longer in use as a station, and ticket offices are now under the platforms nearby.

Krakow's Former Main Railway Station

❸ Jesuit Church

This monumental church was built between 1909 and 1921 to designs by the architect Franciszek Mączyński. He applied a number of historic styles which he modified and combined in new ways. What he created is one of the most interesting ecclesiastical buildings of the first quarter of the 20th century in Poland. Leading artists worked on the interior. Karol Hukan carved sculptures for the altars, while Jan Bukowski painted murals of striking beauty and designed unusual confessionals. The mosaic above the high altar is by Piotr Stachiewicz, and the south portal facing Kopernika Street was designed by Xawery Dunikowski. A small statue of Mączyński on the exterior of the east wall is also by Dunikowski.

★ South Portal
The main entrance to the church is through this monumental portal. Note the exquisite ornaments and figures which are both regarded as outstanding examples of Polish sculpture of the early 20th century.

Mosaic in the Porch
Made of mosaic pieces in vivid colours and set against a shiny background, the figures of Mary and Child have an almost unreal, mystical appearance.

Entrance

Murals decorating the Nave Vaulting
These murals contribute to the rich and monumental character of the interior. They were painted by Jan Bukowski, who also executed decoration in other churches in Krakow, including St Mary's and the Bernardine Nuns' church, as well as the Loretto Chapel by the Capuchin Church.

★ Altar of St Joseph
Altars in the aisles were made by the sculptor Karol Hukan. Of particular interest is the altar of St Joseph, made in 1922 to 1923. It features this figurative group, which is rich in dynamic and wavy forms.

Confessional
The confessionals were designed by Jan Bukowski, Professor of the Industrial School of Art, in the style of the Baroque Revival and are freely decorated with ornaments.

High Altar
The design of the high altar, featuring a half-dome supported by a free-standing colonnade, was influenced by Italian Renaissance architecture. The statues above the altar portray Christ and Jesuit saints.

Statue of Franciszek Mączyński
The Jesuit Church was Mączyński's most important design. His statue, outside the east wall, is by Xawery Dunikowski.

KEY

① **Side porch and tower**

② **Mosaic above the high altar**

Street-by-Street: Matejko Square

Kleparz, an independent settlement north of Krakow, was granted a municipal charter in 1366. It was incorporated into Krakow in 1791. After the introduction of the railway, Kleparz developed rapidly around the railway station. In the heart of the quarter, the empty space in front of the Barbican was transformed into an elegant square welcoming visitors to Krakow, arriving here by rail or approaching the city from the north, via Warszawska Street.

⓾ ★ Grunwald Monument
The making of this monument helped to stimulate patriotic feelings in the late 19th century. It is dedicated "to the ancestors' glory and to the brethren with hope".

⓬ Academy of Fine Arts
The Academy houses a collection of works by its leading professors and students, including a *Self-Portrait* by Jacek Malczewski.

A bust of Jan Matejko,
carved by Jan Tombiński, can be found above the main entrance to the Academy of Fine Arts. Another monument to the artist is located near the Barbican.

Monument to Jan Matejko

Barbican

Tomb of the Unknown Soldier

⓫ National Bank of Poland
The Allegories of Industry and Agriculture, carved by Karol Hukan, decorate the façade of this bank.

0 metres   50
0 yards   50

Key
— Suggested route

⑭ Church of St Vincent de Paul
This church was built from 1875 to 1887 to designs by Filip Pokutyński. The façade was inspired by Italian medieval architecture.

Locator Map
See Street Finder maps 1 & 3

The Church of the Sisters of Charity was built by Filip Pokutyński from 1869 to 1871.

⑨ ★ St Florian's Church
In days gone by life in Kleparz centred around this collegiate church. The effigy of St Florian by Jan Tricius decorates the high altar.

⑬ Polish State Railways Headquarters
This was the most opulent building erected in Krakow at the end of the 19th century.

Elegant town houses at Matejko Square show a range of different architectural styles of the early 20th century.

The Baroque altar of St John of Kęty in St Florian's Church

❾ St Florian's Church
Kościół św. Floriana

ul. Warszawska 1B. **Map** 2 D3. **Tel** 12 422 48 42. 🚌 124, 152, 154, 192. **Open** during services only.

In 1184 Duke Kazimierz the Just received the relics of St Florian from Pope Lucius III and decided to deposit them in Krakow. The horses which drew the carriage carrying the relics of the martyr stopped suddenly in Kleparz, before reaching the city's gate, and refused to move forward. This was interpreted as a miraculous sign indicating where the relics should be placed. The church was, therefore, built on this spot between 1185 and 1212. After the capital was transferred to Warsaw, the church came to prominence as it was used to receive the deceased royalty brought from Warsaw for burial at Wawel. The funeral processions started here.

The church was damaged by frequent invasions and no trace of the medieval architecture has remained. The present interior and its decoration date from 1677 to 1684. The high altar with an effigy of St Florian, painted by Jan Tricius in the late 17th century, as well as an incomplete late-Gothic altar of St John the Baptist are of interest. The exterior was entirely remodelled by Franciszek Mączyński in the early 20th century.

❿ Grunwald Monument
Pomnik Grunwaldzki

Pl. J Matejki. **Map** 2 D3 (6 E1). 🚌 154, 192, 304. 🚋 2, 4, 7, 13, 15, 20, 24.

The monument, featuring King Władysław Jagiełło on horseback, was raised to mark the 500th anniversary of the 1410 victory at Grunwald (Tannenberg in German) over the Teutonic Knights. It was commissioned by the statesman, composer and pianist, Ignacy Jan Paderewski, from the sculptor Antoni Wiwulski.

The monument was inspired by grandiose German monuments of the second half of the 19th century. It was generally well received but some critics mocked the theatrical treatment of the figures. Some even suggested that the only lifelike figure was that of the dead Grand Master Ulrich von Jungingen. The monument was destroyed by the Nazis in 1939 and only reconstructed in 1975 by the sculptor Marian Konieczny.

⓫ National Bank of Poland

ul. Basztowa 20. **Map** 2 D3 (6 E1). **Tel** 12 618 58 00. 🚌 124, 152, 522. 🚋 2, 4, 7, 13, 15, 20, 24. **Open** 7am–5pm Mon–Fri.

The bank, built between 1921 and 1925 by the architects Teodor Hoffman and Kazimierz Wyczyński, exemplifies the Neo-Classical style which became popular during the inter-war years. Neo-Classicism was then applied to important public buildings housing administrative and financial institutions, and was in sharp contrast to the Functionalism favoured in left-wing circles. The exterior sculptural decoration is by Karol Hukan and Stanisław Popławski. Inside, the domed banking hall is worth a visit.

The Academy of Fine Arts in Renaissance Revival style

⓬ Academy of Fine Arts

Pl. J Matejki 13. **Map** 2 D3 (6 E1). **Tel** 12 299 20 14. 🚌 154, 192, 304. 🚋 4, 7, 13, 15, 20. Museum: by appointment only.

The school of Fine Arts in Krakow gained independent status in 1873 through the efforts of the artist Jan Matejko. Three years later the school was allocated a plot in Kleparz by the city's authorities. The building was constructed in 1879 to 1880 to designs by Maciej Moraczewski. The architect adopted the

The imposing building of the National Bank of Poland

Renaissance Revival style for this building, in accordance with the spirit of 19th-century Historicism which favoured such forms for school architecture. On the first floor is a studio where Matejko painted his *Kościuszko at Racławice* and *The Vows of King Jan Kazimierz*.

In 1900 the school gained university status, becoming the Academy of Fine Arts. Some of the best Polish artists were among its students. The building in Kleparz is currently the seat of the Academy's governing body and houses the faculties of painting, printmaking and sculpture.

⓭ Polish State Railways Headquarters

Pl. J Matejki 12. **Map** 2 D3 (6 E1). 🚌 154, 192, 304. 🚊 4, 7, 13, 15, 20. **Closed** to the public.

This imposing building was constructed in 1888 by an unknown Viennese architect who combined the forms of both Romanesque and Baroque Revival into an eclectic whole. It is possibly the only building in Krakow to have been directly influenced by the 19th-century monumental architecture of its Austrian neighbour, Vienna.

⓮ Church of St Vincent de Paul
Kościół św. Wincentego de Paul

ul. Św. Filipa 19. **Map** 2 D3. **Tel** 12 429 25 33. 🚌 124, 502. 🚊 4, 7, 13, 15, 20. **Open** during services only.

The present church was built between 1875 and 1877 and replaced the medieval Church of Saints Philip and James which had been dismantled by the Austrian authorities in 1801. The architect, Filip Pokutyński, was inspired by Italian late-Romanesque architecture. Although modest in design, the church differs from other 19th-century ecclesiastical

The interior of St Vincent de Paul

architecture in Krakow because of its clear, compact and monu-mental forms.

The side altar features a miraculous icon depicting Christ Crucified. This much venerated image was brought after World War II from Milatyn near L'viv.

⓯ Globe House
Dom pod Globusem

ul. Długa 1. **Map** 1 C3. 🚌 124, 502. 🚊 4, 7, 12, 13, 15, 20.

This house was built in 1904 to 1906 for the Chamber of Commerce and Industry. It was designed by the architects Franciszek Mączyński and Tadeusz Stryjeński. The building is considered to be one of the best examples of the Art Nouveau style in Polish architecture. It is an interesting asymmetrical structure dominated by a pyramidal tower topped by a globe. The interior decoration, including murals in the great hall, is mainly the work of Józef Mehoffer.

The Globe House, a prime example of Art Nouveau architecture, topped by a pyramidal tower and globe

Stained-glass windows above the stairs depict allegorical subjects such as the progress of mankind through industry and commerce, thus reflecting the function of the building. The several cast-iron decorations are also of interest. Today, the building houses the publishers Wydawnictwo Literackie.

The façade of the Church of the Nuns of the Visitation

⓰ Church of the Nuns of the Visitation
Kościół Wizytek

ul. Krowoderska 16. **Map** 1 C3. **Tel** 12 632 16 28. 🚊 3, 5, 19. **Open** during services only.

The convent was founded by Bishop Jan Małachowski as a votive offering after he was miraculously saved from drowning in the Vistula. The church is an interesting example of Krakow's Baroque ecclesiastical architecture. It was built from 1686 to 1695 by Giovanni Solari.

The façade is richly decorated with sculptures and ornaments. Some lavish decoration is also characteristic of the interior which, although small, is very elegant. The unusual high altar was made in 1695 by the sculptor Jerzy Golonka. The plasterwork is by Jan Liskowicz. The 18th-century murals decorating the vault have been much altered.

PIASEK AND NOWY ŚWIAT

Piasek, known as Garbary until the 19th century, is located west of the Old Quarter. Its development was hindered in the past by the lack of fortifications and frequent invasions. A number of settlements with independent jurisdictions were located between Garbary and Wawel. They included Groble, Smoleńsko, Wielkorządowa, Wygoda, Retoryka and Rybaki, as well as Nowy Świat which remained under Krakow's jurisdiction.

All these settlements were integrated by the Austrian authorities. By the end of the 19th century Piasek (Sand) and Nowy Świat (New World) began to flourish; wealthy residents moved in, drawn by the pleasant and tranquil atmosphere away from the noisy town centre. As a result, some of the best residential architecture can be found here. It is mostly eclectic in style, dating from the start of the 20th century.

Sights at a Glance

Historic Monuments and Buildings
1 Philharmonic Hall
2 Former Museum of Industry and Technology
6 House of the Singing Frog
7 Europeum
8 Małopolska Garden of Arts
14 Wyspiański Monument
16 School of Chemistry
17 Jagiellonian Library
18 Academy of Mines and Metallurgy, Main Building
21 Spider House

Museums and Galleries
10 Emeryk Hutten-Czapski Museum
12 Józef Mehoffer House Museum
15 National Museum in Krakow, Main Building pp150–51

Churches
3 Church of the Felician Nuns
4 Church of the Merciful God
9 Church of the Sisters of the Sacred Heart of Jesus
11 Capuchin Church
22 Carmelite Church

Historic Streets
5 Retoryka Street
19 Avenue of Three Poets
20 Karmelicka Street

Open Space
13 Błonia Fields

Restaurants see p193
1 Biała Róża
2 CK Browar
3 Dynia Resto-Bar
4 Mamma Mia
5 The Olive
6 Smakołyki
7 Solfeż
8 Someplace Else
9 Zielona Kuchnia

0 metres 200
0 yards 200

See also Street Finder maps 1 & 5

◀ The statue of St Barbara on the roof of the Academy of Mines and Metallurgy

For keys to symbols *see back flap*

Street-by-Street: Piłsudski Street

Józefa Piłsudskiego (formerly Wolska) Street formed part of the route connecting Krakow with Wola Justowska. This route was first recorded in the 16th century. After Nowy Świat and the neighbouring jurisdictions were incorporated into Krakow, it became one of the main avenues in this part of town. The vista formed by the street is closed by the vast Błonia Fields with Kościuszko Mound in the distance, behind which Piłsudski Mound can also be seen. Elegant residential and public architecture developed here by the end of the 19th century. Some of the buildings show Polish architecture at its best.

❾ Church of the Sisters of the Sacred Heart of Jesus
The square in front of this church was once a flood plain of the Rudawa river which was filled in prior to the construction of the convent buildings.

❻ House of the Singing Frog
This house was designed by Teodor Talowski and is decorated with some exquisite, though somewhat overdone, sculptures of fantastic creatures.

JÓZEFA PIŁSUDSKIEGO

RETORYKA

0 metres 50
0 yards 50

Key
— Suggested route

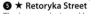

❺ ★ Retoryka Street
The houses designed by Teodor Talowski have a unique "antiquarian" look and contribute to the picturesque character of the street.

⓾ Emeryk Hutten-Czapski Museum
This monster decorates the exhibition pavilion in which Emeryk Hutten-Czapski housed the numismatic collection he brought to Krakow.

Locator Map
See Street Finder maps 1 & 5

❶ Philharmonic Hall
The Hall received a state-of-the-art organ following refurbishment after a fire in 1991.

❷ Former Museum of Industry and Technology
This is one of the most interesting examples of Modernist architecture in Poland.

❸ Church of the Felician Nuns
The church was designed by Feliks Księżarski. Its interior is one of the few examples of Romanesque Revival ecclesiastical architecture in Krakow.

❹ Church of the Merciful God
This memorial plaque of an unknown knight is an exceptional Gothic work surrounded by 19th-century architecture.

The exterior of the Neo-Classical Philharmonic Hall

❶ Philharmonic Hall
Filharmonia

ul. Zwierzyniecka 1. **Map** 1 B5 (5 C3).
Tel 12 422 94 77. 124, 152, 502.
1, 2, 8, 18.

The Society of Friends of Music which was active in Krakow between 1817 and 1884 was regarded as the first philharmonic organization in occupied Poland. The Szymanowski State Philharmonia was established in Krakow in 1945. Walery Bierdiajew, Andrzej Panufnik and Krzysztof Penderecki were among the principal conductors. The orchestra and choir are complemented by the renowned chamber orchestra, Capella Cracoviensis. The Hall is housed in the former Catholic Cultural Institution. It was built between 1928 and 1930 by Pokutyński and Filipkiewicz in the Neo-Classical style which was popular with Polish architects around 1930.

❷ Former Museum of Industry and Technology
Gmach dawnego Muzeum Techniczno - Przemysłowego

ul. Smoleńsk 9. **Map** 1 B5 (5 B3).
124, 152, 502. 1, 2, 8, 18.

This museum was established in 1868 by Andrzej Baraniecki who presented the city with his library and large collection of decorative arts. The museum

ran courses in fine art, as well as a school of painting for women, and workshops on crafts. Collaboration with other institutions at the forefront of modern design was established. The museum published a number of titles, including journals such as *Przegląd Techniczny* (Technical Revue) and *Architekt* (The Architect). It also played an important role in the development of Polish applied art.

The museum was initially housed in the west wing of the Franciscan friary. The new building was constructed in 1908–14 to designs by Tadeusz Stryjeński. Józef Czajkowski designed the elegant façade, which is rich in geometrical forms. The structure of the building, which uses reinforced concrete, was novel at the time and the layout of the rooms was unusual. It is a leading example of Modernist architecture in Poland. The Museum of Industry and Technology was closed down in 1952. Today the Faculty of Industrial Design of the Academy of Fine Arts is housed here.

Façade detail, former Museum of Industry and Technology

❸ Church of the Felician Nuns
Kościół Felicjanek

ul. Smoleńsk 4/6. **Map** 1 B5 (5 B3).
Tel 12 422 08 37. 124, 152, 502.
2, 5, 8, 18. **Open** 8:30am–6pm daily and during services.

The church of the Felician Nuns is one of the largest churches built in Krakow in the 19th century. This basilica in the Romanesque Revival style was built between 1882 and 1884 to designs by Feliks Księżarski, but modified by Sebastian Jaworzyński. The monumental and austere forms are striking, but softened inside through lavish decoration of the altars. The church houses relics of Blessed Maria Angela Truszkowska, the foundress of the Order, who died in 1899.

Altar of Blessed Maria Angela, Church of the Felician Nuns

❹ Church of the Merciful God
Kościół Miłosierdzia Bożego

ul. Bożego Miłosierdzia 1. **Map** 1 B5 (5 B3). 2, 5, 8, 15, 18. **Open** during services only.

In 1555 Jan Żukowski established in Nowy Świat a home for the destitute and a small church. The church was consecrated in 1665. Located outside the city wall, both buildings were badly damaged during a number of invasions. The church has survived. On the outside wall facing Smoleńsk Street, remnants of a Gothic sepulchre, with a kneeling figure of a knight, can be seen.

Among the rather modest Baroque furnishings, the one of most interest is the image of the *Misericordia Domini* (The Suffering Christ and Sorrowful Mary) of 1650, hanging in the chancel.

Adjacent to the church is a presbytery, built in the eclectic style in 1905–6 by Jan Zubrzycki.

❺ Retoryka Street
Ulica Retoryka

Map 1 B5 (5 B3, 4). 🚋 15, 18.

The name of this street comes from the Retoryka jurisdiction, which was established in this area by the Ossolińskis in the first half of the 18th century. In the late 19th century the construction of boulevards began along the Rudawa river, which ran here. They were lined with houses whose architecture was marked by imaginative forms and unusual decoration. In 1910 the river was enclosed in a tunnel beneath street level. The houses designed by Teodor Talowski are most interesting. He used pseudo-antiquarian, intentionally damaged motifs such as mosaics and plaques bearing popular Latin inscriptions for the external decoration. The plaque on his own house reads *festina lente* (hasten slowly) and that on the Ass House, *faber est suae quisque fortunae* (one makes one's own destiny).

The houses in Retoryka Street, designed by Talowski and other leading architects active in Krakow around 1900, are interesting examples of Polish architecture at the dawn of the modern age.

❻ House of the Singing Frog
Dom Pod Śpiewającą Żabą

ul. Retoryka 1. **Map** 1 B5 (5 B3).
🚋 15, 18.

The corner house at No. 1 Retoryka Street is considered

House of the Singing Frog

to be the most interesting of Talowski's designs. It was built in 1889 to 1890. The unusual structure consists of a number of segments varying in height and decoration. It was intended to be viewed at an angle from the adjacent street corner. The name of the house is a joke which refers to both the function and location of the building: it used to house a music school whose singing students were often accompanied by croaking frogs in the nearby Rudawa river.

❼ Europeum

Pl. Sikorskiego 6. **Map** 1 B4 (5 B2).
Tel 12 433 57 60. 🚌 124, 152, 192.
🚋 15, 18, 20. **Open** 10am–6pm Tue–Sat, 10am–4pm Sun. 🎫 free on Sun.

The Europeum is home to the most important assemblage of non-Polish European works of art in the National Museum in Krakow collection. Notable exhibits include works by

Lorenzo Lotto, Pieter Brueghel the Younger and Paolo Veneziano.

The gallery is housed in a renovated 17th-century granary set on a quiet, tree-lined square. At the back of the museum is an intriguing collection of masonry fragments from historic buildings all over the city.

❽ Małopolska Garden of Arts
Małopolski Ogród Sztuki

ul. Rajska 12. **Map** 1 B4 (5 B1).
Tel 12 375 21 50. 🚌 114, 139, 159, 164, 169, 192. 🚋 4, 8, 13, 14.
Open from 9am; closing times vary.
🌐 mos.art.pl

This multifunctional arts complex features several exhibition spaces, a concert hall, a small cinema and a delightful café, all wrapped up in a strikingly contemporary building that consists of a slatted clay façade, glass frame, industrial beams and a garden courtyard. Opened in 2012, the Małopolska Garden of Arts was built on and around buildings belonging to the Juliusz Słowacki Theatre as a joint project by the theatre and the regional government. The semi-enclosed spaces at the front and side of the building are wonderfully peaceful areas in which to sit and relax, and there are always events or exhibitions taking place inside. Many of Krakow's biggest cultural festivals now use the centre as their main venue.

The striking exterior of the Małopolska Garden of Arts

❾ Church of the Sisters of the Sacred Heart of Jesus
Kościół Sercanek

ul. Garncarska 26. **Map** 1 B5 (5 B3).
Tel 12 422 57 66. 🚋 15, 18.
Open during services only.

The Convent of the Sisters of the Sacred Heart of Jesus was built between 1895 and 1900 to designs by Władysław Kaczmarski and Sławomir Odrzywolski. The architects designed the building along Garncarska Street so as to close one side of a square located here. They adjusted the façade of the church and the adjoining buildings of the convent to fit the slight bend in the street. This explains the irregularity of the plan.

The church is eclectic in style. The exterior walls show bare brickwork, ornamented in the Romanesque Revival style, as well as with pseudo-Renaissance *sgraffiti* and Neo-Classical sculptures by Jan Tombiński. Furnishings display Neo-Romanesque forms.

Detail from the Church of the Sisters of the Sacred Heart of Jesus

❿ Emeryk Hutten-Czapski Museum
Muzeum im Emeryka Hutten-Czapskiego

ul. Piłsudskiego 12. **Map** 1 B5 (5 B3).
Tel 12 422 27 33. 🚋 15, 18.
Open Access to the collection for professional researchers only.

This small palace in the Renaissance Revival style was built in 1884 by the architect

The Emeryk Hutten-Czapski Museum, in the Renaissance Revival style

Antoni Siedek for Hubert Krasiński. A few years later the property was purchased by Emeryk Hutten-Czapski who moved from the Vilnius area, bringing with him an exquisite numismatic collection. A pavilion, purpose-built to house this collection, was added in 1896. It was designed by Tadeusz Stryjeński and Zygmunt Hendel. The inscription decorating the pavilion reads *Monumentis Patriae naufragio ereptis* (To the national heritage salvaged from destruction). In 1903 the Czapskis bequeathed the palace and collection to the city of Krakow.

Today the palace is the seat of the directors of the National Museum and houses the Museum's special holdings. A collection of salvaged architectural fragments can be found outside.

⓫ Capuchin Church
Kościół Kapucynów

ul. Loretańska 11. **Map** 1 B4 (5 B2).
Tel 12 422 18 03. 🚌 124, 152, 192, 502. 🚋 2, 4, 8, 13, 14, 15, 18.
Open 9:30am–4:30pm and 5–7pm daily as well as during services.

The Capuchin friars arrived in Krakow in 1695. They began constructing the church and friary a year later. The work was supervised at first by Carlo Ceroni, who was later succeeded by Martino Pellegrini. The architecture and furnishings, the latter dating from 1775, reflect the strict rule of the Order which espouses extreme poverty. Hence the simplicity and functionalism

of the architecture and the modest composition of the altars made of painted timber and lacking decoration. The altars, however, feature good paintings. They include *The Annunciation* by Pietro Dandini, *St Erasmus and St Cajetan*, two 18th-century effigies by Łukasz Orłowski, and *St Francis of Assisi* by Szymon Czechowicz. A number of sepulchres are of interest. A wooden crucifix in front of the church indicates the tomb of the Confederates of Bar who fell in a rebellion against the Russians in 1768.

Between 1712 and 1719 an external Loreto Chapel was built to a design by Kacper Bażanka; this is linked to the church through a cloister. The chapel houses a Neo-Classical altar with a miraculous statue of the Madonna of Loreto and a beautiful tabernacle. The latter was also designed by Bażanka. An animated Christmas crib is erected here every year, featuring historic Polish characters.

The interior of the Loreto Chapel by the Capuchin Church

⑫ Józef Mehoffer House Museum
Muzeum Józefa Mehoffera

ul. Krupnicza 26. **Map** 1 B4 (5 B2). **Tel** 12 433 58 80. 🚌 124, 152, 173, 179, 502, 512. 🚋 2, 4, 8, 12, 13, 15, 18, 24. **Open** 10am–4pm Wed–Sun. 🎟️ free Sun.

Stanisław Wyspiański was born in this house in 1869. In 1930 it was bought by Józef Mehoffer (1869–1946), one of the foremost Modernist artists in Poland. He was also a painter and a stage and interior designer. In 1968 the house was acquired by the National Museum and the Józef Mehoffer House Museum was established. The interiors have been preserved in the tasteful way they were arranged by the artist himself. Many of his works, including paintings, stained glass, cartoons for stained glass and murals, are on display.

Portrait of Mrs Mehoffer by Józef Mehoffer

⑬ Błonia Fields

Map 1 A5. 🚌 114, 134, 152, 164, 173, 179, 192, 292. 🚋 15, 18.

The Błonia Fields formed part of the grounds owned by the Convent of Premonstratensian (Norbertine) Nuns in Zwierzyniec and were originally used as pastures. In 1366 the nuns made a rather bad deal with the city's authorities and exchanged Błonia for a house in Floriańska Street. The house proved to be unprofitable and was eventually destroyed by fire. This gave rise to a joke about the nuns who had exchanged pastures for a bonfire. For centuries the nuns tried in vain to regain the land. The Błonia Fields remain the property of the City of Krakow.

Błonia were used in the past as a venue for mass religious and national celebrations. The first football match in Krakow took place here in 1894. Pope John Paul II said a Holy Mass here on four occasions. Today it is a wildlife sanctuary in the centre of Krakow and a popular place for recreation. It should, however, be avoided on days when football matches between Wisła and Cracovia take place.

⑭ Wyspiański Monument
Pomnik S. Wyspiańskiego

Map 1 A5 (5 A3). 🚌 114, 164, 173, 179.

The monument was unveiled in 1982 to mark the 75th anniversary of the death of the great artist and playwright of the so-called Young Poland movement (Polish Modernism). The sculptor, Marian Konieczny, depicted Stanisław Wyspiański surrounded by the characters from two of his plays, *The Wedding* and *November Night*. The monument was badly received and prompted unfavourable interpretations. Its location, right behind the parking place in front of the National Museum, proved to be particularly unfortunate as the figures seem to emerge from behind parked cars. The agitated gestures of the figures have even been interpreted as an expression of their astonishment at the fast rate of automobile development.

⑮ National Museum in Krakow, Main Building

See pp150–51.

⑯ School of Chemistry
Zespół Szkół Chemicznych

ul. Krupnicza 44. **Map** 1 A4 (5 A2). **Tel** 12 422 32 20. 🚌 114, 164, 169, 173, 179. **Closed** to the public.

In 1834 the Institute of Technology was established in Krakow, funded by the bequest of the architect Szczepan Humbert. It was later transformed into the State School of Industry. In 1912 the school moved to a new building designed by Sławomir Odrzywolski. This irregular brick structure, decorated with Art Nouveau ornaments, now houses the School of Chemistry.

Wyspiański Monument

⑮ National Museum in Krakow, Main Building

The modern building of the National Museum in Krakow was designed by Czesław Boratyński, Edward Kreisler and Bolesław Schmidt in 1934 but the building was not completed until 1989. Permanent galleries display Polish painting and sculpture of the 20th century, decorative arts and arms and other mementos of the Polish Army. Temporary shows are also organized here. The art collection is one of the largest in Poland and includes works by leading Modernist artists, as well as some outstanding works from the period between the two World Wars. Post-1945 art, however, predominates.

★ *Polonia*, a Cartoon for Stained Glass
Stanisław Wyspiański's cartoons for stained-glass windows in the Cathedral symbolically depict visions of the past but also relate to modern issues.

First floor

Nike of the Legions
This is one of Jacek Malczewski's symbolic *tours de force*. Nike, the goddess of victory, is sitting by the body of a legionary whose face resembles Józef Piłsudski.

The Uniform of Józef Piłsudski
"The uniform of the grey rifleman" reminds one of the tragic but nevertheless victorious history of the Polish Legions between 1914 and 1917.

Audiovisual room

Ground floor

Library and Reading Room

Mace
This gilded "buzdygan" mace belonged to Grand Hetman Stanisław Jabłonowski, who fought in the Battle of Vienna in 1683.

Main entrance

Education Room

Second floor

Emballage (1975)
This work by Tadeusz Kantor is an artistic
interpretation of Jan Matejko's great history
piece depicting *The Prussian Homage*.

Execution (1949)
The art of Andrzej
Wróblewski, who
died prematurely, is
a personal analysis
of the tragic
war years.

Self-Portrait with Masks
This self-portrait by Wojciech
Weiss (1875–1950) dates from
the early years when the artist
remained under the influence
of Symbolism.

★ **A Design for Mickiewicz's
Statue in Vilnius**
This monumental statue by the
Cubist artist Zbigniew Pronaszko
(1885–1958) was never executed
and exists only as a model.

Key

- Temporary exhibitions
- Arms and Uniforms in Poland
- Gallery of Polish Art of the 20th Century
- Gallery of Decorative Arts
- Non-exhibition space

Gallery Guide

*Temporary displays and the exhibition "Arms and
Uniforms in Poland" are located on the ground floor.
The display on the first floor is dedicated to decorative
arts and temporary exhibitions. The Gallery of Polish
Art of the 20th Century is housed on the second floor.*

⑰ Jagiellonian Library
Biblioteka Jagiellońska

ul. Oleandry 3. **Map** 1 A4 (5 A2). **Tel** 12 633 09 03. 🚋 15, 18. 🚌 114, 144, 164, 169, 173, 179, 194. **Open** 8:15am–8:50pm Mon–Fri, 9am–4pm Sat.

For many centuries the Library of the Jagiellonian University was housed in the Collegium Maius (see pp108–9). The new building was constructed between 1931 and 1939 to designs by Wacław Krzyżanowski. It has impressive modern forms and a spacious and functional interior. It is not only the success of the design but also the high quality of craftsmanship and the use of luxurious materials that make this building an outstanding example of Krakow's architecture in the interwar years.

During the 1990s work was undertaken on a new wing of the Library, designed by Romuald Loegler. This was completed in 2001, when the University celebrated the 6th centenary of its re-establishment. The additional wing matches the forms of the old building and is one of the most interesting examples of architecture of the 1990s.

The Library's holdings include 25,000 priceless manuscripts and 100,000 rare books and prints.

⑱ Academy of Mines and Metallurgy, Main Building

Al. Mickiewicza 30. **Map** 1 A3, 4 (5 A1). **Tel** 12 617 33 33. 🚌 114, 144, 164, 169, 173, 179, 194. **Open** 7:30am–8pm daily.

The Academy of Mines was established in Krakow in 1919. In 1922 the Faculty of Metallurgy was added. After 1945 the Academy was transformed into a large and well-equipped technological university. It has its own nuclear reactor and modern acoustic laboratory. The enormous main building, with 110,000 sq m (1,183,600 sq ft)

Statues in front of the Academy of Mines and Metallurgy

of floor space, was built between 1923 and 1935. It was designed by Sławomir Odrzywolski and Wacław Krzyżanowski in a Neo-Classical style that is particularly prominent in the façade and portico. The statues of miners and steel workers in front of the building are by Jan Raszka.

In German-occupied Poland the building became the seat of the Governor-General. A museum housed in Building C-1 is dedicated to the history of the Academy.

⑲ Avenue of Three Poets
Aleje Trzech Wieszczów

Map 1 A3, 1 A4, 1 B2, 1 C2. 🚌 114, 129, 139, 144, 164, 173, 179.

In the mid-19th century an earthen embankment was constructed along what is today this avenue, and in 1887 to 1888 a railway line was laid for trains connecting Krakow to Płaszów. East of the embankment, new streets were laid out and new houses constructed in the eclectic and Art Nouveau styles. When in 1910 the borders of Krakow were extended, the railway and the embankment were dismantled. Their site was replaced by a wide avenue comprising a dual carriageway with a belt of greenery in the middle. Each of the sections of the avenue was named after a Romantic poet: Krasiński, Mickiewicz and Słowacki. The intention was to transform the avenue into Krakow's Champs Elysées.

An illuminated page in the Behem Codex, Jagiellonian Library

A view looking down Karmelicka Street

⑳ Karmelicka Street
Ulica Karmelicka

Map 1 B3, 5 (B1, C1). 🚌 114, 159, 164, 169, 179. 🚋 4, 8, 13, 14.

Karmelicka Street formed part of the old route connecting Krakow to Czarna Wieś and Łobzów. Formerly known as Czarna, Karmelicka was always the main street in the Garbary quarter. The Carmelite Church and, at No. 12, the Town Hall of Garbary were built here. Initially the street was divided into two parts: the wider part stretched from the Cobblers' Gate to a small bridge, beyond which the street narrowed considerably. This explains why the Carmelite friary building projects into the present-day street.

By the end of the 19th century Karmelicka became one of the most elegant streets in Krakow. Splendid houses were built to designs by Maksymilian Nitsch, Teodor Talowski and Filip Pokutyński. The writers Stanisław Przybyszewski and Tadeusz Boy-Żeleński were among the celebrated residents.

㉑ Spider House
Dom pod Pająkiem

ul. Karmelicka 35. **Map** 1 B3 (5 B1). 🚋 4, 8, 13, 14. **Closed** to the public.

This house was built in 1889 by Teodor Talowski, one of the leading architects in Krakow in the late 19th century. His intention was to give this irregular structure "an ancient appearance" by adding a "Gothic" round corner tower and a high gable in the style of Netherlandish Mannerism. By using different architectural styles of the past he wanted to pretend that the house had been rebuilt many times. He inserted, for example, a parapet modelled on the Renaissance Cloth Hall into the crenellated "Gothic" frieze. The decoration is rich in inventive detail.

㉒ Carmelite Church
Kościół Karmelitów

ul. Karmelicka 19. **Map** 1 B3 (5 C1). **Tel** 12 632 67 52. 🚌 114, 139, 159, 164, 169, 192. 🚋 4, 8, 13, 14. **Open** 9:30am–4:30pm and 5–7pm daily and during services.

According to a legend, Duke Władysław Herman cured his skin disease by rubbing sand on the infected areas. He took the sand from a site miraculously indicated by the Virgin Mary.

This site was therefore named Piasek (sand), and a votive church founded by the duke was built in 1087. Thus was born the legend of the Madonna of the Sand.

The church was actually founded by Queen Jadwiga in 1395. It was almost entirely destroyed during the Swedish invasion in the 17th century and its remnants were incorporated into the new Baroque church which was consecrated in 1679. The magnificent high altar, made in 1698 to 1699, and lavishly decorated with acanthus leaves, is worth noting. The splendid stalls and the balcony with the organ, both by Jan Hankis, are also of interest. An icon of the Madonna of the Sand, painted directly on the wall, is much venerated.

The Calvary Chapel in the side wall of the Carmelite Church

Queen Jadwiga (Hedwig)

Queen Jadwiga (c. 1374–99) was famous for her piety and charity. She contributed to the development of the Academy of Krakow. Venerated since the Middle Ages, she was finally canonized in 1997. A touching legend links Jadwiga to the Carmelite Church. It tells the story of a mason employed at the construction of the church who lamented to Jadwiga about his poverty and lack of money to buy medicine for his wife. The Queen removed a gold brooch from her shoe and offered it to the man. The imprint of her foot can still be seen today.

The imprint of Queen Jadwiga's foot

FURTHER AFIELD

Lesser Poland is the most densely populated and richest region of the former Polish-Lithuanian Commonwealth. Until the 17th century the local nobility held the highest offices and played an important political role at the royal court of Krakow, influencing matters of state. The nobles spent their time carrying out official duties in the capital as well as staying in their country estates, where they built castles, churches and monasteries. They introduced the art and culture of Krakow to the rest of Lesser Poland. In the centuries that followed, Krakow continued to dictate

the local fashion and was a centre of artists for the whole province. Krakow's strong influence over neighbouring regions contributed to their unique artistic climate, in which the elitist merged with the vernacular, often with surprising effects. To appreciate the long tradition of Krakow's links with the area, visitors should consider excursions out of town. They are ideal for those who are interested in historic or traditional architecture and places of historical interest, as well as those who like to relax in beautiful natural surroundings.

Sights at a Glance

1 Nowa Huta
2 Mogiła
3 Polish Aviation Museum
4 Branice
5 Niepołomice
6 Staniątki
7 Wieliczka
8 Ojców

9 Schindler's Factory
10 Museum of Contemporary Art in Krakow (MOCAK)
11 Grodzisko
12 Pieskowa Skała
13 Tyniec
14 Wadowice
15 *Auschwitz (Oświęcim) (pp162–5)*
16 Kalwaria Zebrzydowska

Key

- City centre
- Motorway
- Major road
- Minor road
- Railway line

0 km   10
0 miles   5

◀ The clock tower at the castle of Pieskowa Skała

For keys to symbols *see back flap*

The Socialist Realist architecture of Nowa Huta

❶ Nowa Huta

🚌 117, 132, 138, 139, 142, 148, 149, 163, 174. 🚃 4, 15, 17, 21, 22.

The Communist authorities in Krakow suffered a crushing defeat in the 1946 referendum. This was blamed upon an inappropriate social balance within the class-based society. In order to "rearrange" this balance, they undertook a programme of quick industrialization of the Krakow region to increase the working-class population. In 1948 a contract was signed between Poland and the Soviet Union for a giant steelworks named after Lenin. The construction of a new town named Nowa Huta (New Steelworks) began in 1949. It was designed by Tadeusz Ptaszycki in the Socialist Realist style.

The housing estate, Centre, built between 1949 and 1955, is an interesting example of urban planning. In this "model Communist town" there was no room for churches. However, the people of Nowa Huta demanded one, so despite official intentions, the construction of churches began in the 1970s. Among these, the well-known Ark of God (see p39) is an outstanding piece of modern sacred Polish architecture. During the period of Martial Law (1981–3), the workers residing in Nowa Huta clearly demonstrated that they were not the best allies of the Communists, and the town became notorious for riots.

The Lenin Steelworks have been renamed Sendzimir.

❷ Mogiła

7 km (4 miles) east of Krakow. 🚌 123, 153, 163. 🚃 15. Cistercian Church: Klasztorna 11. **Tel** 12 644 23 31. **Open** 6am–7pm daily.

Mogiła village developed around the Cistercian Abbey. The Cistercians were brought to Poland in 1222, or 1225, by Iwo Odrowąż, the Bishop of Krakow. The new monastery was named *Clara Tumba* ("Bright Tomb", Jasna Mogiła, in Polish) because of the proximity of the reputed burial place of the legendary princess Wanda.

This Romanesque church followed the strict building regulations of the Cistercian order. The chancel ended with a flat perpendicular wall, and pairs of chapels with a square ground-plan were added to the transept. In 1447 the church was destroyed by fire. Gothic forms were introduced during its rebuilding. Stanisław Samostrzelnik decorated the interior with murals in the first half of the 16th century. These Renaissance paintings are complemented by 18th-century furnishings. The Baroque façade was added by Franz Moser as late as 1779–80. Other wall paintings in the church were made by Jan Bukowski in the early 20th century.

The Gothic cloister built in the time of Kazimierz the Great is the most beautiful part of the Abbey. It leads to the Chapter House, which features murals painted in the 19th century by Michał Stachowicz. These illustrate scenes from the life of Wanda. Not far from the abbey is the Church of St Bartholomew. Built in 1466, it is one of the oldest timber churches in Poland.

❸ Polish Aviation Museum

Al. Jana Pawła II 39. 🚃 5, 9, 10, 15, 40, 73. **Tel** 12 640 99 60. **Open** 9am–7pm Tue–Sun. 🎟 free Tue. 📷 🖳 muzeumlotnictwa.pl

This museum is located on the historic Rakowice-Czyżyny airfield, one of the oldest military airfields in Europe (established in 1912) and the second largest in Poland prior to World War II. The collection consists of more than 200 aircraft, including pre-war Polish fighter planes, Spitfires, German Albatrosses and Soviet Kakaruzniks. Also in the museum are 22 rare aeroplanes that were once part of Hermann Göring's personal collection.

The Renaissance Old Manor in Branice

❹ Branice

12 km (7.5 miles) east from Krakow. Manor: Branice 131.

Branice is situated not far from Niepołomice and is worth visiting for its two manors ▪ which exemplify the small-scale residential architecture of the gentry of Lesser Poland. The Old Manor, later converted into a store, was built around 1603 for the Castellan of

Żarnów, Jan Branicki, by an architect from the circle of Santi Gucci. The exterior of the manor is decorated with sgraffiti and topped with a parapet. The doors and fireplace inside are lavishly decorated with imaginative Mannerist ornaments carved in stone.

The New Manor was built in the early 19th century in Classical style. Its high hipped roof, and the entrance marked by a small portico supported by columns, make this building characteristic of Polish architecture of this type. Both manors are set in a picturesquely landscaped park, laid out in the 19th century.

Next to Branice is the village of Ruszcza with the Church of St George. The church was built around 1420 by the Royal Master of the Pantry, Wierzbięta of Branice. His Gothic memorial plaque and the Baroque high altar are both of interest.

❺ Niepołomice

24 km (15 miles) southeast of Krakow.
🚌 minibus from Krakow's Main Railway Station. 🚆 from Krakow's Main Railway Station. Church: **Open** 7am–6pm daily. Castle: **Tel** 12 281 30 11. **Open** 10am–5pm daily. 📷

The royal grounds in Niepołomice, situated on the outskirts of a vast woodland, were much favoured by Polish kings. They came here to rest and hunt, and developed magnificent buildings in the town they owned. The Gothic church in Niepołomice was founded by King Kazimierz the Great between 1350 and 1358. Like other sacred buildings founded by this sovereign, this church had two aisles separated by pillars.

It was later rebuilt in the Baroque style. Fragments of the rich stone decoration from the interior of the medieval church have survived and are displayed in the Old Sacristy. Outstanding Gothic paintings made between 1370 and 1375 by an Italian master, commissioned by Princess

Elżbieta (daughter of Władysław the Short), are also in the Old Sacristy.

Next to the church are two mausolea of noble families, both in the form of chapels covered by domes. Built in 1596, the Branicki Chapel is the earlier of the two. It features an ornamental tomb made by the Italian architect and sculptor Santi Gucci in the Mannerist style. In the Chapel of the Lubomirski family, built in 1640, wall paintings depicting scenes from the life of St Carlo Borromeo are of interest. Late-Baroque altars were added in the 18th century.

The hunting lodge in Niepołomice was originally built by Kazimierz the Great. It was transformed by Zygmunt August into a magnificent residence. The new castle was constructed between 1550 and 1571. Its regular plan and the central, square courtyard differ from other royal Renaissance houses in Poland. In 1637 massive stone arcades were added to the courtyard. Part of the castle is used to house the Museum of Hunting.

The dense forest (Puszcza Niepołomicka), a favourite hunting ground of Polish

Façade of the palace in Niepołomice, a residence of Polish kings

kings, stretches right behind the town. Brown bears, bison, lynx, wildcat and deer are known to have inhabited it. The forest is not so magnificent as it used to be, though wild areas have been preserved, including the bison sanctuary in the Proszowo forest.

Belfry by the Church of the Benedictine Nuns in Staniątki

❻ Staniątki

24 km (15 miles) southeast of Krakow.
🚆 from Krakow's Main Railway Station and Krakow-Płaszów. Church: **Open** during services only.

The Convent and Church of the Benedictine Nuns in Staniątki is not far from Niepołomice. The convent was founded in 1228 by Klemens of Ruszcza, Castellan of Krakow. The Church of St Mary and St Adalbert, dating from the same period, is Poland's oldest hall-church (a type of church in which the aisles and nave are of the same height).

The church is a brick structure. Its rather modest decoration is carved in stone. The interior was refurbished completely in the 18th century. The lavishly decorated organ gallery, added in 1705, and wall paintings executed in 1760 by the Rococo artist Andrzej Radwański of Krakow, are of great interest.

❼ Wieliczka

12 km (7.5 miles) southeast of Krakow. 🚌 Luxbus coaches from Krakow's Main Railway Station. 🚆 from Krakow's Main Railway Station and Krakow-Płaszów. Salt Mines: ul. Daniłowicza 10. **Tel** 12 278 73 02. 📷 **Open** Apr–Oct: 7:30am–7:30pm daily; Nov–Mar: 8am–5pm daily. **Closed** 1 Jan, Easter, 1 Nov, 24–25 & 31 Dec. 🅆 **kopalnia.pl**

Wieliczka developed and was granted a municipal charter in 1290 due to its rich deposits of salt. Salt was probably excavated here as early as the 11th century. The Latin name for Wieliczka was *Magnum Sal* (Great Salt) and indicated the importance of this mine in comparison to a smaller one in nearby Bochnia. According to a legend, the salt in Wieliczka constituted the dowry of St Kinga (Cunegunda) when she marrried Duke Bolesław the Chaste. The salt dowry was supposedly transposed magically from Hungary to Krakow for the wedding.

The salt in Wieliczka was re-garded for centuries as a major natural asset of the Kingdom of Poland. A vast network of underground galleries was created here over the centuries. Salt was also used as a building material in the carving of underground chapels and altars in front of which the miners prayed for God's protection against accidents.

The Wieliczka Salt Mine Museum is housed inside the mine. The exhibits on display illustrate the old mining methods and tools. A unique underground sanatorium is also housed here.

The small chapel overhanging the mountain river in Ojców

❽ Ojców

24 km (15 miles) northwest of Krakow. 🚌 from Krakow's Main Coach Station. Ojców National Park Museum: **Tel** 12 389 20 40. **Open** Apr–Oct: 9am–4:30pm daily; Nov–Mar: 8am–3pm Tue–Fri. Castle Tower: **Open** 13 Apr–11 Nov: from 10am; closing times vary.

The valley of the Prądnik river is the most beautiful part of the local uplands. The river eroded a deep gorge through the limestone. The steep cliffs are overgrown with trees through which stunning rock formations can be seen.

Kazimierz the Great had a number of hill-top castles built in the area to guard the western border of his Kingdom. The one in Ojców was one of the most important fortresses in Poland, but only remnants have survived. In 1956 part of the Prądnik valley was transformed into the Ojców National Park.

After the discovery of the healing properties of the local springs in the mid-1800s, the village at the foot of the castle was transformed into a spa: therapy clinics were set up and luxurious hotels built. The Łokietek Hotel, once the most sumptuous of all the buildings, now houses the museum of the Ojców National Park. During the Partition era, the Tsarist authorities denied planning permission for a church. So only a small timber chapel was built in 1901 to 1902 overhanging the Prądnik river.

❾ Schindler's Factory

ul. Lipowa 4. 🚆 3, 6, 7, 9, 11, 13, 20, 23, 24, 50, 51. **Tel** 12 257 10 17. **Open** Apr–Oct: 10am–8pm daily (to 4pm Mon, to 2pm first Mon of month); Nov–Mar: 10am–6pm daily (to 2pm Mon). 🎟 free Mon. 📷

Located in the former industrial district of Zabłocie, Schindler's Factory is a symbol of humanitarian courage. In 1943, the factory's German owner, Oskar Schindler *(see p127)*, protected his Jewish workers by claiming that they were essential to the running of his business. The factory, now a branch of the Historical Museum of Krakow, is one of the most visited museums in Poland. The "Krakow during the Nazi Occupation 1939–1945" exhibition illustrates everyday life in the city during World War II using original documents, radio and film recordings, photos and multimedia installations. Visitors follow a trail through time, from the Nazi invasion to the Soviet occupation, delving into specific aspects such as the fate of the city's Jews and the resistance movements.

❿ Museum of Contemporary Art in Krakow (MOCAK)

ul. Lipowa 4. 🚆 3, 6, 7, 9, 11, 13, 20, 23, 24, 50, 51. **Tel** 12 263 40 00. **Open** 11am–7pm Tue–Sun. 🎟 free Tue.

Popularly know as MOCAK, this energetic and constantly evolving institution has carved

The Chapel of St Kinga in Wieliczka salt mine

The exterior of MOCAK, housed on the site of the former Schindler's Factory

out an important place for itself in the city's cultural landscape since opening in 2011. The building is the result of a remodelling of parts of Schindler's Factory and features both intimate spaces and open galleries. The MOCAK hosts exhibitions of the most striking contemporary Polish art.

⓫ Grodzisko

28 km (17 miles) northwest of Krakow. 🚆 from Krakow's Main Railway Station. Church: **Open** 9–10am Sun.

Grodzisko is situated on the opposite bank of the Prądnik river from Ojców. The Convent of the Poor Clares was established here in 1262. Blessed Salomea, the sister of Duke Bolesław the Chaste, was the first Mother Superior. The nuns moved to Krakow in 1320 and the convent fell into ruin. The cult of the Blessed Salomea developed over time, and in 1677 Canon Sebastian Piskorski transformed Grodzisko into a sanctuary devoted to this pious nun. He designed a complex hermitage consisting of a church and a number of chapels enclosed within a wall. There are several charming Baroque touches, like the elephant bearing an obelisk, an idea borrowed from the Italian architect Bernini.

⓬ Pieskowa Skała

35 km (22 miles) northwest of Krakow. 🚌 from Krakow's Main Coach Station. Castle: **Tel** 12 389 60 04. **Closed** for renovation until Apr 2016. 🏛 free Wed.

The castle in Pieskowa Skała was built by King Kazimierz the Great in the 14th century as part of the defence system on the Krakow-Częstochowa Uplands. It became private property in 1377.

Between 1542 and 1544, enlargement of the castle was undertaken by Stanisław Szafraniec and his wife, Anna Dębińska. The commission was probably given to the Italian architect Nicolo da Castiglione.

The castle houses a museum of the history of Polish interiors from medieval times to the "19th century. Some pieces of furniture, tapestries and decorative objects, as well as works of art, are on display.

⓭ Tyniec

10 km (6 miles) west of Krakow. 🚌 112. Benedictine Abbey: Benedyktyńska 37. **Tel** 12 688 54 52. **Open** 10am–6pm daily. 🌐 **tyniec. benedyktyni.pl/en**

The Benedictine Abbey at Tyniec is situated on a rocky escarpment by the Vistula, west of Wawel. The monks were brought to Krakow in 1044, probably by King Kazimierz the Restorer. A Romanesque basilica was built here soon after. Only parts of the walls and a few architectural fragments of this basilica have survived. The new church and monastery were built in the 15th century. The church was remodelled in the early 17th century in the Baroque style, and magnificent stalls were added to the chancel. Large altars in black marble were made in the 18th century.

In the 12th and 13th centuries, during the period when Poland was fragmented into principalities, Tyniec was transformed into a fortress and played an important role during the struggles for the crown of the suzerain province of Krakow. By the end of the 16th century the fortifications were extended. A number of gates linked through an angled corridor were introduced as part of a defence system modelled on Wawel. Tyniec was a strategic site and as a result often came under attack from the enemy.

Today, the Benedictine Abbey is a picturesque sight.

Benedictine Abbey in Tyniec on the Vistula

The Church of the Presentation of the Virgin Mary in Wadowice

⓮ Wadowice

40 km (25 miles) southwest of Krakow. 🚌 from Krakow's Main Coach Station. Family House of John Paul II: **Tel** 033 823 2662. **Open** daily. May–Sep: 8:30am–5:30pm, Nov–Mar: 9am–2:30pm, Apr & Oct: 9am–4:30pm.

Wadowice was first recorded in 1327, but the town came to international attention in 1978 when Karol Wojtyła, born here on 18 May 1920, was elected Pope. Almost immediately the town became a place of mass pilgrimage and the local sites associated with the Pope include the Baroque Church of the Presentation of the Virgin Mary in Market Square, where he was baptised, and his family home, which now houses a museum dedicated to the pontiff.

Another site associated with John Paul II is the monumental votive Church of St Peter the Arch-shepherd which was built on the outskirts of Wadowice in thanksgiving for the Pope's survival of an assassination attempt on 13 May 1981. Designed by Ewa Węcławowicz-Gyurkovich and Jacek Gyurkovich, the walls of its nave seem to give way under the power of light, symbolizing the triumph of good over evil.

The town has had a chequered history, especially in the last century. While under German occupation during World War II, it was renamed Frauenstadt and the entire Jewish population was either executed or sent to nearby Auschwitz *(see below)*.

Wadowice has since been growing as a tourist centre, replacing the local industries, which collapsed in the newly democratic economy during the 1990s.

⓯ Auschwitz (Oświęcim)

See pp162–5.

⓰ Kalwaria Zebrzydowska

30 km (19 miles) sw of Krakow. 🚌 from Main Coach Station or Krakow-Dębniki. 🚆 from Krakow's Main Railway Station or Krakow-Płaszów. Bernardine Church: **Open** 6am–7pm daily.

Calavaries, or Ways of the Cross, were introduced in the 16th century and were built throughout Europe to commemorate the Passion and Death of Christ. The landscaping of Calvary grounds had to imitate the topography of Jerusalem. They consisted of structures commemorating the "tragedy of Salvation" and imitations of holy sites connected to the Virgin Mary.

Poland's first Calvary was built by Mikołaj Zebrzydowski from 1600 onwards. He located the chapels representing the Stations of the Cross along Christ's route to Golgotha on the Żary Hill near his residence in Zebrzydowice.

Mystery plays enacting Christ's Passion are staged in Kalwaria during Holy Week. The "funeral of the Virgin" takes place on the feast of the Assumption. Crowds of pilgrims arrive to venerate the miraculous icon of the Mother of God, whose cult in the Bernardine Church goes back to the 17th century. Kalwaria is one of the main religious centres in Lesser Poland.

The Baroque façade of the early 17th-century Bernardine Church in Kalwaria Zebrzydowska

Kalwaria Zebrzydowska

The most interesting chapels in the Kalwaria Zebrzydowska are those designed by Paulus Baudarth, a Flemish architect and goldsmith. He was commissioned to design many chapels, and avoiding repetition must have been a difficult task. He applied many different ground-plans, including a Greek cross, a circle and even a triangle. In some chapels he resorted to truly Baroque ideas, and based the plans on the shape of a heart or rose.

㉜ Chapel of the Second Fall
This chapel resembles a gate and has decoration carved in stone.

㉖ Herod's Palace
The design of this chapel, featuring recesses and mansard roofs, was inspired by the architecture of old Polish manors.

Key

- **▪ ▪ ▪** Path of Jesus
- ▪ ▪ ▪ Paths of the Virgin Mary

Sights on the Way of the Cross

① St Raphael's Chapel
② Chapel of the Throne
③ Chapel of the Joyful Patriarchs
④ Chapel of the Triumphant Apostles
⑤ Chapel of St John Nepomuk
⑥ Bridge of Angels
⑦ Chapel of Farewell
⑧ Church of the Sepulchre of the Virgin Mary
⑨ Gethsemane
⑩ Chapel of the Arrest of Christ

⑪ Church of the Ascension
⑫ Jewish Chapel
⑬ Bridge over the Cedron
⑭ East Gate
⑮ Bethsaida
⑯ Apostles' Chapel
⑰ Chapel of the Veneration of the Soul of the Virgin
⑱ Angels' Chapel
⑲ House of Annas
⑳ The Cenacle
㉑ House of Mary
㉒ House of Caiaphas

㉓ Chapel of the Fainting Virgin
㉔ Pilate's Town Hall
㉕ The Holy Steps
㉖ Herod's Palace
㉗ Chapel of the Taking up of the Cross
㉘ Chapel of the First Fall
㉙ Chapel of the Heart of Mary
㉚ Chapel of Simon of Cyrene
㉛ St Veronica's Chapel
㉜ Chapel of the Second Fall
㉝ Chapel of the Sorrowful Women

㉞ Chapel of the Third Fall
㉟ Chapel of the Stripping of Christ
㊱ Church of the Crucifixion
㊲ Chapel of the Anointment
㊳ Chapel of the Holy Sepulchre
㊴ Hermitage of St Mary Magdalene
㊵ Hermitage of St Helen
㊶ Chapel of the Madonna of Sorrows

⑮ Auschwitz I

For most people, Auschwitz represents the ultimate horror of the Holocaust. The Nazis began the first mass transportation of European Jews to Auschwitz in 1942 and it soon became the centre of extermination. Over the next three years, at least 1.1 million people, a quarter of those who died in the Holocaust, were killed at Auschwitz and the neighbouring Birkenau camp *(see pp164–5)*, also known as Auschwitz II. Today, the grounds and buildings of both camps are open to visitors, as a museum and a poignant memorial. Auschwitz is now a UNESCO World Heritage site.

Exhibitions
The daily horrors of life in the camp are today displayed in some of the barracks.

The Camp

Auschwitz I opened in 1940 on the site of former Polish army barracks. Originally built to incarcerate Polish political prisoners, further buildings were added in the spring of 1941 as the number of prisoners dramatically increased. Camp administration was also based at Auschwitz I.

0 metres ——————— 100
0 yards ——————— 100

Gas Chambers and Crematoria
The entire Auschwitz complex had seven gas chambers and five crematoria. Six of the gas chambers were in Birkenau but the first was at Auschwitz, operating from 1941.

The Two Camps

Though part of the same camp complex, Auschwitz and Birkenau are in fact 3 km (2 miles) apart. The small Polish

town of Oświęcim was commandeered by the Nazis and renamed Auschwitz. Birkenau was opened in March 1942 in the village of Brzezinka, where the residents were evicted to make way for the camp. There were an additional 47 sub-camps in the surrounding area.

Aerial view of the complex taken by the Allies in 1944. The yellow dotted line marks Birkenau; the blue shows Auschwitz I.

KEY

① **SS Guard house and office of the camp supervisor**

② **"Arbeit Macht Frei" entrance**: the words above the infamous entrance to Auschwitz translate as "Work makes you free". This was certainly not the case for the prisoners transported here, who were often worked to death.

③ **Block 11 was the central jail** that housed prisoners from all over the camp complex.

④ **Store containing the poison, Zyklon B**, first used at Auschwitz to kill prisoners.

⑤ **Camp kitchen**

⑥ **Present-day Information Centre for visitors**

The "Wall of Death"
This is a reconstruction of the wall near Block 11 used for the summary executions by shooting. Usually covered in flowers, it now serves as a place of remembrance.

VISITORS' CHECKLIST

Practical Information
Oświęcim. **Road map** D5. **Tel** 33 844 81 00. W **auschwitz.org**
Open Dec–Feb: 8am–3pm; Mar & Nov: 8am–4pm; Apr & Oct: 8am–5pm; May & Sep: 8am–6pm; Jun–Aug: 8am–7pm.
Closed 1 Jan, Easter Day, 25 Dec. Call to arrange, fee applies.

Transport
to Oświęcim, then 24, 25, 26, 27, 28, 29. Shuttle bus to Birkenau (every 15 mins in high season; from Information Centre).

Maksymilian Kolbe
The camp jail, in Block 11, was used for those who broke camp rules. Few emerged alive. Father Kolbe (see p37) died here after sacrificing his life for another inmate's.

Roll Call Square
Roll call took place up to three times a day and could last for hours. Eventually, due to the increasing numbers of prisoners, roll call was taken in front of individual barracks.

1939	1940	1941	1942	1943	1944	1945
1939 1 Sep, Hitler invades Poland.	**1940** First deportation of German Jews into Nazi-occupied Poland.	**1941** Hitler reported to have ordered the "Final Solution".	**1942** First section of Birkenau camp completed		**1944** As the Soviet Army closes on Auschwitz, the SS begin destroying all evidence of the camp.	**1945** 27 Jan, Soviet soldiers liberate the few remaining prisoners at Auschwitz.
1940 Oświęcim chosen as the site of the Nazis' new concentration camp.	**1941** Himmler makes first visit to Auschwitz and orders its expansion.	**1941** First gas chamber goes into operation.	**1942** Beginning of mass deportation to Auschwitz.	**1943** Four gas chambers built for mass murder. **1945** 18 Jan, 56,000 prisoners evacuated on "Death March".		**1945** 7 May, Germany surrenders to the Allies.

Auschwitz II–Birkenau

Birkenau was primarily a place of execution. Most of Auschwitz's machinery of murder was housed here. In the six gas chambers in use at different stages of the camp's construction, over one million people were killed, 98% of whom were Jewish. Victims included people from over 20 nations. Birkenau was also an enormous concentration camp, housing 90,000 slave labourers by mid-1944 and providing labour for many of the factories and farms of southwestern, Nazi-occupied Poland. The gas chambers were quickly destroyed by the Nazis shortly before the Soviet Army liberated the camp in January 1945.

Hell's Gate
In 1944 the numbers arriving began to increase dramatically. A rail line was extended into the camp. The entrance gate through which the trains passed was known as "Hell's Gate".

Visiting Birkenau
There is little left of the camp's buildings today; its main purpose is for remembrance. Most visitors come to pay their respects at the Monument to the Victims of the Camp, on the site of the gas chambers.

The Unloading Ramp
This was possibly the most terrifying part of the camp. It was here that SS officers separated the men from the women and children, and the SS doctors declared who was fit for work. Those declared unfit (as many as 70 or 80 per cent) were taken immediately to their death.

The Camp

Birkenau was the largest concentration camp in Nazi-occupied Europe. In 1944 the camp had more than 90,000 prisoners, the majority of whom were exterminated. From the unloading ramp to the gas chambers, the crematoria to the ash dumping grounds, the whole process of murder was carried out systematically and on an enormous scale. This reconstruction shows the camp at its peak in 1944, when as many as 5,000 people could be killed every day.

The Liberation of the Camps

With the war all but lost, in mid-January 1945 the Nazi authorities gave the order for all the camps to be destroyed. Such was the speed of the collapse of the German army, however, that only part of Birkenau was destroyed. Between 17–21 January more than 56,000 inmates were evacuated by the Nazis and forced to march west; many died en route. When the Soviet army entered the camps on 27 January 1945, they found just 7,000 survivors.

Survivors of Auschwitz II-Birkenau, filmed by Soviet troops

Kanada

"Kanada" was the nickname of the barracks where property stolen from prisoners was stored. It was the preferred place to work at Auschwitz II-Birkenau as it offered opportunities for inmates to pilfer items to barter for food or medicine later.

The Sauna

New arrivals selected for work were deloused and disinfected in this building, which became known as the "sauna". Periodic disinfections of existing prisoners were also carried out here.

| 0 metres | | 200 |
| 0 yards | | 200 |

The Ash Pond

Tons of ash – the remains of hundreds of thousands of Auschwitz victims – were dumped in ponds and troughs dug around the outskirts of the camp.

KEY

① **Towers and barbed wire** isolated the camps from the outside world.

② **Large gas chambers and crematoria (from 1943)**

③ **Area of expansion**, nicknamed "Mexico", never completed.

④ **Wooden barracks**, with 500–600 people living in each.

⑤ **Hell's Gate**

Barracks

The conditions of the living quarters at the camps were terrible. With little or no sanitation, poor nutrition and no medical care, diseases such as typhus spread rapidly. This image shows a typical wooden barracks at Birkenau shortly after liberation.

A Two-Hour Walk around Planty

The Planty green belt in Krakow has replaced the city's medieval fortifications, built between the late 13th and 15th centuries. They were demolished early in the 19th century and the small stretch of wall by Floriańska Street is the only fragment to have survived. The gardens of Planty were landscaped to include a network of radiating lanes and beautiful vistas. In the second half of the 19th century the well-kept Planty became a popular venue for socializing. After a period of regeneration the Planty now features period fencing, benches and street lamps.

One of many fountains in the Planty gardens

Wawel to the University

The walk begins by the Coat of Arms Gate at Wawel. Walk downhill and cross the street to enter the so-called Wawel gardens. The Gothic Revival Seminary building will be on your right, and a sculpture depicting *Owls* can be seen on your left ①.

Continue down through the park some 40 m (130 ft) towards a little square decorated with a statue of the renowned translator of French literature into Polish, Tadeusz Boy Żeleński, carved by Edward Krzak ②. Turn right and after some 50 m (165 ft) you will reach the wall enclosing the gardens of the Archaeological Museum (see p85). Mounted in the wall are small plaques, overrun with greenery, commemorating the contributions made by the honorary Committee for the Renovation of Krakow's Monuments.

Carry straight on and cross Poselska Street. Those interested in archaeology may turn right to visit the museum. On the other side of the street is a plinth indicating the site of one of many medieval towers which formed part of the defence wall. The outline of the wall is marked by sandstones which you can see positioned along the lanes. Take a sharp left turn and walk

down 20 m (65 ft) to a little square where, hidden behind trees, is a statue made in 1884 of Grażyna and Litawor ③, two characters from a poem by Adam Mickiewicz.

From this statue, take a right turn to return to the main lane. You will notice the buildings of the Franciscan Church (see pp88–9) and the Episcopal Palace (see p106). Go straight ahead and cross Franciszkańska Street to enter the University Gardens. Walk down the main lane along the wall of the Episcopal Palace, passing by the end of Wiślna Street. Some 150 m (492 ft) further down, by Jagiellońska Street, is an 18th-century statue of the Virgin Mary of Grace ④, which originally was in the graveyard of the Church of St Mary. After another 40 m (130 ft), you may choose to rest, looking at the Kościuszko Mound which can be seen through Józefa Piłsudskiego Street in the distance. Then carry on, passing by the façade of the Collegium Novum, the main university building. An oak planted in 1918, known as the Oak of Liberty, can be seen in front of the college. A red-brick paved

① *Owl* (1964) by Bronisław Chromy

0 metres		300
0 yards		300

pattern in the square imitates the curves of Copernicus's astrolabe. The statue of the astronomer ⑤ *(see p106)*, surrounded by trees, is to the left of Collegium Novum and in front of the Witkowski College. Further down, you will pass by the Collegium Nowodvorianum *(see pp106–7)* and after some 50 m (165 ft) cross St Anne's Street. The university Collegiate Church of St Anne *(see pp110–11)* will be on your right.

Planty in autumn, with visitors strolling along a path

beautiful statue of Artur Grottger ⑥ made in 1901 by Wacław Szymanowski. Cross St Thomas's Street (ulica św. Tomasza) and after some 300 m (985 ft) turn left. In this "corner" of the Planty is the statue of Lilla Veneda ⑦, the leading character in a play by Juliusz Słowacki. Walk some 200 m (655 ft) down one of the lanes which run alongside Basztowa Street. The next monument you will notice is that of Queen Jadwiga and King Władysław Jagiełło ⑧. It was raised to commemorate the fifth centenary of the union between Poland and Lithuania in 1386. After crossing Sławkowska Street, you will find on your left a large pond where in summer swans can be seen. You can cross a little bridge over the pond and this will lead you to a statue of the Harpist ⑨. Continue down the main lane. Pass by the remains of the defence wall with St Florian's Gate *(see p113)* to finally reach the Barbican *(see p116)*.

Krakow's Main Railway Station to Stradom

Walk some 300 m (985 ft) through the so-called Station Gardens. The major attractions here are the Słowacki Theatre *(see p117)* and the Church of the Holy Cross *(see p117)*.

Continue to the subway entrance by which the Straszewski Obelisk ⑩ is located. Florian Straszewski was the man who laid out Planty. Behind the Church of the Holy Cross is a statue of the playwright Michał Bałucki ⑪. Walk another 300 m (985 ft) cross Mikołajska Street to enter the "Na gródku" Gardens. The Church of the Dominican Nuns *(see p117)* will be on your right. Continue down the lane and cross Sienna Street. The Dominican Church *(see pp118–19)* will be on your right. You will pass by an unusual statue of Colonel Narcyz Wiatr-Zawojny ⑫, who was shot dead in 1946 by the secret police (UB). The statue was made in 1992 by Bronisław Chromy. Stroll another 500 m (0.3 mile) downhill to enter the so-called Stradom Gardens and the end of the walk.

Key

••• Walk route

Palace of Art to the Barbican

Continue some 100 m (330 ft) and cross Szewska Street. The "Bunker of Art" *(see p107)* will be on your right. A little further down, some 20 m (65 ft) after crossing Szczepańska Street, continue to walk down the Planty's main lane. You will pass a little square where you will see the Palace of Art *(see p107)* on the right, while on your left will be a most

⑦ Statue of Lilla Veneda by Alfred Daun

Tips for Walkers

Starting point: At the foot of Wawel, by Kanonicza Street.
Length: approx. 5 km (3 miles).
Getting there: Bus Nos. 128, 304, 522; the nearest stop is by Straszewskiego Street.
Stopping-off points: Café at the "Bunker of Art" near the Collegium Novum. There are benches near the Barbican and throughout the park.

A One-Hour Walk around Zwierzyniec

In the 12th century Zwierzyniec was a small village, founded as the endowment to the Premonstratensian nuns, whose convent was located by the Rudawa river, a tributary of the Vistula. Polish sovereigns used to take a rest in the royal gardens located in this village. Henri de Valois is reputed to have organized orgies here to the outrage of his subjects. The richest Krakovians followed in the kings' footsteps by establishing their country residences in Zwierzyniec. Despite being incorporated into Krakow in the early 20th century, Zwierzyniec has managed to retain its original village character.

⑤ Salwator Cemetery

② Altar in St Margaret's Chapel

Salwator

After arriving at the tram depot, walk to the Church of the Premonstratensian Nuns ①. The church was founded in the second half of the 12th century but its appearance today is a result of a remodelling under-taken between 1595 and 1638. The Neo-Classical decoration of the choir is most interesting. It was created between 1775 and 1779 to designs by Sebastian Sierakowski. The convent building next to the church is one of the largest in Poland. It is worth visiting for its courtyard. After leaving the church, go up

the chapel. The Church of the Holy Redeemer ③ is further uphill. According to Polish chroniclers, it was built immediately after

the steep Św. Bronisławy Street. The Chapel of St Margaret ②, built in 1690, will be on your left. Those who died of the plague were buried by

0 metres   300
0 yards   300

Key

••• Walk route

The Kościuszko Mound and Zwierzyniec seen from Wawel

Poland had accepted Christianity in 966, by Duke Mieszko I. The duke presented the church with a miraculous crucifix. Evidence shows, however, that the church was actually constructed later and consecrated in 1148. Despite extensive remodelling, the church has retained much of its Romanesque character. An interesting painting of 1605 by Kasper Kurch depicts a most unusual scene of the crucified Christ shaking off his shoe in order to pass it to a poor fiddler playing under the Cross. A 17th-century pulpit has also survived by the church, as well as a number of interesting tombs from the first half of the 19th century.

A residential estate ④ established in the early 20th century is located near the church. Its Art Nouveau architecture is worth seeing.

Salwator Cemetery

Walk down Anczyca Street and turn right into Aleja Jerzego Waszyngtona (Washington Avenue). The small Salwator Cemetery ⑤ consecrated in 1865 is located on the outskirts of the Salwator estate. A chapel, built in 1888 to 1889 in the Neo-Gothic style to a design by architect Sebastian Jaworzyńsk can be seen in the middle of the cemetery. A great number of tombs of those who made important contributions to Polish culture can be found here.

Kościuszko Mound

The tree-lined Aleja Jerzego Waszyngtona will lead you to the Kościuszko Mound on Sikornik Hill. At its foot, the Chapel of St Bronisława ⑥ marks the site of the hermitage of the eponymous nun. The chapel was built between 1856 and 1861 by Feliks Księżarski in the Neo-Gothic style. The Kościuszko Mound ⑦ was

⑥ Chapel of the St Bronisława at the foot of the Kościuszko Mound

erected between 1820 and 1823 to commemorate the leader of the insurrection of 1794. This monument to the hero in the struggle for Polish independence was inspired by the mounds of two mythical Polish rulers, Krak and Wanda, which are located in the environs of Krakow. The construction of the mound became a patriotic endeavour and the monument itself a destination for national pilgrimages arriving in Krakow. Fortifications ⑧ at the foot of the Kościuszko Mound were constructed after 1850 by the Austrians as part of a project which aimed to transform Krakow into a massive fortress. The fortress is currently used as a hotel and houses the popular RMF FM radio station. A bus stop, which serves the city centre, is situated by the entrance to the hotel.

① Church and Convent of the Premonstratensian Nuns at Salwator

Tips for Walkers

Starting point: The Salwator tram depot.
Length: 2.5 km (1.6 miles).
Getting there: The walk starts from the tram depot in Salwator. You can get there by tram Nos. 1, 2 and 6. Return by bus No. 100 which stops at the foot of the Kościuszko Mound.
Stopping-off points: Benches to relax can be found on Aleja Jerzego Waszyngtona. There is a café and restaurant in the Hotel "Pod Kopcem" on the same street.

For keys to symbols see back flap

A Walk in Las Wolski

Las Wolski (the Wolski Wood) is the largest green area in Krakow. It has partly retained its original character as a forest, while the remaining ground is maintained as a park. Paths and lanes wind up and down this hilly terrain, leading to many wild spots of surprising beauty created either artificially or naturally. The lovely architecture of the Camaldolese Monastery and Decius Villa, both on the outskirts of the park, are worth exploring. The walk route described below includes sights in the Wolski Wood and the surrounding neighbourhood.

The park by the Decius Villa

① Entrance to the Camaldolese Monastery

Srebrna Góra (Silver Mount)
The walk begins at the bus stop at the intersection of Aleja Wędrowników (Wędrowników Avenue) and Księcia Józefa Street. Walk some 500 m (0.3 mile) down Aleja Wędrowników then turn right into Aleja Konarowa (Konarowa Avenue).

Climb up the Silver Mount to visit the Camaldolese Monastery ①. The monastery of this strict Reformed Benedictine order was built between 1605 and 1642 by two outstanding architects, Valentin of Säbisch and Andrea Spezza, among others. The stone-clad façade of the church is particularly impressive. The austerity of the interior is in striking contrast with the lavishness of the decoration of the chapels, which feature stuccowork by Giovanni Falconi. The so-called Royal Chapel, dating from 1633 to 1636, is very beautiful. The stairs on either side of the high altar lead down to the crypt which houses a catacomb. This subterranean gallery has recesses excavated in the sides for tombs of the deceased monks. Next to the catacomb is the *ossuarium*, a common grave containing bones removed from the recesses in the catacomb. The hermitages are closed to visitors but can be seen from the ossuary chapel.

Women are allowed into the church on a few festive days only.

② The Wolski Wood, a favourite place for walks

0 metres 400
0 yards 400

Key

••• Walk route

Wolski Wood (Las Wolski)
Leave the monastery by Aleja Konarowa (Konarowa Avenue), the same route by which you arrived, then turn right into Wędrowników Avenue which is the main lane of Wolski Wood ②. This wood was transformed into a public park in 1917 through the efforts of Juliusz Leo, the President of the City of Krakow. Turn right again into a path which leads to Aleja Żubrowa (Bison Avenue). After a few minutes' walk the entrance to the Zoo ③ will be in front of you. The Zoo was established in 1929. It differs from other zoological gardens owing to its location in the middle of a forest. Leave the Zoo via Al Do Kopca (Towards the Mound Avenue) which will take you to the Marshal Piłsudski Mound ④ on top of Sowiniec Mount. The mound was

constructed between 1934 and 1936 as a monument commemorating the Poles who fell during the long struggle for independence from the three powers that partitioned Poland between 1772 and 1918. The mound is called "a Tomb of Tombs" and contains ashes from many battlefields. Walk down the mound and continue along Aleja Panieńskich Skał (Virgin Rocks Avenue) toward the Sanctuary of the Virgin Rocks ⑤ where you will find picturesque limestone formations. According to a legend, this was the place where the Premonstratensian nuns of Zwierzyniec took refuge and hid from the Tatars. A 16th-century timber church ⑥ at the end of the avenue was moved here from Komorowice.

Wola Justowska
Continue walking along Aleja Panieńskich Skał and turn right at the T-junction into Aleja Kasztanowa (Chestnut Avenue).

⑤ A statue of the Virgin in Panieńskich Skał

Wola Justowska, a fashionable district of Krakow, begins here. Carry on until you see the Decius Villa (Willa Decjusza) ⑦ ahead. Justus Decius was Secretary to King Zygmunt the Old. In 1530 he transformed a late-Gothic manor, dating from the 15th century, into a Renaissance residence. The villa was extended in the first half of the 17th century and a loggia added, offering a view over the area. The Villa houses the European Academy, which is dedicated to the study of European cultural heritage. A nearby bus stop serves the city centre.

Tips for Walkers

Starting point: The bus stop at the intersection of Księcia Józefa Street with Wędrowników Street.
Getting there: Bus routes 109, 209, 229, 239 and 269 will take you to Srebrna Góra. Take bus 134 by the entrance to the Zoo or bus routes 102, 134, 152 and 192 from Wola Justowska to return to the city centre.
Stopping-off points: There are benches to relax on throughout the Wolski Wood. Restaurants are at the foot of Srebrna Góra and near the Zoo and there is a café in the Villa of Decius.
Note: Women are only permitted into the Camaldolese Church on 7 Feb, 25 Mar, Easter Sun, Whit Sun; Whit Mon, Corpus Christi; 19 Jun, Sun after 19 Jun, 15 Aug, 8 Sep, 8 Dec and 25 Dec.

⑦ A suburban residence known as the Villa of Decius

For keys to symbols *see back flap*

WHERE TO STAY

Krakow is home to some of Poland's best hotels. Besides the big international names, such as Radisson Blu and Sheraton, visitors will also find many independent hotels famed for their architecture, for traditions extending back to the 19th century, and for their *fin-de-siècle* atmosphere. The best of these have managed to recapture the magnificence that was lost during the period of Communist rule. Many of the hotels in the older parts of the city have been renovated, and new establishments have sprung up on the city's fringes and around the river. The number of backpacker hostels has also mushroomed, ensuring that there is a broad choice of accommodation for all budgets. Visitors can still expect to pay a premium for an Old Quarter location, but the competition helps keep prices in check. From all the hotels in Krakow, this section highlights some of the best; they have been listed according to theme, location and price on pages 180–83.

Where to Look

Most of Krakow's hotels are located in the Old Quarter, near the main Market Square; in the former Jewish district of Kazimierz; and in the city-centre districts that surround these two areas. All of these districts are within walking distance of each other, and finding accommodation that is close to the action is never too difficult. Accommodation located outside these central areas is usually linked to the centre by reasonably swift bus or tram services; there are no parts of Krakow where visitors will feel isolated or cut off.

Hotels

Krakow is one of the most atmospheric places to stay in the whole of Central Europe. The city boasts an impressive number of historic, mostly 19th-century hotels, especially grand old establishments like Pod Różą, Pollera, Francuski

Elegant, flower-filled room at the Polski Hotel Pod Białym Orłem *(see p180)*

and Elektor *(see p180)*, which have preserved the decor and atmosphere of the Belle Époque. There are also many luxury hotels – notably Copernicus *(see p182)*, Stary and Pałac Bonerowski *(see p183)* – that have made good use of old buildings, adapting medieval and Renaissance town houses to the needs of the modern hospitality industry, while leaving much of the original exposed-brick and stone features intact. Modern five-star chains such as Radisson Blu and Sheraton are also present in Krakow, alongside many of the more budget-oriented chains such as Ibis, Best Western, Novotel and Campanile. Recent years have seen the emergence of a breed of boutique and design hotels, such as Pugetów and andel's *(see p182)*, that aim to make best use of the local artistic traditions; and there is also a healthy quantity of B&Bs, offering charming, characterful and informal accommodation in the heart of the city.

Making a Reservation

Most of Krakow's hotels, apartments and hostels are featured on international booking sites such as **Booking**, **Airbnb** and **Hostelworld**.

Neo-Classical building housing the Fortuna B&B *(see p181)*

◀ Outdoor dining area at the Noworolski café on Market Square

Reservations can also be made by contacting the establishment directly by phone or email. Early booking is advisable for most of Krakow's hotels, especially during high summer, when finding vacancies may be quite a challenge. Peak times are July and August, the period around the May Day public holiday and New Year's Eve. However, it is worth noting that the tourist season lasts all year round, and only autumn and winter see a decline in the number of tourists. Krakow also sees a constant flow of international conferences, meetings and festivals. Finding a hotel on arrival may prove difficult at any time.

Communal lounge area at the Metropolitan Boutique Hotel *(see p183)*

Facilities

Most hotels offer ensuite rooms with satellite or cable television. The provision of Wi-Fi Internet access is also pretty standard throughout the Polish hotel industry. Even in the better hotels, bathrooms may feature a shower rather than a bathtub, so if you specifically want a bathtub, you should enquire about this when booking. Rooms in the more expensive hotels may have a mini-bar, 24-hour room service and laundry service; some hotels have facilities such as business centres with computers and fax machines. Fitness facilities are increasingly common, but only a handful of hotels in the luxury bracket offer spas or swimming pools. Tourist information is sometimes available at the reception desk, as well as ticket booking facilities for various events.

Check-out time is generally noon, but luggage can usually be left at reception. Hotel personnel frequently speak both English and German.

Discounts

Hotels often advertise rate cuts and budget specials on Internet booking sites. In general, prices tend to fluctuate according to the season, and most hotels in Krakow reduce their prices in autumn and winter. Throughout the year, business and conference hotels, which are often full on weekdays, usually reduce their prices at weekends. There are not many single-bed hotel rooms available for solo travellers, so negotiate a discount when offered a double room for single use.

Wherever you are thinking of staying, it is always worth asking for a discount, and you stand a good chance of getting one if you are planning a longer stay.

Hidden Extras

In accordance with Polish law, the prices quoted or displayed in hotels have to include tax and service. In most places, they also include breakfast, but this is not always the

Swimming pool at the contemporary Galaxy hotel *(see p181)*

case, so check in advance. Telephone calls from hotel rooms are never included (even in the best hotels), and they are far more expensive than elsewhere. As an alternative, use one of the numerous card-operated public telephones around town. Phonecards for these are available from newsagents and tobacco kiosks as well as post offices, where you will also find public telephones. Some of the telephone booths situated on the street are specially adapted for wheelchair users.

Although free Wi-Fi Internet access is increasingly standard in the hospitality industry, some hotels (mostly in the business category) may charge for this service; again, it is wise to ask in advance.

Despite these hidden extra costs, Polish hospitality almost always extends to providing guests with a free supply of mineral water. Regardless of the standard of hotel, a fresh bottle of sparkling water is usually left in your room every day. As a rule, if it is not in the mini-bar, it is free.

Tips are not offered to hotel staff, except at the most exclusive hotels where it is customary to offer 10 per cent. You may, however, choose to give less depending on the service you have received. Be aware that saying "thank you" when paying a bill is automatically taken to mean "keep the change".

Travelling with Children

Children are welcome everywhere in Poland. Most hotels offer additional beds for children, and usually no extra charge is made for this as long as the child is under the age of seven or eight. Check when making your reservation. In hotel restaurants there should be no problem in ordering children's portions, and most places also have high chairs. Only the very best hotels offer baby-sitting facilities as part of their service.

Disabled Travellers

Since Poland is a member of the European Union (EU), all hotels must fall in line with EU legislation. This means that any new hotels must include a certain number of rooms for disabled travellers, while all existing hotels must adapt their rooms and common areas to the needs of disabled guests within a strict timeline. The latter part of this legislation has not been strictly enforced, however, and many hotels in Krakow, especially those in the Old Quarter, which have no space for lifts, remain devoid of any facilities for the disabled. As a rule, the newer the hotel (or the more recently it has been renovated), the more likely you are to find suitable access. It is advisable to contact the hotel beforehand to check which facilities for the disabled they have.

Cheerful decor in the communal lounge at the Flamingo Hostel *(see p183)*

Rooms and Apartments to Let

Many rooms and apartments in Krakow are rented out to tourists for short- or long-term stays. Accommodation of this type can be found in all areas of the city. Apartments in the Old Quarter are often located in beautifully renovated old buildings and are usually more expensive than those further out. Apartments tend to have a fully equipped kitchenette and a TV; many also have Wi-Fi access. Some of the more expensive apartments are cleaned daily or every few days.

Rooms and apartments are often rented out directly by the owner via accommodation websites such as Booking or Airbnb. A number of agents, such as **Krakow Apartments**, **Old City Apartments** and **Sodispar**, rent out holiday apartments in central locations.

B&Bs

There is a small but growing number of bed-and-breakfasts in Krakow, catering for travellers who want something a bit more informal than the average hotel, with the added benefit of friendly and helpful hosts. Krakow's B&Bs tend to have a bit more character than contemporary hotels, frequently featuring homely decor that is in keeping with the often very old buildings in which they are situated. Some of the more characterful B&Bs in Krakow include La Fontaine, Tango House, Wielopole, Klezmer-Hois

and Kolory *(see p181)*. Be aware that rooms might be on the small side. While most B&Bs offer rooms with ensuite bathrooms, some will offer a mixture of ensuite rooms and rooms with shared facilities. Some B&Bs will have someone at reception 24 hours a day, while others may be staffed only at specific daytime hours. Always confirm your arrival time by email or phone to make sure somebody will be there to meet you.

Hostels

There is a huge number of backpacker hostels in Krakow, most of which offer cheap, simple dorm accommodation in fun, informal surroundings. Beds in hostels can be booked via the hostels' own websites or on specialist websites such as Hostelworld. Many hostels offer doubles, triples and quads as well as dorms, and they are increasingly popular with couples and families who enjoy the social aspects of backpacker culture but who want a private room.

Hostels in Krakow vary a great deal in terms of character: some have a bar on site and encourage late-night socializing, while others offer a bit more peace and quiet. The type of atmosphere favoured will be clear from the description on each hostel's website. Many hostels have invested a lot of money in contemporary design and comforts, and are similar in style to small boutique hotels.

Brightly coloured room at the Secret Garden Hostel *(see p183)*

Breakfast is available at some Krakow hostels, but not all – this can be checked when making your booking. Due to their popularity, it is advisable to book hostels at least two or three days in advance.

Camping

There is a modest handful of suburban campsites in Krakow, and although they are a fair way from the centre, all are well served by public transport. **Krakowianka** (open from May to September) is a tranquil suburban site next to the wooded Solvay Park, just off the Zakopane road, 6 km (4 miles) south of town. During the summer months there is an open-air swimming pool for the use of the campers, and the Solvay shopping mall is a short walk away; however, there's nothing else of sightseeing or recreational interest in this part of town. **Smok** (open all year) is a privately run site 4 km (2.5 miles) west of town, on the main Oświęcim road, in a pleasant suburban setting with plenty of greenery around.

Recommended Hotels

The places to stay listed on pages 180–83 are the best from a range of accommodation

A room in the moden Wyspiański hotel *(see p182)*

types, from charming B&Bs and backpacker hostels to luxury establishments, chains, boutique hotels and the grand, historic hotels for which Krakow is renowned. They are listed by price within each area, be that the narrow alleys of the Old Quarter, bohemian Kazimierz or the pleasant leafy streets just outside the city centre. These lodgings have been featured for their excellent service, wide-ranging facilities or unique character.

Throughout the listings certain hotels have been highlighted as DK Choice. These offer a particularly special experience, such as a beautiful location, spectacular views, a historical setting, outstanding service, a

romantic atmosphere or a combination of these qualities. Whatever the reasons, the DK Choice label is a guarantee of an especially memorable stay. Many of these establishments are popular so it is advisable to book well in advance.

DIRECTORY

Internet Booking Sites

Airbnb
W airbnb.com

Booking
W booking.com

Hostelworld
W hostelworld.com

Rooms and Apartments

Krakow Apartments
Tel 502 501 812.
W krakow-apartments.com

Old City Apartments
Tel 606 941 483.
W oldcityapartments.eu

Sodispar
Tel 12 423 42 44.
W sodispar.pl

Campsites

Krakowianka
ul. Żywiecka Boczna 2.
Tel 12 268 11 33.
W krakowianka.com.pl

Smok
ul. Kamedulska 18.
Tel 12 429 72 66.
W smok.krakow.pl

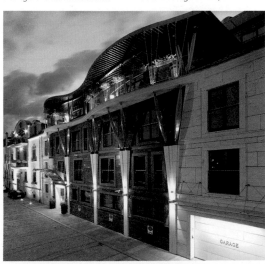

Sleek exterior of the Art Hotel Niebieski, located by the river *(see p183)*

Where to Stay

Historical

Okół and Stradom Quarters

Rezydent zł zł
ul. Grodzka 9
Tel *12 429 54 10* **Map** 6 D3
W rezydent.krakow.pl
Behind its medieval façade, the Rezydent's rooms and suites offer good value for a three-star hotel.

Royal zł zł
ul. Św. Gertrudy
Tel *12 421 35 00* **Map** 6 D5
W hotelewam.pl
Stay in comfortable rooms at the foot of the Wawel Royal Castle in this hotel housed in a 19th-century Art Nouveau building.

Wawel zł zł zł
ul. Poselska 22
Tel *12 424 13 00* **Map** 6 D3
W hotelwawel.pl
In a 16th-century building, the Wawel mixes the old with the new. The large, well-appointed rooms have Art Nouveau-style decor. There is a wellness centre.

Old Quarter

Amadeus zł zł
ul. Mikołajska 20
Tel *12 429 60 70* **Map** 6 E2
W hotel-amadeus.pl
This four-star hotel in a lovely mansion has plush, antique furnishings and a retro feel.

DK Choice

Elektor zł zł
ul. Szpitalna 28
Tel *12 423 23 17* **Map** 6 E2
W hotelelektor.pl
One of the grand old ladies of the Kraków hotel scene, the Elektor preserves an old-world charm. The staff will fall over themselves to help guests, royalty or otherwise: illustrious patrons have included Prince and Princess Takamodo of Japan, King Harald V of Norway and Princess Maha Chakri Sirindhorm of Thailand.

Francuski zł zł
ul. Pijarska 13
Tel *666 195 831* **Map** 6 D1
W hotel-francuski.com
This hotel retains an air of pre-World War I opulence and features retro furnishings and a fine restaurant.

Pod Różą zł zł
ul. Floriańska 14
Tel *12 424 33 00* **Map** 6 E2
W podroza.hotel.com.pl
Balzac and Liszt have stayed in the elegant, high-ceilinged rooms at this hotel, Krakow's oldest.

Pollera zł zł
ul. Szpitalna 32
Tel *12 422 10 44* **Map** 6 E2
W pollera.com.pl
An Art Nouveau classic in the heart of the Old Quarter.

Polski Hotel Pod Białym Orłem zł zł
ul. Pijarska 17
Tel *12 422 11 44* **Map** 6 E1
W podorlem.com.pl
Located next to St Florian's Gate, this comfortable hotel provides traditional accommodation.

Saski zł zł zł
ul. Sławkowska 3
Tel *12 421 42 22* **Map** 6 D2
W hotelsaski.com.pl
A traditional hotel in a 16th-century house, with elegant, retro furnishings and old-school service.

Wit Stwosz zł zł zł
ul. Mikołajska 28
Tel *12 429 60 26* **Map** 6 E2
W hotelws.pl
Housed in an old townhouse just off the main Market Square, this plush hotel has attentive service.

Kazimierz Quarter

Regent zł zł
ul. Bozega Ciala 19
Tel *12 430 62 34* **Map** 4 D2
W rhotels.com.pl
A stylish hotel in a 19th-century building with spacious rooms.

Wrought-iron sign outside the Polski Hotel Pod Białym Orłem

Price Guide
Prices are based on one night's stay in high season for a standard double room, inclusive of service charges and taxes.
zł under 300zł
zł zł 300zł to 500zł
zł zł zł over 500zł

Wesoła, Kleparz and Biskupie

Europejski zł
ul. Lubicz 5
Tel *12 423 25 12* **Map** 6 F1
W he.pl
Founded in the 19th century, this friendly family-run hotel is near the railway station.

Polonia zł zł
ul. Basztowa 25
Tel *12 422 12 33* **Map** 6 F1
W hotel-polonia.com.pl
An Art Nouveau gem dating to World War I, the Polonia is a grand place to stay.

Red Brick Apartments zł zł
ul. Kurniki 3
Tel *12 628 66 00* **Map** 2 D3
W redbrick.pl
These self-catering units in a restored 19th-century building sleep two to six people. Perfect for families or groups.

Piasek and Nowy Świat

Maltanski zł zł zł
ul. Straszewskiego 14
Tel *12 431 00 10* **Map** 5 C4
W donimirski.com
A boutique hotel with luxurious but understated rooms in a restored Neo-Classical building.

Further Afield

Dwór w Tomaszowicach zł zł zł
ul. Krakowska 68, Tomaszowice
Tel *12 419 20 00*
W dwor.pl
In a Neo-Classical manor house, this hotel blends luxury with a rural atmosphere.

B&B

Okół and Stradom Quarters

Globus zł zł
ul. Dietla 91
Tel *12 350 62 65* **Map** 6 F4
W globuskrk.pl
In a converted town house, Globus offers rooms and apartments with elegant decor.

Wielopole   zł zł
ul. Wielopole 3
Tel *12 422 14 75*   **Map** 6 E3
W wielopole.pl
A small, friendly B&B in a 19th-
century building.

Old Quarter
Dom Polonii   zł
Rynek Główny 14
Tel *12 422 61 58*   **Map** 6 D2
W wspolnota-polska.krakow.pl
In a classic town house, this
guesthouse has three large
rooms and friendly staff.

La Fontaine   zł
ul. Sławkowska 1
Tel *12 422 65 64*   **Map** 6 D2
W bblafontaine.com
La Fontaine offers cosy rooms and
family-sized apartments.

Tango House   zł
ul. Szpitalna 4
Tel *12 429 31 14*   **Map** 6 E2
W tangohouse.pl
Choose from eight double rooms
and two self-catering studios.

Kazimierz Quarter
Abel   zł
ul. Jozefa 30
Tel *12 411 87 36*   **Map** 4 D1
W abelkrakow.pl
The characterful, individually
furnished rooms here all have
en-suite bathrooms.

Alef   zł
ul. Św. Agnieszki 5
Tel *12 424 31 31*   **Map** 3 C1
W alef.pl
Wooden antique beds, retro
furnishings and a hearty breakfast feature at this popular B&B.

Klezmer-Hois   zł
ul. Szeroka 6
Tel *12 411 12 45*   **Map** 4 E1
W klezmer.pl
This characterful guesthouse is
full of 19th-century artifacts.

DK Choice
Kolory   zł
ul. Estery 10
Tel *12 421 04 65*   **Map** 4 D1
W kolory.com.pl
The bright, homely rooms at
Kolory are decorated with Polish
folk art. It is in the centre of the
nightlife zone, so ask for a room
at the back of the building to
minimize street noise. Breakfast
is served in Les Couleurs café on
the ground floor, whose
croissants and coffee rank
among the best in Krakow .

The sauna room at the Galaxy hotel

Tournet   zł
ul. Miodowa 7
Tel *12 292 00 88*   **Map** 4 D1
W nocleg.krakow.pl
Tournet offers simply furnished,
well-maintained rooms on one of
Kazimierz's quieter streets.

Eden   zł zł
ul. Ciemna 15
Tel *12 430 65 65*   **Map** 4 D1
W hoteleden.pl
Offering large but simple rooms,
Eden also has a kosher restaurant
and a healing salt grotto.

Wesoła, Kleparz and Biskupie
Jordan   zł
ul. Długa 9
Tel *12 430 02 92*   **Map** 1 C3
W nocleg.jordan.pl
Above a travel agent, Jordan
offers simple, pleasant rooms on
a lively shopping street near
colourful markets.

Piasek and Nowy Świat
Fortuna   zł zł
ul. Czapskch 5
Tel *12 422 31 43*   **Map** 5 B3
W hotel-fortuna.com.pl
In a charming building, Fortuna
has decent-sized rooms and
large bathrooms. Friendly service.

Modern
Okół and Stradom Quarters
**Best Western Krakow
Old Town**   zł zł
ul. Św. Gertrudy
Tel *12 422 76 66*   **Map** 6 E4
W bwkrakow.pl
This four-star hotel is well placed
for visiting the Old Quarter.

Old Quarter
Floryan   zł zł
ul. Floriańska 38
Tel *12 431 14 18*   **Map** 6 E2
W http://floryan.com.pl
At the top of a historic town
house, this highly individual hotel
has contemporary design and an
intimate vibe.

Unicus Hotel   zł zł
ul. Św. Marka 20
Tel *12 433 71 11*   **Map** 6 E2
W hotelunicus.pl
In a historic building, Unicus is
contemporary on the inside, with
a grey and brown colour scheme.

Kazimierz Quarter
Columbus   zł zł
ul. Starowiślna 57
Tel *12 252 75 50*   **Map** 4 E1
W hotelcolumbus.pl
The Columbus has rooms decked
out in warm colours, attentive
staff and a good buffet breakfast.

Galaxy   zł zł
ul. Gęsia 22a
Tel *12 342 81 00*   **Map** 4 F1
W http://galaxyhotel.pl
A hotel with designer rooms in
bright colours, Galaxy also has a
pool and a spa centre.

Karmel   zł zł
ul. Kupa 15
Tel *12 430 67 00*   **Map** 4 D1
W karmel.com.pl
A welcoming guesthouse
with high-ceilinged rooms, the
Karmel features an antique-
meets-modern decor.

Kazimierz   zł zł
ul. Miodowa 16
Tel *12 421 66 29*   **Map** 4 D1
W hk.com.pl
The comfortable modern rooms
in this contemporary building
feature stained-glass windows
with scenes from local history.

For more information on types of hotels *see pages 176–9*

zł zł

Map 3 C2

…sja.pl
…eter side of Kazimierz,
… hotel has Art Nouveau-
…d decor in warm colours.

Vesoła, Kleparz and Biskupie

Ibis Budget Stare Miasto zł
ul. Pawia 11
Tel 12 355 29 50   Map 2 D3
W ibisbudget.com
Next to the main railway station,
this no-frills hotel has well-
equipped but functional rooms.

Atrium zł zł
ul. Krzywa 7
Tel 12 430 02 03   Map 1 C3
W hotelatrium.com.pl
A good option near the railway
station, Atrium offers 50 rooms
and two suites with kitchenettes .

Batory zł zł
ul. Sołtyka 19
Tel 12 294 30 30   Map 2 E5
W hotelbatory.pl
This brightly decorated hotel in a
quiet location has friendly staff
and a cosy atmosphere.

Puro Hotel zł zł
ul. Ogrodowa 10
Tel 12 314 21 00   Map 2 D3
W purohotel.pl
Opposite the railway station
and the Galeria shopping centre,
Puro has sleek, minimalist but
well-equipped rooms with
large windows.

Wyspiański zł zł
ul. Westerplatte 15
Tel 12 422 95 66   Map 6 F2
W hotel-wyspianski.pl
This large, functional hotel is a
reliable option, offering three-star
comforts close to the Old Town.

DK Choice

andel's zł zł zł
ul. Pawia 3
Tel 12 660 00 10   Map 6 F1
W andelskrakow.com
Jutting out into the plaza in
front of the main railway station
like an ocean liner, andel's
offers design-conscious,
supremely comfortable rooms
in harmonious colours. It is a
place for spending quality
time in rather than just
sleeping, though its location
opposite Planty Park and the
Old Quarter makes it a perfect
sightseeing base.

Piasek and Nowy Świat

Kossak zł zł
Pl. Juliusza Kossaka 1
Tel 12 379 59 00   Map 5 B4
W hotelkossak.com
A smart hotel with contemporary
design touches. Rooms on the
upper floor offer good views of
the castle and the river.

Logos zł zł
ul. Szujskiego 5
Tel 12 631 62 00   Map 1 B4
W hotel-logos.pl
The stylish Logos offers large
rooms with great bathrooms.
There are sauna and spa facilities.

Further Afield

Dom Goscinny Przegorzaly zł
ul. Jodłowa 13
Tel 12 429 71 15
W dg.uj.edu.pl/przegorzaly
This student campus on the
fringes of Las Wolski forest offers
tourist accommodation over the
summer. Rooms are bright and
plain; the surroundings, peaceful.

Ruczaj zł
ul. Ruczaj 44
Tel 12 269 10 00
W ruczajhotel.pl
Rooms have large windows and
enormous beds at this charming
hotel in a leafy suburb. It has a
sauna and solarium.

Teresita zł
ul. Schweitzera 3
Tel 12 657 94 77
W teresita.pl
Kitsch decor and loud colours
make the gypsy-themed Teresita
a fun place to stay, with simple
but comfortable rooms.

Chopin zł zł
ul. Przy Rondzie 2
Tel 12 299 00 00
W vi-hotels.com
This functional hotel, a 20-minute
walk from the city centre, offers
brightly coloured rooms, efficient
staff and good facilities.

Ibis Krakow Centrum zł zł
ul. Syrokomli 2
Tel 12 299 33 00
W accorhotels.com
Just a short tram ride from the
city centre, this hotel offers
spacious, comfortable rooms.

Novotel Centrum zł zł zł
ul. T. Kościuszki 5
Tel 12 299 29 00   Map 5 C5
W accorhotels.com
Bright rooms, great service and
a generous buffet breakfast are
the main draws here. There is a
gym, sauna and swimming pool.

The sleek reception area of the luxurious
Art Hotel Niebieski in Zwierzyniec

Luxury

Okół and Stradom Quarters

Copernicus zł zł zł
ul. Kanonicza 16
Tel 12 424 3400   Map 6 D4
W copernicus.hotel.com.pl
In a Renaissance town house, this
hotel features beautiful historic
interiors and spacious rooms.

Pugetów zł zł zł
ul. Starowislna 15a
Tel 12 432 4950   Map 6 E4
W donimirski.com/hotel-pugetow
This hotel has original artworks
and sumptuous rooms.

Queen Boutique Hotel zł zł zł
ul. Dietla 60
Tel 12 433 3333   Map 6 E5
W queenhotel.pl
In a 19th-century town house,
this hotel offers plush rooms with
contemporary furnishings.

Senacki zł zł zł
ul. Grodzka 51
Tel 12 422 7686   Map 6 D4
W hotelsenacki.pl
This hotel with well-equipped
rooms is in a historic building.

Old Quarter

Grodek zł zł
ul. na gródku 4
Tel 12 431 9030   Map 6 E3
W donimirski.com/hotel-grodek
Adjoining a Dominican convent,
the opulent 5-star Grodek offers
high-end comfort.

Grand zł zł zł
ul. Sławkowska 5–7
Tel 12 424 0800   Map 6 D2
W grand.pl
A historic hotel with antique
furnishings and superb amenities.

Pałac Bonerowski zł zł zł
ul. Św. Jana 1
Tel *12 374 13 00* **Map** 6 D2
W palacbonerowski.pl
This 16th-century mansion retains some historic features. The bathrooms are totally modern.

DK Choice

Stary zł zł zł
ul. Szczepańska 5
Tel *12 384 08 08* **Map** 6 D2
W stary.hotel.com.pl
In a 15th-century merchant's house, Stary retains many original features, such as exposed brick and stone, high ceilings and wall paintings. Furnishings are contemporary and bathrooms have the highest quality marble. Amenities include a swimming pool, saunas and a spa centre that boasts salt inhalation among its treatments.

Wentzl zł zł zł
Rynek Główny 19
Tel *12 430 26 64* **Map** 6 D3
W wentzl.pl
Elegant rooms here have views over the main Market Square.

Kazimierz Quarter

Metropolitan Boutique Hotel zł zł zł
ul. Berka Joselewicza 19
Tel *12 442 75 00* **Map** 4 D1
W hotelmetropolitan.pl
This plush, modern hotel offers large rooms in soothing colours and a generous buffet breakfast.

Wesoła, Kleparz and Biskupie

Komorowski zł zł zł
ul. Długa 7
Tel *505 989 371* **Map** 1 C3
W hotelkomorowski.com
Ideal for a romantic break, this boutique guesthouse has rich colours and lavish furnishings.

Piasek and Nowy Świat

Amber Design zł zł zł
ul. Garbarska 8–10
Tel *12 421 06 06* **Map** 5 C1
W hotel-amber.pl
Murals inspired by the Art Nouveau artist Stanisław Wyspiański adorn the rooms here.

Sheraton zł zł zł
ul. Powiśle 7
Tel *12 662 10 00* **Map** 5 B4
W sheraton.pl/krakow
The Sheraton offers high-end comfort and service by the river.

Further Afield

Art Hotel Niebieski zł zł zł
ul. Flisacka 3
Tel *12 297 40 00*
W niebieski.com.pl
Large rooms have all mod cons at this tranquil hotel by the river.

Qubus zł zł zł
ul. Nadwiślańska 6
Tel *12 374 51 00* **Map** 4 E2
W qubushotel.com
Large and superbly equipped, this hotel south of the Vistula is perfect for exploring Kazimierz.

Sympozjum zł zł zł
ul. Kobierzyńska 47
Tel *12 261 86 00*
W sympozium.com.pl
A popular conference hotel with great dining and a lively bar.

Hostel

Okoł and Stradom Quarters

DK Choice

Mundo Hostel zł
ul. J. Sarego 10
Tel *12 422 61 13* **Map** 6 E4
W mundohostel.eu
Rooms at this boutique hostel have a geographic theme and contain ethnic-influenced *objets d'art* and textiles. There is a communal kitchen. A quieter option than some of the other backpacker places in town.

Old Quarter

Flamingo Hostel zł
ul. Szewska 4
Tel *12 422 00 00* **Map** 6 D2
W flamingo-hostel.com
A firm favourite, this hostel is off the main square, on a lively street.

Tulip Hostel zł
Pl. Wszystkich Świętych 6
Tel *513 399 690*
W tuliphostel.pl
Tulip has two-, three- and four-bed rooms with wooden floors. There is a fully equipped kitchen.

Tutti Frutti zł
ul. Floriańska 29
Tel *12 428 00 28* **Map** 6 E2
W tuttifruttihostel.com
A mixture of dorms and four-bed rooms is on offer at this central but relaxing hostel.

Kazimierz Quarter

Goodbye Lenin zł
ul. Berka Joselewicza 23
Tel *12 421 20 30* **Map** 4 E1
W goodbyeleninhostel.com
In a ramshackle old house adorned with Pop Art murals, this is an enjoyable, sociable hostel.

Secret Garden Hostel zł
ul. Skawińska 7
Tel *12 430 54 45* **Map** 3 C2
W thesecretgarden.pl
Hidden away in a quiet corner of Kazimierz, this hostel offers bright dorms and double rooms, and a relaxing vibe. Closed 24–27 Dec.

Wesoła, Kleparz and Biskupie

Greg & Tom Hostel zł
ul. Pawia 12–17
Tel *12 422 41 00* **Map** 6 F1
W gregtomhostel.com
This hostel has dorms and double rooms with neat furnishings and a fully equipped kitchen .

Mosquito Hostel zł
Rynek Kleparski 4–6
Tel *12 430 14 61* **Map** 1 C3
W mosquitohostel.com
Mosquito offers a mixture of dorms and private rooms.

An elegant room at the Metropolitan Boutique Hotel

For more information on types of hotels *see pages 176–9*

ERE TO EAT AND DRINK

has always been known as a good
or eating out. Even during the
munist era, when Polish restaurants were
torious for having very little on the menu,
rakow's culinary culture survived unscathed.
Now one of the busiest tourist destinations
in the country, Krakow boasts hundreds of
restaurants, many of the highest quality.
Traditional Polish food is at its best here –
whether in the budget canteen restaurants
where customers queue up to order at the
counter, or in the finer restaurants serving
traditional specialities like roast duck with
apples. There is a growing number of haute
cuisine restaurants offering Mediterranean,
French and contemporary Polish cooking,
often blended with Asian influences. Italian,
Asian, Mexican and South American eateries
can all be found in Krakow. Some of the best
eateries in the city are listed on pages 190–93.

Restaurants

Those who enjoy good food
in a pleasant atmosphere will
not be disappointed in Krakow.
Many of the city's restaurants
are housed in historic buildings
or medieval cellars, usually
painstakingly restored and
tastefully furnished. Eateries
in the bohemian quarter of
Kazimierz frequently opt for
a range of retro styles, with
candles on the table and
antique furniture. Restaurants
on the main Market Square and
on Szeroka Street in Kazimierz
have large areas of outdoor
seating, although pavement
terraces are a rarity elsewhere.
Evenings and weekends tend to
be particularly busy, so booking
a table in advance is advisable.
Wherever you go, restaurants
are not too formal, and there
is no real dress code.

Canteen Restaurants and Vodka-and-Herring Bars

Much of the best local food
can be enjoyed in a *jadłodajnia*
(also known as a *bar mleczny* or

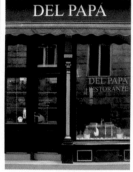

Del Papá, considered by many to be one of
Krakow's best Italian restaurants *(see p192)*

"milk bar"), a budget canteen
restaurant where customers
order at the counter, choosing
from a menu of inexpensive
soups, *pierogi*, potato pancakes,
pork chops and other Polish
staples. The decor is often plain
in these places, but prices are
rock bottom – visitors can enjoy
a three-course meal for as little
as 20zł. *Jadłodajnias* often close
early – usually late afternoon
or early evening, or when the
food has sold out.

The Krakow dining scene is
witnessing a rise in the number
of vodka-and-herring bars,
some of which are open
round the clock. These places
sell spirits and traditional bar
snacks (marinated herring
being one ubiquitous favourite)
for very little money.

Street Food

Krakow pretzels, or *obwarzanki*,
are sold by street vendors
throughout the city and make
an excellent snack. Very much
a local speciality, they are
traditionally coated with salt
crystals, poppy seeds or sesame
seeds. You will also see street
sellers offering delicious hunks of
oscypek, smoked sheep's cheese
from the Tatra Mountains.

Arguably Poland's favourite
street snack, the *zapiekanka* is
a halved baguette covered in
meat, cheese and vegetables,
then toasted. *Zapiekanki* are
sold from fast-food kiosks all
over the city, notably on plac
Nowy, the centre of nightlife
in Kazimierz.

Another ubiquitous feature
of the Krakow street-food scene
is the grilled sausage. The best
sausages are sold at the
outdoor grill on plac Nowy
in Kazimierz and at the kiosk
near the Market Hall in
Grzegórzecka Street, where
they are available until 3 o'clock
in the morning.

Eating at Night

The majority of restaurants in
Krakow close around midnight
but several establishments in

The chic outdoor area at Someplace Else, within the Sheraton Hotel *(see p193)*

Pimiento Argentino, with decor in the style of an Argentinian hacienda *(see p191)*

Kazimierz are open till 1 or 2am. Several vodka-and-herring bars in the Old Quarter stay open round the clock. Plenty of street-food outlets keep going beyond midnight, and it is usually possible to pick up a pizza slice or a *zapiekanka* in the Old Quarter or in Kazimierz well into the early hours.

Prices and Tips

The price of food in Krakow's restaurants is below the European average. A three-course meal without alcohol will cost about 100zł per person in all but the most expensive places. However, drinking alcohol with your meal will add a substantial amount to your bill.

Credit cards are becoming ever more popular and should be readily accepted by all the larger restaurants and those located on the main tourist trail. Signs on windows or doors indicate which cards are accepted by the establishment.

All over Poland a customary tip amounts to about ten per cent of the bill.

Vegetarian Food

The majority of restaurants in Krakow serve at least a handful of vegetarian dishes. Traditional local specialities, such as *pierogi* (dumplings) filled with wild mushrooms,

cheese, sauerkraut or fruit, are very popular, as are all kinds of savoury pancakes, omelettes and *knedle* (potato dumplings). A choice of many colourful and tasty salads is available in all restaurants. Beetroot, carrots, cabbage, cauliflower, celeriac and leeks are traditional Polish favourites. Broccoli, aubergines, celery, endives and courgettes have also been introduced to Polish cuisine. Vegetarian food is available not only from most ethnic restaurants, but also from salad bars, which are very popular and also serve freshly pressed fruit and vegetable

juices. In some restaurants you can create your own salad from a selection of ingredients.

Recommended Restaurants

The restaurants listed on pages 190–93 have been selected to give a cross-section of the most noteworthy places to eat in Krakow. Whether located in the lively main Market Square, the medieval brick cellars of the Old Quarter and Okół or the former Jewish quarter of Kazimierz, they all have an evocative ambience.

The listings cover a vast variety of eateries and cuisine types, from traditional Polish canteens to pizzerias and ethnic restaurants, from places specializing in fish and seafood to designer bistros, and from characterful cafés to smart, elegant restaurants offering fine dining.

Throughout the listings some establishments have been labelled as DK Choice. These stand out from the crowd and offer something particularly special, such as superb local specialities, excellent value for money, a beautiful location, a historical setting, a romantic atmosphere, particular charm or a combination of these factors.

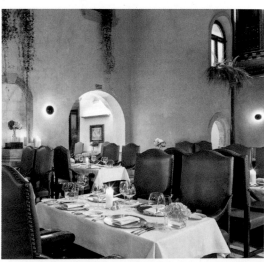

The elegant dining area at Copernicus *(see p190)*

The Flavours of Krakow

Polish cuisine, like that of many central European countries, makes heavy use of meat, especially pork, which is often served quite plainly with potatoes or rice and cabbage. However, because of the long Baltic coastline in the north of the country, fish is also likely to feature on many menus. Carp, trout and herring are particular favourites. Around Krakow, in the south, the local forests yield a bounty of quality game, with duck being very popular. The legacy of former rule by Austria is also evident in the south, especially in some of the sophisticated cakes and pastries.

Pickled herring

Barbecuing meat at a street celebration on Palm Sunday

Meat

Pork (*wieprzowina*) is the most popular meat by far in Poland. It usually comes as a steak (*kotlet schabowy*) or on the bone (*golonka wieprzowa*) and also appears in soups, sausages and as hams. Polish hams are generally cured and have a rich, sweet flavour. Ham is mainly served cold as an appetizer with cheese and pickles, though it may also be eaten for breakfast. Poland also produces high quality veal (*cielęcina*), which is often dished up with a rich mushroom sauce (*cielęcina po staropolsku*) or with cabbage and raisins.

Poultry and Game

Chicken (*kurczak*) is a staple food in Poland and drumsticks (*podudzie*) are especially popular. Chicken livers (*wątróbka*), served with a fruit sauce, are considered a delicacy.

A wide variety of game roams the forests of southern Poland. Pheasant (*bażant*), duck (*kaczka*), goose (*gęś*), venison (*comber*), rabbit (*królik*) and hare (*zając*) are found on many local menus. Availability varies with the season; autumn is the best time to enjoy game.

Parówka (pork frankfurters)
Wiejska (garlic and herb sausage)
Gruba krakowska (smoked garlic sausage)
Chicken kabonos (air-cured sausage with caraway seeds)
Podwawelska (smoked sausage)
Smoked pork loin
Zagòrska (smooth textured, smoked sausage)

Selection of typical Polish sausages and cured meat

Local Dishes and Specialities

Many classic Polish dishes are offered at restaurants all over the country, but fish also features prominently on northern menus, while those of the the the south offer a range of game. The most varied and cosmopolitan cuisine is found in large cities, such as Warsaw and Krakow, where top chefs run the kitchens of some of the grand hotels. The national dish, *bigos*, comes from eastern Poland. It is hearty and warming for the long, bleak winters found there, as is another dish from this chilly region, *pierogi* (pasta dumplings, stuffed with meat, cheese or fruit). Both are influenced by the food of neighbouring Russia. Polish cakes and desserts also tend to be heavy and rich, although most originate in the warmer south, once ruled by Austria.

Green cabbage

Bigos Chunks of meat and sausage are simmered with sauerkraut, cabbage, onion, potatoes, herbs and spices.

A colourful display of locally grown vegetables at a city market stall

Fish

Fish features strongly on menus in northern Poland, where herring (śledź) is a central part of the diet. It comes pickled, in oil, with onions, with soured cream – in fact, with just about everything. Rolmops po kaszubsku (marinated herring wrapped around pickled onion, then spiked with cloves and dipped in soured cream) are widely enjoyed. Other popular fish are freshwater trout (pstrąg) – served simply grilled with boiled potatoes; carp (karp) – often accompanied by horseradish sauce; and salmon (łosoś). A treat in early summer is smoked salmon served with spears of fresh asparagus (łosoś wędzony ze szparagami), which is then in season.

Vegetables

Poland produces many fine quality vegetables. The hardy cabbage (kapusta) remains the country's top vegetable. It is used in so many ways, including raw in salads and simply boiled to partner meat or fish. Cabbage soup

Polish pretzels on sale in a Krakow bread shop

(kapuśniak) and sauerkraut are on every menu. Potatoes are also a staple. They come boiled, baked and mashed, though rarely roasted. Peppers are popular too, often served stuffed with rice and minced meat or pickled in summer salads. Root vegetables such as carrots, parsnips, swede (rutabaga), turnips and beetroot make their way into a range of dishes. Mushrooms grow wild all over Poland and come both cooked and pickled as a tasty addition to many meals.

SNACKS

Sausages A wide range of smoked and unsmoked varieties are on offer at the profusion of street stalls and snack bars that can be found on most city streets.

Precles (pretzels) Another favourite street snack, these are popular, freshly baked, at train and bus stations first thing in the morning.

Zapiekanki Often referred to as Polish-style pizzas, these are tasty, open-top baguettes, spread with cheese and tomato, then toasted and served piping hot. They are also a common item on street-stall menus.

Smalec This snack consists of fried lard, liberally sprinkled with sea salt, and eaten with chunks of crusty bread. It can be found as a bar snack in most pubs and makes a good accompaniment to beer.

Pierogi These ravioli-style dumplings may be stuffed with meat, sauerkraut, mushrooms, cheese or fruit.

Barszcz This beetroot soup, flavoured with lemon and garlic, may be served clear or with beans or potatoes.

Poppy seed roll A rich yeasted dough is wrapped around a sweet poppy-seed filling and baked until lightly golden.

What to Drink in Krakow

In Krakow, as indeed anywhere in Poland, you may try many different brands of exquisite vodkas, both clear and flavoured. Beer is becoming ever more popular and its production is growing rapidly. There are many bars in Krakow that offer a large selection of beers, especially beers brewed in Poland. Poland does not produce quality wines but shops and restaurants offer a large selection of brands imported from all over the world, especially from throughout Europe and the New World.

Vodka

Vodka distilled from potatoes or grain is a Polish speciality. Such brands as clear *Wódka Wyborowa* and dry but flavoured *Żubrówka* are both world-famous. The variety of vodka brands produced in Poland may be bewildering. Clear *Cracovia*, which has been produced in Krakow for some years, is very popular. *Starka* is definitely the oldest brand among quality vodkas. For centuries *starka* was made from unrectified grain spirit, which was aged for at least six years in reused oak wine-casks. The casks used to be buried for ageing, but this is no longer the case. Krakow *Starka* was once regarded as the "queen" of all *starkas*, but has lost this status.

Starka krakowska vodka

Dzięgielówka, a dry vodka flavoured with angelica root

Cracovia, one of the best Polish clear vodkas

Polish distilleries have been decentralized, but have retained the recipes imposed during Communist rule. Above all the lack of an *appellation contrôlée* has resulted in the fact that, if you buy a *Starka krakowska* (Krakow starka), be prepared to accept that it may have been produced elsewhere. (Another example is the renowned Goldwasser liqueur which was unique to Gdańsk but is now produced in Poznań.) *Starka bankietowa* is aged for longer and is definitely one of the best. It is sold in crystal-glass bottles and is a luxurious drink difficult to find elsewhere.

Good kosher plum vodka is distilled in Poland. *Śliwowica łącka* is the best and most famous of all plum vodkas. Paradoxically, it is produced illegally owing to the lack of proper regulations. It is home-made in the small village of Łącko in the mountain region, some 70 km (43 miles) south of Krakow. Śliwowica Łącka is not available from off-licences (liquor stores) but is offered in many households in Krakow.

A vodka glass

Amaretto liqueur	Plum Łąck brandy	Passover Plum vodka	Senator vodka	Krakus vodka	Harnaś vodka

Żywiec logo with the date of establishment

A dancing couple in traditional costumes from the Krakow region

Żywiec Beer Label

Many brands of beer are produced by the Żywiec Brewery, but bottles with the couple dressed in traditional Krakow costumes sell best.

Brackie beer from Żywiec

Lezajsk beer from Żywiec

Beer from the Okocim Brewery

Beer

Polish breweries have developed rapidly over the years. The production of quality beer has grown and been modernized. Figures show that Poles are drinking more and more beer and less strong alcohol.

Pre-1939 advertisement of the Okocim Brewery

Beers from Okocim and Żywiec are traditionally the most popular in Krakow. Kracovians are still very aware that both breweries were established in Galicia. The Okocim brewery was founded by the Goetz family who were raised to the rank of hereditary barons by Emperor Franz Joseph. The Żywiec brewery was set up and owned, until World War II, by the Habsburg Archdukes. The grim paradox was that this Żywiec branch of the Habsburgs, who took up Polish citizenship after World War I, had their brewery confiscated by the Nazis after they refused to sign the *Volkslist*. After World War II the Communists nationalized Żywiec as a former German property. Heineken, the Dutch brewer, acquired a majority

holding in the enterprise a few years ago, and the brewery is now one of the most technologically advanced in Europe.

Wine

Although vineyards were cultivated in the Krakow area quite successfully, they disappeared in the 15th century. Large quantities of quality wine were produced until World War II in the Zaleszczyki region on the then Romanian border. Today only a few vineyards can be found near Zielona Góra in the far west of the country, which means that Poland's wine production is negligible. Any visitor to Krakow wishing to drink wine will find a large selection of imported wines both in shops and restaurants.

Wine comes from many countries, including France, Italy, Spain and Austria, as well as California, Australia, Chile and New Zealand. Hungarian wine, however, is to be recommended in Krakow. This is not only because of its budget price. For centuries Krakow was a place where Tokay wines were stored for ageing, in barrels housed in large cellars beneath Market Square, before being exported all over the world.

Non-Alcoholic Drinks

Mineral water, sparkling and still, is the most popular non-alcoholic drink. Many brands of mineral water come from the springs in the mountain foothills or highlands not far from Krakow. Fruit juices are also popular. Apple and blackcurrant juices are Polish specialities.

Apple juice

Blackcurrant juice

Where to Eat and Drink

Wawel Hill

Pod Basztą zł
Traditional Polish **Map** 3 C1
Zamek Wawel 9
Tel *12 422 75 28*
This stalwart has a well-earned
reputation for good authentic
Polish cooking and reasonable
prices despite its very touristy
Wawel Hill location.

Okół and Stradom Quarters

Balaton zł
Hungarian **Map** 1 C5 & 6 D4
ul. Grodzka 37
Tel *12 429 51 41*
A plain-looking restaurant,
Balaton has been around for a
long time and still serves the best
goulash soups and *pörkölts*
(paprika-rich stews) in town.
Savour them with wine from the
excellent Hungarian list.

Smak Ukrainski zł
Ukrainian **Map** 1 C5 & 6 D4
ul. Kanonicza 15
Tel *12 421 92 94*
Hearty meat-and-potato dishes
and dumplings from Poland's
eastern neighbour are served by
costumed staff in a lively cellar.
Wash them down with a
selection of Ukrainian beers.

Il Calzone zł zł
Italian **Map** 2 D5 & 6 E3
ul. Starowiślna 15a
Tel *12 429 51 41*
This is the restaurant to visit for a
range of high-quality fish and
pasta dishes, plus a long menu
of inexpensive pizzas. There is a
terrace for outdoor dining.

DK Choice

Miód Malina zł zł
Traditional Polish **Map** 6 D4
ul. Grodzka 40
Tel *12 430 04 11*
Occupying lovely barrel-vaulted
rooms decorated in raspberry
shades of red, Miód Malina
("Honey Raspberry") is one of
the most welcoming places to
eat in Krakow. Traditional Polish
festive fare is the main focus,
with generous portions of
meat and poultry followed
by delicious desserts.

Pod Baranem zł zł
Polish **Map** 2 D5 & 6 E4
ul. Św Gertrudy 21
Tel *12 429 40 22*
There are few better places in
Krakow for Polish cuisine with a
modern European twist, made
with locally sourced ingredients.

Sakana Sushi Bar zł zł
Asian **Map** 2 D5 & 6 E4
ul. Św. Gertrudy 7
Tel *12 429 30 86*
Enjoy a range of sushi, tempura
dishes and soba noodles at one
of Krakow's best Asian restaurants.

Trattoria La Campana zł zł
Italian **Map** 1 C5 & 6 D4
ul. Kanonicza 7
Tel *12 430 22 32*
This is a great place for a romantic
dinner. Ingredients in the dishes
are imported from Italy.

Copernicus zł zł zł
Fine dining **Map** 1 C5 & 6 D4
ul. Kanonicza 16
Tel *12 424 34 21*
This atmospheric hotel restaurant
specializes in superlative modern
Polish cuisine and lots of game.

The sunny alfresco dining area at Pimiento Argentino

Price Guide
Prices are for a three-course meal per
person, with a half-bottle of house wine,
including tax and service.

zł   under 50zł
zł zł   50zł to 80zł
zł zł zł   over 80zł

Pod Aniołami zł zł zł
Traditional Polish **Map** 6 D3
ul. Grodzka 35
Tel *12 421 39 99*
Classic Polish recipes, superbly
prepared, are served in
meticulously restored medieval
cellars that were once home to
goldsmiths' workshops.

Old Quarter

DK Choice

Ambasada Śledzia zł
Polish **Map** 6 D3
ul. Stolarska 8/10
Tel *662 569 460*
An outstanding example of the
vodka-and-snack bars cropping
up all over Poland, the "Herring
Embassy" serves traditional
Polish bar food, such as
marinated fish and potato pie
meat in aspic at rock-bottom
prices. Drinks are similarly good
value; no wonder the outdoor
terrace is constantly full.

Camelot zł
Café-patisserie **Map** 6 D2
ul. Św. Tomasza 17
Tel *12 421 01 23*
This mildly bohemian café with
a cabaret club downstairs is
famous for its good coffee, fine
cakes and delicious apple pie.

Chimera zł
Polish **Map** 5 C2
ul. Św. Anny 3
Tel *12 292 12 12*
At this buffet restaurant in a
medieval cellar, you pay
according to the size of your
plate. It is ideal for sampling a
variety of different dishes.
Vegetarian options aplenty.

Green Day zł
Vegetarian **Map** 6 E2
ul. Mikołajska 14
Tel *12 431 10 27*
A good-value buffet restaurant,
Green Day serves all kinds of
meat-free fare, including filling
soups, generous salads and tasty
savoury pancakes.

Noworolski zł
Cafe-patisserie **Map** 6 D2
Rynek Główny 1/3
Tel *12 422 47 71*
This beautifully preserved Art Nouveau treasure attracts both locals and visitors eager for a cup of coffee and a slice of something sweet. Try the *sernik* (cheesecake).

DK Choice

La Petite France zł
Cafe-patisserie **Map** 6 E2
ul. Św. Tomasza 25
Tel *12 370 20 74*
A combined delicatessen and café, this ideal lunchtime spot is dominated by the aroma of fresh cheeses and charcuterie. As well as strong coffee, La Petite France serves some of the finest quiches in Poland and delicious gourmet sandwiches. With only eight tables and a few bar stools, it's a cosy, intimate space.

U Babci Maliny zł
Traditional Polish **Map** 6 D1
ul. Sławkowska 17
Tel *12 422 76 01*
Krakow has no shortage of queue-at-the-counter budget restaurants, and this is one of the best, serving all manner of classic Polish fare in a folksy bench-filled basement.

Zapiecek zł
Traditional Polish **Map** 6 D1
ul. Sławkowska 32
Tel *12 422 74 95*
This is something of a temple to the humble *pierogi* (stuffed dumplings), which are served with a range of fillings. The savoury, sweet and baked versions are all well represented.

Chłopskie Jadło zł zł
Traditional Polish **Map** 6 D2
ul. Św. Jana 3
Tel *12 429 51 57*
Polish classics dominate the menu at this characterful, folk-styled restaurant, with plenty of meat dishes in heavy sauces. There is also a long list of typical Polish alcoholic spirits.

CK Dezerter zł zł
Eastern European **Map** 1 C5
ul. Bracka 6
Tel *12 422 79 31*
Large portions of meaty Polish and Austro-Hungarian classics are served at this charming restaurant. The soups are terrific, and cabbage has never tasted as good as in the sauerkraut here.

Diners enjoying their meal accompanied by live music at CK Dezerter

Czerwone Korale zł zł
Traditional Polish **Map** 6 D1
ul. Sławkówska 13–15
Tel *12 430 61 08* **Closed** *lunch Sat & Sun*
Decorated with dolls in Polish costume and pictures of folk-dancing villagers, this is the perfect place to feast on traditional fare. All dishes are reasonably priced.

Farina zł zł
Seafood **Map** 6 D1
ul. Św. Marka 16
Tel *12 422 18 60*
An informal, Mediterranean-themed restaurant that specializes in fish and seafood. Fine white fish is served grilled, pan-fried or baked.

Hawelka zł zł
Traditional Polish **Map** 6 D2
Rynek Główny 34
Tel *12 422 06 31*
For fine Polish cuisine in a historic setting, it is difficult to do better than Hawelka, which has been serving roast duck and other classics since 1876 and is somewhat a local institution.

Leonardo zł zł
Italian **Map** 6 E2
ul. Szpitalna 20-22
Tel *12 429 68 50*
Exquisite cuisine, including superb pasta dishes, is served in this basement dining room decked out to look like a Mediterranean piazza.

Marmolada zł zł
Tradtional Polish **Map** 6 D3
ul. Grodzka 5
Tel *12 396 49 46*
Classic Polish cuisine and Italian pizzas are on the menu at this smart restaurant. A profusion of candles and cut flowers provide a soothing ambience. There is live classical music on Saturday and Sunday evenings.

Miód i Wino zł zł
Traditional Polish **Map** 6 D1
ul. Sławkowska 32
Tel *12 422 74 95*
Enjoy classic Polish food in a traditional setting, with waiting staff in folk costumes and wooden-bench seating. This is a good place for meat-heavy feasting washed down with local beer.

Pimiento Argentino zł zł
Argentinian **Map** 6 D3
ul. Stolarska 13
Tel *12 422 66 72*
Meat-lovers will relish the steaks freshly imported from Argentina at this grill restaurant. The menu includes everything from beef empanadas to ribeye steaks. South American wines complete the picture.

Restauracja we Francuskim zł zł
Contemporary Polish **Map** 6 D1
ul. Pijarska 13
Tel *666 195 831*
This hotel restaurant with understated decor is famous for reinventing European classics (such as Wiener Schnitzel and beef Stroganoff) with great skill. Waiters dressed in white serve the freshly prepared dishes at your table.

Resto Illuminati zł zł
International **Map** 6 D3
ul. Gołębia 2
Tel *12 430 73 73* **Closed** *lunch (Jul & Aug)*
Boasting exposed-brick interiors, Iluminati is a good restaurant to sample the best of modern Polish cuisine. Traditional meat and poultry dishes are cooked with a Mediterranean twist. There is often live piano music in the evenings.

Amadeus zł zł zł
International **Map** 6 E2
ul. Mikołajska 20
Tel *12 423 03 40*
International and Polish dishes take pride of place on the menu of this restaurant in the hotel of the same name. The service is outstanding; the wines exemplary. The decor is themed on Wolfgang Amadeus Mozart.

Aqua e Vino zł zł zł
Italian **Map** 6 D1
ul. Wiślna 5/10
Tel *12 421 25 67*
The dishes at this outrageously trendy restaurant appear as carefully designed as the interior. Expect imaginative takes on classic recipes made from fresh ingredients, and superb desserts.

For more information on types of restaurants *see pages 184–5*

DK Choice

Cyrano de Bergerac   zł zł zł
Fine dining   Map 6 D1
ul. Sławkowska 26
Tel 12 411 72 88
If prices are high, the diners
who book days in advance here
don't seem to mind. This is a
world-class French restaurant,
set in two elegant rooms, with a
quiet patio for the summer. The
food is exquisite (leave room for
the extravagant desserts), and
the service impeccable. Look
out for affordable set-menu
lunches on weekdays.

Da Pietro   zł zł zł
Italian   Map 6 D2
Rynek Główny 17
Tel 12 422 32 79
The quality food here is made
with ingredients imported from
Italy. The unrivalled main-square
location is reflected in the prices.

Del Papá   zł zł zł
Italian   Map 6 D2
ul. Św. Tomasza 6
Tel 12 421 83 43
This is one of Krakow's best
Italian eateries, with a menu that
features classic meat dishes as
well as Mediterranean seafood.

Grodek   zł zł zł
Fine dining   Map 6 E3
ul. Na Grodku 4
Tel 12 431 90 30
Polish and International cuisine
prepared with flair is served in
the brick-lined basement of the
historic Grodek hotel.

Pod Różą   zł zł zł
International   Map 6 E2
ul. Floriańska 14
Tel 12 424 33 81
Under a glass-covered atrium
at the Pod Różą hotel, this
restaurant combines tradition
and creativity in its dishes.
Game is a speciality.

Szara   zł zł zł
International   Map 6 D2
Rynek Główny 6
Tel 12 421 66 69
An imposing place with vaulted
ceilings, crisp linens and a grand
menu that spans the globe, Szara
has a reputation for quality.

Tetmajerowska   zł zł zł
Traditional Polish   Map 6 D2
Rynek Główny 34
Tel 12 422 06 31
From the elegant decor to the
sublime service, everything at this
modern restaurant contributes to
a special experience.

The courtyard at Del Papá, perfect for
alfresco dining in warm weather

Trzy Rybki   zł zł zł
Fine dining   Map 6 D2
ul. Szczepańska 9
Tel 12 384 08 01
The cosy flagship restaurant of
the Stary hotel offers a seasonally
changing menu of European fare.

Wentzl   zł zł zł
International   Map 6 D3
Rynek Główny 19
Tel 12 429 52 99
Savour Polish and European food
in a historic room with oak floors,
high ceilings and lavish fabrics.

Wierzynek   zł zł zł
Traditional Polish   Map 6 D3
Rynek Główny 15
Tel 12 424 96 00
Claiming to be the oldest
restaurant in Krakow, Wierzynek
serves sumptuous Polish fare in
elegant, wooden-beamed rooms.

Kazimierz Quarter

Dawno temu na Kazimierzu   zł
Traditional Polish   Map 4 E1
ul. Szeroka 1
Tel 12 421 21 17
Enjoy classic Polish and Jewish
fare in a room full of retro
furnishings and memorabilia.

Fabryka Pizzy   zł
Italian   Map 4 D2
ul. Jozefa 34
Tel 12 433 80 81
The "Pizza Factory" serves some
of the tastiest and best-value
thin-crust pizzas in Poland, plus
a good selection of pasta dishes.

Manzana   zł
Mexican   Map 4 D1
ul. Miodowa 11
Tel 12 422 22 77
This is the place for tacos, burritos,
fajitas and other Mexican classics.
It also has the biggest selection
of tequila in Krakow.

DK Choice

Pierogi Mr Vincent   zł
Polish   Map 4 D2
ul. Bozego Ciała 12
Tel 506 806 304
Pierogi (stuffed pastry pockets)
are among Poland's most
emblematic dishes, yet they
rarely receive the culinary
attention they deserve. This tiny
restaurant offers only *pierogi*
with all kinds of creative fillings,
including exotic spicy versions.

Polakowski   zł
Polish   Map 4 D1
ul. Miodowa 39
Tel 12 421 21 17
This popular order-at-the-
counter restaurant offers the best
in Polish cooking, including *bigos*,
pierogi and *żurek* (rye soup), plus
pancakes and Jewish specialities.

Zazie Bistro   zł
French   Map 4 D2
ul. Józefa 34
Tel 500 410 829
Everything from onion soup and
bouillabaisse to mussels with fries
is served at this bistro. With
low prices and little space, it's
often busy.

Genji Sushi Premium   zł zł
Japanese   Map 6 E5
ul. Dietla 55
Tel 12 429 59 59
This restaurant offers a full range
of Japanese dishes. The decor is
Far Eastern too, with one room
carpeted in dried rushes.

Horai   zł zł
Asian   Map 4 D2
pl. Wolnica 4
Tel 12 430 03 58
The menu at Horai spans the
entire Asian continent, with solid
standards across the board. The
Thai curries are especially strong.

Trezo   zł zł
Traditional Polish   Map 4 D1
ul. Miodowa 33
Tel 12 374 50 00
Classic meat, poultry and fish
dishes are presented with style in
an interior that mixes modern
minimalism with exposed brick.
Live music at weekends.

Klezmer Hois   zł zł zł
Jewish   Map 4 E1
ul. Szeroka 6
Tel 12 411 16 22
Quality Jewish and Central
European fare is served in
this restaurant filled with bric-a-
brac. There is Klezmer
music nightly.

For key to prices *see page 190*

DK Choice

Studio Qulinarne   zł zł zł
Contemporary Polish Map 4 D2
ul. Gazowa 4
Tel *12 430 69 41*
Studio Qulinarne uses
traditional Polish ingredients,
Mediterranean style and the
odd touch of Oriental spice to
conjure up an original menu.
Game and seafood feature
strongly. The bright interior is
filled with bookshelves and
wine bottles; the garden is
one of Krakow's loveliest.

Wesoła, Kleparz and Biskupie

Trzy kroki w szaleństwo   zł zł
International   Map 2 E4
ul. Lubicz 28
Tel *12 430 04 38*
An attractive brick-lined cellar is
the setting for this contemporary
restaurant, offering inventive
pasta and fish dishes, steaks and
delicious desserts.

Jarema   zł zł zł
Eastern European   Map 2 D3 &
6 F1
pl. Matejki 5
Tel *12 429 36 69*
Cuisine from the eastern margins
of what used to be the Polish–
Lithuanian commonwealth are
on the menu here, including
plenty of hearty meat dishes
sourced from old recipe books.

Piasek and Nowy Świat

Mamma Mia   zł
Italian   Map 5 C1
ul. Karmelicka 14
Tel *12 430 04 92*
A classy pizzeria that draws local
families in droves, Mamma Mia
opts for authenticity rather than
experimentation in its traditional
pizza toppings. There are also
many pasta alternatives.

Smakołyki   zł
Traditional Polish   Map 5 C4
ul. Straszewskiego 28
Tel *12 430 30 99*
Located opposite the main
university building, this
contemporary, bright canteen
restaurant is the ideal place to
try filling, inexpensive Polish
favourites such as potato
pancakes, stuffed cabbage
leaves and borscht.

CK Browar   zł zł
Traditional Polish   Map 6 D1
ul. Podwale 6–7
Tel *12 429 25 05*
This large brewery-restaurant is
an excellent place to enjoy local
favourites such as sausages and
bigos, plus the house-brewed ales.

Dynia Resto-Bar   zł zł
International   Map 5 B2
ul. Krupnicza 20
Tel *12 430 08 38*
The "Pumpkin" excels in pasta
dishes, salads and fresh cakes. It
has a wonderful walled garden.

Someplace Else   zł zł
Mexican   Map 3 B1 & 5 B4
ul. Powiśle 7
Tel *12 662 10 00*
The bar of the Sheraton offers an
affordable menu of Mexican
specialities, plus burgers and
chicken wings. Sporting events
are shown on the big screen.

Zielona Kuchnia   zł zł
Organic   Map 1 B3
ul. Grabowskiego 8/9
Tel *12 634 55 22*   **Closed** *Sat, Sun*
The emphasis at this sleek eco-
restaurant is on organic produce
and naturally reared meats. There
are also vegetarian options.

Biała Róża   zł zł zł
International   Map 1 C5 & 5 C4
ul. Straszewskiego 16
Tel *12 421 51 90*
This convivial restaurant between
the Philharmonic Hall and Wawel
Hill serves Polish classics with
French and Italian influences.

The Olive   zł zł zł
Mediterranean   Map 3 B1 & 5 B4
ul. Powiśle 7
Tel *12 662 16 60*
The Sheraton Hotel's showpiece
restaurant offers refined Polish
and Mediterranean fare, especially
fish and seafood. Good wine list.

Solfeż   zł zł zł
International   Map 1 C5 & 5 C4
ul. Straszewskiego 17
Tel *12 618 88 88*
Enjoy inventive European cuisine
and attentive service in the
elegant Radisson Hotel.

Further Afield

Stylowa   zł
Traditional Polish
osiedle Centrum C bl. 3 (Aleja Róża)
Tel *12 644 26 19*
One of the few restaurants in
Nowa Huta, Stylowa is like a step
back in time, with its 1980s decor
and old-fashioned (but delicious)
meat-and-potatoes menu.

U Ziyada   zł zł
International
ul. Jodłowa 13
Tel *12 429 71 05*
Perched high on a hill, this café-
restaurant on the edge of Las
Wolski forest has superb views
across the Vistula River and
serves quality Polish, European
and Kurdish cuisine.

Zakładka   zł zł
French   Map 4 E3
ul. Józefińska 2
Tel *12 442 74 42*   **Closed** *Mon lunch*
Just across the river from the
Kazimierz Quarter, this bistro
offers a creative and seasonally
changing menu. You can also
pop in simply for a sandwich
and a glass of wine.

Villa Decius   zł zł zł
Fine dining
ul. 28 Lipca 1943 17a
Tel *12 425 33 90*
A luxurious restaurant in a
park-fringed Renaissance villa,
Decius serves classic Polish
and other European cuisines
with old-school finesse.

The airy interior of The Olive, located inside the Sheraton Hotel

For more information on types of restaurants *see pages 184–5*

Cafés and Bars

Krakow's cafés are an important part of everyday life and are often institutions in their own right. It would be unthinkable to deny a Krakovian his or her daily 15 minutes or so spent chatting with a friend or reading a newspaper in a café. The majority of cafés have regular customers, who come year in, year out to their chosen place, every day except at weekends.

Cafés

Situated in the heart of the city, **Kawiarnia Noworolski** is one of the longest established cafés. It is housed in the Cloth Hall, with its entrance facing the Mickiewicz Monument. It dates back to the end of the 19th century. The interior, modelled on Viennese cafés, has preserved its original appearance. A visit to the **Jama Michalika** *(see p116)*, renowned for the Zielony Balonik (Green Balloon) Cabaret, is a must. However, the Art Nouveau rooms offer a feast for the eye rather than the palate. They are now often deserted, possibly because of a total ban on smoking (smoke would damage the historic interior).

The **Pożegnanie z Afryką** (Out of Africa) is the best place for lovers of good coffee. The coffee served here will satisfy even the most demanding customer. Situated in St Thomas Street (ul. Św. Tomasza), it is a coffee bar and shop. A variety of brands are available here, which can be prepared in small espresso machines. The smell is so fantastic that it is hard to resist buying or trying a cup. There are many outlets of Pożegnanie z Afryką in other cities throughout Poland but the company started in Krakow and has its headquarters here.

The **Café Zakopianka** occupies meticulously restored 19th-century premises right on the Planty Park and has a distinctly Parisian feel and live music. If you want to travel back in time and see how a patisserie looked in the early 19th century, then **Europejska** in Market Square is the place to visit, to see the original period furnishing.

This café was established by a Swiss man, Lorenzo Paganino Cortesi, in 1823, but the name Redolfi refers to its second owner, also Swiss. Lunch is also served here.

Krakow's very large student population is one of the main reasons the city's cafés continue to thrive and haven't become gentrified curiosities for tourists. Students of all subjects, ranging from art to philosophy and astrophysics, can be found lounging around in the cafés that surround the old university buildings. These include **Nowa Prowincja**, with its legendary hot chocolate, and **Café Gołębia 3**, a down-at-heel hangout where you could meet anyone from a professor of literature to the CEO of one of the city's many hi-tech startups. Apple cake *(szarlotka)* is the usual order, and provides delicious fuel for conversation.

Tasty canapés served on bread from the highlands and tea with home-made raspberry syrup are just two specialities of the **Café Camelot**. The walls here are decorated with pictures by the celebrated Polish naive artist Nikifor. The **Dym** (Smoke) is next door, serving delicious Pischinger cake as well as beer and spirits.

Street Cafés

Most of the eateries in Market Square (Rynek Główny) open street bars and cafés in the spring and summer. The square is thus transformed into a huge open-air café for thousands of customers.

A little away from the square, the corner of ul. Św. Tomasza and ul. Św. Jana is a tiny pavement café paradise.

The street café set up by the **Black Gallery** is very busy at night, sometimes till the early hours. An enormous parachute will protect you from rain, and the house drink Kamikaze, a deceptive mixture of Blue Curacao, vodka and lemon juice, may well help you not notice any change in the weather.

If you decide to eat at one of the outdoor restaurant tables, expect a lunch rather than a full dinner menu. Dishes served outside are less elaborate. Bear in mind that the journey from the kitchen to the table is a long one and makes serving an exotic *flambé* lobster, for example, almost impossible.

All sorts of street buskers roam and play in and around the street cafés. They request gratuities but you are not obliged to give any. It is worth listening to the gypsy band, with a partially paralysed fiddler in a wheelchair, who plays his violin holding it like a double-bass.

Bars

An increasing number of bars have opened in Krakow. They are often called "pubs" as in England. They are housed in cellars and are open till late, and live music is played in many. The **Free Pub** in the Old Quarter and **Singer** in Kazimierz were the first and remain firm favourites. Hot hangouts for the younger crowd include **Pauza**, **Alchemia**, **Kitsch** and **Piękny Pies**.

The **Pod Złotą Pipą** is popular with more conservative customers. The place is nostalgically decorated in the Austro-Hungarian style and features many portraits of His Imperial Majesty Franz Joseph and the Empress Sissi. White sausage with cabbage and peas is served here, and to accompany this you may order authentic Czech Budweiser on draught. The fruits of Poland's rocketing craft-beer revival can be sampled at **Omerta** and the appropriately named **House of Beer**.

DIRECTORY

Afera
ul. Sławkowska 13.
Map 1 C4 (6 D1).
Tel 12 421 17 71.

Albo Tak
ul. Mały Rynek 4.
Map 2 D4 (6 E3).
Tel 12 421 11 05.

Alchemia
ul. Estery 5.
Map 4 D1.
Tel 12 421 22 00.

Antycafe
ul. Sławkowska 12.
Map 1 C4 (6 D2).
Tel 506 48 18 88.

Aperitif
ul. Sienna 9.
Map 1 C4 (6 D3).
Tel 12 432 33 33.

Ariel
ul. Szeroka 18.
Map 4 E1.
Tel 12 421 79 20.

Arlekin
Rynek Główny 24.
Map 1 C4 (6 D2).
Tel 12 430 24 57.

Black Gallery
ul. Mikołajska 24.
Map 2 D4 (6 E2).
Tel 12 423 00 30.

Bomba
Plac Szczepański 2/1.
Map 1 C4 (5 C1).
Tel 782 60 19 99.

Bunkier Café
Plac Szczepański 3A.
Map 1 C4 (5 C1).
Tel 12 431 05 85.

Café Camelot
ul. Św. Tomasza 17.
Map 1 C4 (6 D2).
Tel 12 421 01 23.

Café Czekolada
ul. Bracka 4.
Map 1 C4 (6 D3).
Tel 12 430 24 08.

Café Gołębia 3
ul. Gołębia 3.
Map 1 C4 (5 C3).
Tel 12 430 24 19.

Café Manekin
ul. Św. Tomasza 25.
Map 2 D4 (6 E2).

Café Numero
Rynek Główny 6.
Map 1 C4 (6 D2).
Tel 12 421 13 05.

Café Zakopianka
ul. Św Marka 34a.
Map 1 C4 (6 D1).
Tel 12 421 40 45.

Carpe Diem
ul. Floriańska 33.
Map 2 D4 (6 E2).
Tel 12 431 22 67.

Charlotte
Plac Szczepański 2.
Map 1 C4 (5 C1).
Tel 600 807 880.

Dym
ul. Św. Tomasza 13.
Map 1 C4 (6 D2).
Tel 12 429 66 61.

Dynia Resto Bar
ul. Krupnicza 20.
Map 1 B4 (5 A2).
Tel 12 430 08 38.

Europejska
Rynek Główny 35.
Map 1 C4 (6 D2).
Tel 12 429 34 93.

Free Pub
ul. Sławkowska 4.
Map 1 C4 (6 D2).
Tel 0802 90 82.

Le Fumoir
ul. Sławkowska 26.
Map 1 C4 (6 D2).
Tel 12 429 54 28.

Hamlet
ul. Miodowa 9.
Map 4 D1 (6 F5).
Tel 12 422 12 11.

Hot Chili
ul. Pijarska 9.
Map 1 C4 (6 D1).
Tel 12 422 12 92.

House of Beer
ul. Św. Tomasza 35.
Map 1 C4 (6 D2).
Tel 12 794 222 136.

Jama Michalika
ul. Floriańska 45.
Map 2 D4 (6 E2).
Tel 12 422 15 61.

Jazz Rock Café
ul. Sławkowska 12.
Map 1 C4 (6 C1).
Tel 511 433 506.

Kawiarnia Noworolski
Rynek Główny 1,
Cloth Hall.
Map 1 C4 (6 D2).
Tel 12 422 47 71.

Kitsch
ul. Grodzka 20.
Map 1 C5 (6 D4).
Tel 12 518 879 055.

Krzysztofory
ul. Szczepańska 2.
Map 1 C4 (6 D2).

Lamus
ul. Karmelicka 54.
Map 1 B3.

Manggha
ul. Marii Konopnickiej 26.
Map 2 D5 (6 E3).
Tel 12 267 27 03.

Nowa Prowincja
ul. Bracka 3–5.
Map 1 C5 (6 D3).
Tel 12 430 59 59.

Omerta
ul. Kupa 3.
Map 4 D1.
Tel 12 501 508 227.

Pauza
ul. Floriańska 18.
Map 2 D4 (6 E2).
Tel 12 422 48 66.

Piękny Pies
ul. Bożego Ciała 9.
Map 4 D2.

Pierwszy Lokal
ul. Stolarska 6.
Map 1 C5 (6 D3).
Tel 12 431 24 41.

Pod Białym Orłem
Rynek Główny 45.
Map 1 C4 (6 D2).
Tel 12 421 57 97.

Pod Papugami
ul. Św. Jana 18.
Map 1 C4 (6 D2).
Tel 12 422 82 99.

Pod Złotą Pipą
ul. Floriańska 30.
Map 2 D4 (6 E2).
Tel 12 421 94 66.

Poezja Smaku
ul. Jagiellońska 5.
Map 1 C4 (6 D2).
Tel 12 292 80 20.

Pożegnanie z Afryką
ul. Św. Tomasza 21.
Map 1 C4 (6 E2).
Tel 12 644 47 45.

Ratuszowa
Rynek Główny 1.
Map 1 C4 (6 D2).
Tel 12 421 13 26.

Royal Art Café
ul. Św Gertrudy 29.
Map 2 D5 (6 E4).

Senacka
ul. Grodzka 51.
Map 1 C5 (6 D4).
Tel 12 422 76 86.

Singer
ul. Estery 20.
Map 4 D1.
Tel 12 292 06 22.

Stare Mury
ul. Pijarska 21.
Map 2 D4 (6 E1).
Tel 12 421 38 98.

U Literatów
ul. Kanonicza 7.
Map 1 C5 (6 D4).
Tel 12 421 86 66.

U Louisa
Rynek Główny 13.
Map 1 C4 (6 D3).
Tel 12 617 02 22.

Vis-a-vis
Rynek Główny 29.
Map 1 C4 (6 D2).
Tel 12 422 69 61.

Wiśniowy Sad
ul. Grodzka 33.
Map 1 C5 (6 D3).
Tel 12 430 21 11.

Yummie
Rynek Główny 25.
Map 1 C4 (6 D2).
Tel 12 421 34 44.

SHOPS AND MARKETS

Krakow has always been a favourable place for merchants and recent reforms have stimulated trade. Unlike in other Polish cities, most of the prewar buildings in Krakow have remained in private hands. After 1989 the number of new shops opening surged with house owners either opening shops themselves or letting premises out. A profusion of shop-signs appeared on façades, inner courtyards and basements. Quality soon took over and big Western names also began to appear. Today one can hardly tell the difference between a Krakow shop and its Viennese or Parisian counterpart. The area around Market Square is especially good for shopping. It offers a variety of elegant shops, little traffic and many cafés. Markets and street stalls offer a different kind of shopping and a lively atmosphere. There is something for everyone.

Shopping Hours

In Poland, unlike in many other Western European countries, there is no law regulating the hours of trade. Each shop owner decides for themselves when to open and close their shop, and this is regarded as a necessary part of a free-market economy. Grocers open in Krakow at 6 or 7am and close at 7pm at the earliest. Many remain open until 10pm or longer, and a dozen or so shops are open 24 hours. Other types of shops are generally open between 10am and 7pm on weekdays, but on Saturdays close at 2 or 3pm. All shops within the Planty green belt tend to trade on Sundays for similar periods to those on Saturdays. All shops are customarily open on the Sunday preceding Christmas and Easter Day. Supermarkets are at their busiest on Friday afternoon and evening. The great number of tourist shops in the centre attract customers all

Pictures for sale, displayed on the wall near St Florian's Gate

the time regardless of the day of the week but Saturdays are possibly the busiest.

How to Pay

Cash is the most popular form of payment throughout Poland. The situation is different in major cities, where most of the shops in the city centre do accept major credit cards, as indicated by stickers displayed in their windows. Supermarkets and department stores also accept credit cards as well as cheques, but the latter must be issued by a Polish bank. All the prices displayed are inclusive of VAT.

Department Stores and Shopping Malls

Jubilat, built in the mid-1970s, is the largest department store in Krakow. The food department is on the ground floor, and on the other floors you will find household goods, furniture and electrical appliances, clothes, shoes and cosmetics, as well as toys and books. The large **Galeria Krakowska** shopping mall is located by the main train station, and there is another large mall, **Galeria Kazimierz**, on

A collectors' fair in Market Square

the opposite side of town. Both contain dozens of stores, including international names, and at least one large supermarket. A little out of town, but served by many bus routes, is a large branch of the **Factory** clothes discount store.

Right on the Market Square (Rynek Główny) is the **Pasaż 13** shopping centre. Converted from a beautiful old townhouse, it has 17 designer and boutique shops, plus a restaurant.

Krakow now has at least eight large shopping malls further out from the centre, with more opening all the time. They include mega supermarkets, DIY stores and all the usual services you would expect elsewhere in Europe.

Dolls in regional costumes sold in the Cloth Hall

Jewellery shop on Floriańska Street

Markets and Fairs

Krakow's markets are never called bazaars as in other Polish towns. Here the term bazaar has a pejorative connotation. In Krakow locals go to the "square" to buy fruit and vegetables, cheese, meat, fish or other produce from the stallholders.

The Old Kleparz market is the nearest to the city centre. The New Kleparz market sells not only food but also flowers and clothes, while every Tuesday and Friday you will find stalls selling brooms, clay pots and wickerware. The market in Grzegórzecka Street by the Market Hall is the biggest

and full of stalls selling meat, fruit and vegetables. On Sundays you have the added attraction of book and antique stalls.

The unique atmosphere of the New Market in Kazimierz was used to good effect in the filming of *Days and Nights (Noce i dnie)*, a Polish film after a well-known novel by Maria Dąbrowska of the same title. The late 19th-century round butchers stalls, which are centrally located, are still in use. These stalls are surrounded by vegetable and fruit stands. On Sundays this place becomes an extensive flea market, where among other things you can buy famous Harris tweed jackets from Scotland and woollen coats and Tyrolean tunics from Austria. The Tomex Market in

Nowa Huta is dominated by sellers from the former Soviet Union. The so-called Tandeta Market sells mostly clothes. Although *tandeta* means rubbish in Polish, this term is used in Krakow to mean an ordinary clothes market and has no derogatory meaning.

Sales

Seasonal sales are now quite common in a number of larger shops but, in terms of the selection of goods on offer and the prices, they are not as attractive as those in other Western European countries. Goods are no longer reduced because they are imperfect or no longer in fashion, as used to be the case, but because of promotions, end of season sales or the arrival of new collections.

A flower stall in Market Square

Shopping in Krakow

If you are a Western visitor you can expect to be able to find everything in Krakow you can buy at home. It is no longer necessary to bring items for everyday use. On the other hand you should not expect luxury Western merchandise, such as perfumes, alcohol, designer clothes and shoes and other branded items, to be cheaper in Poland. You may, however, find bargains in shops and galleries selling handicrafts, silver jewellery, contemporary paintings and prints, as well as leather goods, bric-à-brac and coffee-table books.

Book and Record Shops

There are many excellent bookshops in Krakow. **Massolit Books** sells second-hand and new books in English. It also features a café that serves teas and superb cakes. It's common to find people pouring over books in here for hours on end. This is typical of Krakow, where the way of life is still heavily influenced by artists, professors and students. Massolit also hosts literary readings, art exhibitions and musical events.

Empik, one of Poland's leading book retailers, has nine branches in Krakow, with the two biggest in the Galeria Krakowska and Kazimierz malls. Galeria Krakowska is also home to **The American Bookstore**, which sells only English-language books.

For visitors with more literary tastes, the prestigious **Znak** bookshop in Kościuszki Street has a large selection of foreign titles. Academic books and fiction can be bought at the **Ossolineum** and Elefant bookshops. The **Księgarnia Muzyczna Kurant** in Market Square specializes in music books, scores and recordings. The shop of the **Polskie Wydawnictwo Muzyczne** (Polish Music Publishers) has a similar assortment with an emphasis on classical music. Among many shops in the centre selling CDs and cassettes, the one in Poselska Street offers a particularly good selection of jazz and classical recordings. It also has a useful sale-or-return section. The music shop found in Mikołajska Street specializes in jazz.

Antiques

Krakow is possibly the best place in Poland for antiques because the city was saved from destruction during World War II and Krakovians did not have to migrate. Foreigners are advised that exporting pre-1945 antiques from Poland is illegal without special permission, which is very difficult to obtain (see p210). As far as valuable works of art are concerned, as well as those which form part of the cultural heritage, such as paintings, furniture, jewellery, old prints, rare books and maps, this law is rigorously observed, but less so in the case of objects of lesser value and bric-à-brac, which are plentiful in Krakow.

Antique dealers are mainly located in the area around the Planty gardens. Occasional antique markets take place in Market Square. Every Sunday, sellers of collectors' items and second-hand books put up their stalls by the Market Hall in Grzegórzecka Street. They are worth visiting.

Folk Art

The annual folk Art Fair in Market Square takes place in September. Dozens of stalls are set up, selling sculpture, earthenware, woven rugs and wood carvings made in various parts of Poland.

The stalls in the **Cloth Hall** offer a large selection of crafts and are a must for the tourist. You will find here colourful, embroidered traditional costumes of the Krakow and Podhale regions, as well as walking sticks from the highlands, crafted with an axe-like handle; ornate chess sets and jewellery boxes, devotional statues and Jewish objects all carved in wood; paper cutouts, painted Easter eggs, traditional dolls and much more.

Crafts and Contemporary Art

The stands in the Cloth Hall also sell silver jewellery, amber *objets d'art*, leather items and fabrics for the home. Shopping in this Renaissance hall has the added bonus of sustaining a trading tradition that goes back to the 16th century. The charming **Kramy Dominikańskie** (Dominican Stalls) also specialize in crafts. The **Galeria Osobliwości** (Gallery of Curiosities) in Sławkowska Street sells rare and unusual objects. The **Calik** Gallery is famous for Christmas decorations and attracts customers from all over the world.

Krakow is a good centre for Polish contemporary art, which is enjoying an ever-greater demand. Works by contemporary artists can be found in the **Starmach Gallery**, **Zderzak**, **Space Gallery**, **Galeria Mariana Gołogórskiego**, **Dominik Rostworowski Gallery**, **Kocioł Artystyczny** and many others. The open-air gallery by St Florian's Gate is the place for lovers of images of sunsets and sunrises, galloping horses or large-scale nudes. This kind of painting is displayed on the city wall throughout the year. Fans of satirical drawings by **Andrzej Mleczko** will find a visit to his gallery in St John's Street (Św. Jana) a must.

Clothes and Shoes

Jeans can be found in abundance in almost any clothes shop and those who prefer the well-known brands can go to the shops of **Levi Strauss**, **Diesel**, **Wrangler** or Lee. There are also shops that sell the leading brands of sports shoes: **Reebok** and **Puma**.

Timberland has fashion for the young, while designer menswear is available from **Pierre Cardin**. Polish brands, such as **Vistula**, offer less expensive suits for men, and **Wólczanka** specializes in shirts. **IDEA FIX** is a hothouse of Polish design, mixing fashion, art, music and photography. **Linen Dream** sells unique shawls, tunics and coats made by Polish artisans with organic materials.

Promod offers a good selection of clothes and shoes from both leading foreign brands and designers as well as Polish names.

The **Zebra** chain of shops is best for Italian shoes and the **Nico** store is great for Italian fashion for the whole family – men, women and children.

Food Shops and Off-Licences (Liquor Stores)

The only supermarket in the centre of Krakow is in the **Galeria Krakowska** mall. The Delikatesy general grocery store next to the Hawełka Restaurant is the largest in Market Square. Its selection of alcoholic drinks is particularly good. Apart from a number of small shops close to Market Square there are several self-service ones.

The large supermarkets such as **Real** and **Tesco** are located away from the centre and cater for shoppers who come by car. There are supermarkets on most of the housing estates, catering for local needs.

Most Krakovians purchase their fruit and vegetables from local stalls and markets. The Old Kleparz market is the closest to the city centre just a few minutes' walk away. The selection of coffee brands available from the charming **Pożegnanie z Afryką** (Out of Africa) is hard to beat. Julius Meinl's famous Viennese coffee is only available from the Meinl supermarket in the Azory (Azores) housing estate. The little and delightfully decorated **Pod Aniołami** (Angels) shop sells exquisite cold meats prepared according to old Polish recipes, *bundz* and

oszczypek cheese from the highlands, as well as country-style bread baked in log-fired ovens. Wines are also sold here but the largest selection from around the world can be found in the off-licence (liquor store) **In Vino Veritas**, as well as in the drinks department at the Galeria Krakowska. Those who favour strong spirits may choose the **Polmos** shop, where they can not only buy but also sample drinks at the bar.

Lovers of chocolate will be welcomed in the **Wawel** shop in Market Square, selling goods from the local sweet factory, Zakłady Przemysłu Cukierniczego. Many patisseries throughout Krakow offer a wonderful selection of cakes and pastries. The best doughnuts can be bought at **Michałek** and nougat at **Cichowski**. Look out for *kremówka*, a delicious puff-pastry cake filled with custard and available in the city's main patisseries. Note that what is known as *kremówka* in Krakow, in Warsaw is called *napoleonka*.

Other language differences between Mazovia and Lesser Poland include the names given to fruits of the forest, blueberries are called *borówki* in Krakow and Galicia, and *czarne jagody* in the Warsaw region. All berries, including the non-edible varieties, are called *jagody* in Krakow; *brusznice* is the name given to small red berries, which are called *borówki* in Warsaw, but in both regions *żurawiny* is the name for cranberries.

There are further differences in bread terminology which will probably confuse first-time visitors to the city. A long white loaf of bread called *weka* in Krakow is known as Wrocław bread in Warsaw.

Cosmetics

All chemists (drug stores) and supermarkets sell basic cosmetic goods, but expensive international brands are best purchased from specialist shops where expert advice is also available. **Guerlain** and Yves Rocher have their own outlets and beauty clinics.

Well-known foreign brands of perfumes, such as Gucci, Biagotti, Trussardi, Bulgari, Carolina Herrera and Burberry are available from the large **Marionnaud** shop or from **Sephora**. Another place to find a good selection of brands is in hotel shops.

Pharmacies

The majority of drugs are available from Polish chemists on prescription only. Prescriptions issued by overseas doctors are generally accepted without any problem. Non-prescription drugs and medicines are readily available throughout the city. In the city centre, there are many chemists in the following streets, among others: **Szczepańska, Grodzka** or **Dunajewskiego**. If you need some medication after normal opening hours, then go to one of the chemists that are open 24 hours; their addresses are displayed in all the chemists' shop windows. A 24-hour telephone service (12 94 39) will provide you with general medical information, including the location of the nearest hospital with an accident and emergency unit.

Florists

Krakow would not be Krakow without the flower stalls by the Mickiewicz statue in Market Square. On the day of the great poet's birthday, these street vendors have made it a tradition to lay flowers at the base of the statue in tribute. They also regularly make a gift of flowers to visiting foreign VIPs. On warm summer days you can buy flowers till late into the evening. There are many flower stalls to be found in New Kleparz market. Of the specialist florist shops, **Niezapominajka** (Forget-me-not) is particularly well known. Alternatively, you can buy bunches of flowers in one of the many 24-hour shops and at petrol stations.

DIRECTORY

Department Stores and Shopping Malls

Factory Outlet
ul. Różańskiego 32.
Tel 12 297 35 00.

Galeria Kazimierz
ul. Podgórska 34.
Map 4 F1.
Tel 12 433 01 01.

Galeria Krakowska
ul. Pawia 5.
Map 2 D3 (6 F1).
Tel 12 428 99 00.

Jubilat
al. Krasińskiego 1–3.
Map 1 B5 (5 B4).
Tel 12 619 33 00.

Pasaż 13
Rynek Główny 9.
Map 1 C4 (6 D2).
Tel 12 422 77 13.

Book and Record Shops

American Bookstore
ul. Pawia 5 (Galeria Krakowska).
Map 2 D3 (6 F1).
Tel 12 628 75 73.

Empik
ul. Pawia 5 (Galeria Krakowska).
Map 2 D3 (6 F1).
Tel 12 451 03 85.

Inter Book
ul. Karmelicka 27.
Map 1 B3.
Tel 12 632 10 08.

Księgarnia Muzyczna Kurant
Rynek Główny 36.
Map 1 C4 (6 D2).
Tel 12 422 98 59.

Massolit Books
ul. Felicjanek 4.
Map 1 B5 (5 B4).
Tel 12 432 41 50.

Ossolineum
ul. Św. Marka 12.
Map 2 D4 (6 E2).
Tel 12 422 58 44.

Polskie Wydawnictwo Muzyczne (Polish Music Publishers)
al. Krasińskiego 11a.
Map 1 B5 (5 B4).
Tel 12 422 70 44 ext.121.

Znak
ul. Sławkowska 1.
Map 1 C4 (6 D2).
Tel 12 422 45 48.

Rare and Second-Hand Books

Antykwariat AB
Rynek Główny 43.
Map 1 C4 (6 D2).
Tel 12 421 69 03.

Antykwariat księgarski
ul. Stolarska 8/10.
Map 1 C5 (6 D3).
Tel 12 422 62 88.

Bibliofil
ul. Szpitalna 19.
Map 2 D4
(6 E2). **Tel** 12 422 18 61.

Krakowski Antykwariat Naukowy
ul. Św. Tomasza 8.
Map 1 C4 (6 D2).
Tel 12 421 21 43.

Rara Avis
ul. Szpitalna 11.
Map 2 D4 (6 E2).
Tel 12 422 03 90.

Antiques

Antique
ul. Św. Tomasza 19.
Map 1 C4 (6 D2).
Tel 503 517 171.

Connaisseur
Rynek Główny 11.
Map 1 C4 (6 D2).
Tel 12 503 517 171.

Desa
ul. Floriańska 13.
Map 1 C4 (6 D2).
Tel 12 422 27 06.

ul. Grodzka 8.
Map 1 C5 (6 D4).
Tel 12 421 54 54.

Galeria Kersten
ul. Sławkowska 5/7.
Map 1 C4 (6 D1).
Tel 12 424 08 49.

Sopocki Dom Aukcyjny
Rynek Główny 45.
Map 1 C4 (6 D2).
Tel 12 429 12 17.

Folk Art

Cloth Hall
Rynek Główny 1/3.
Map 1 C4 (6 D2).

Crafts and Contemporary Art

Autorska Galeria Andrzeja Mleczki (Mleczko Gallery)
ul. Św. Jana 14.
Map 1 C4 (6 D2).
Tel 12 421 71 04.

Bunkier Sztuki
Pl. Szczepański 3A.
Map 1 C4 (5 C2).
Tel 12 422 10 52.

Calik
Rynek Główny 7.
Map 1 C4 (6 D2).
Tel 12 421 77 60.

Dominik Rostworowski Gallery
ul. Św. Jana 20.
Map 1 C4 (6 D2).
Tel 12 423 21 51.

Galeria Jana Siuty
ul. Sławkowska 14.
Map 1 C4 (6 D1).

Galeria Mariana Gołogórskiego
ul. Grodzka 29.
Map 1 C5 (6 D4).
Tel 12 421 44 19.

Galeria Osobliwości
ul. Sławkowska 16.
Map 1 C4 (6 D1).
Tel 12 429 19 84.

Galeria Związku Polskich Artystów Plastyków (Gallery of the Association of Polish Artists)
ul. Łobzowska 3.
Map 1 C3 (5 C1).
Tel 12 632 46 22.

Kocioł Artystyczny
ul. Sławkowska 14,
1st floor.
Map 1 C4 (6 D2).
Tel 12 429 17 97.

Kramy Dominikańskie
ul. Stolarska 8/10.
Map 1 C5 (6 D3).
Tel 12 422 19 08.

Mocak
ul. Lipowa 4.
Map 3 F2.
Tel 12 263 40 01.

Pryzmat
ul. Łobzowska 3.
Map 1 C3 (5 C1).
Tel 12 632 46 22.

Space Gallery
ul. Św. Marka 7.
Map 1 C4 (6 D1).
Tel 12 432 29 20.

Starmach Gallery
ul. Węgierska 5.
Map 4 E3.
Tel 12 656 43 17,
12 656 49 15.

Zderzak
ul. Floriańska 3.
Map 1 C4 (6 D2).
Tel 12 429 67 43.

Clothes and Shoes

Diesel
Rynek Główny (Pasaż 13).
Map 1 C4 (6 D2).
Tel 12 617 02 16.

IDEA FIX
ul. Bocheńska 7 .
Map 4 D2.
Tel 12 422 12 46.

Levi Strauss
ul. Floriańska 9.
Map 1 C4 (6 D2).
Tel 12 428 15 73.

Linen Dream
ul. Grodzka 63.
Map 1 C5 (6 D4).
Tel 790 46 61 03.

Nico
ul. Modlnica 214.
Tel 12 637 03 95.

Pierre Cardin
ul. Kamieńskiego 11
(Bonarka City Center).
Map 4 D5.
Tel 506 457 825.

Promod
ul. Floriańska 18.
Map 1 C4 (6 D2).
Tel 694 462 950.

Puma
ul. Pawia 5.
Map 2 D3 (6 F1).
Tel 12 628 76 35.

Reebok
ul. Pawia 5.
Map 2 D3 (6 F1).
Tel 12 628 76 48.

Timberland
ul. Szewska 20.
Map 1 C4 (5 C2).
Tel 12 432 84 40.

Troll
ul. Pawia 5.
Map 2 D3 (6 F1).
Tel 12 628 78 67.

Vistula
ul. Pawia 5 (Galeria Krakowska).
Map 2 D3 (6 F1).

Wólczanka
Pl. Mariacki 1.
Map 1 C4 (6 D2).
Tel 12 421 83 16.

Wrangler
ul. Pawia 5.
Map 2 D3 (6 F1).
Tel 12 428 99 00.

Zebra
Rynek Główny 7.
Map 1 C4 (6 D2).
Tel 12 421 40 34.

Food Shops

Carrefour
ul. Witosa 7.
Tel 12 639 48 00.

Chichowsky
ul. Starowiślna 21.
Tel 12 421 02 27.

Krakowski Kredens
ul. Grodzka 7.
Map 1 C5 (6 D4).
Tel 12 423 81 59.

Michałek
ul. Krupnicza 6.
Map 1 B4 (5 C2).
Tel 12 422 47 05.

Pod Aniołami
ul. Grodzka 35.
Map 1 C5 (6 D4).
Tel 12 421 39 99.

Polo Market
ul. Św. Gertrudy 5.
Map 2 D5 (6 E4).
Tel 518 014 075.

Pożegnanie z Afryką
ul. Św. Tomasza 21.
Map 2 D4 (6 D2).
Tel 12 644 47 45.

Real
ul. Bora Komorowskiego 37. Tel 12 617 06 00.

Tesco
ul. Dobrego Pasterza 67.
Tel 12 412 75 34.

ul. Kapelanka 54.
Map 3 A3.
Tel 12 255 25 00.

ul. Włoska 2.
Tel 12 655 76 71.

ul. Wybickiego 10.
Tel 12 633 43 99.

Wawel
Rynek Główny 33.
Map 1 C4 (6 D2).
Tel 12 423 12 47.

Cosmetics

Guerlain
ul. Św. Jana 20.
Map 1 C4 (6 D2).
Tel 12 422 39 45.

Marionnaud
ul. Szpitalna 34.
Map 2 D4 (6 E2).
Tel 12 421 30 55.

Sephora
ul. Floriańska 19.
Map 1 C4 (6 D2).
Tel 12 421 24 24.

Off-Licences (Liquor Stores)

Baryłeczka
ul. Szczepańska 9.
Map 1 C4 (5 C2).
Tel 12 429 62 67.

Dom Wina
ul. Starowiślna 66.
Map 2 D5 (6 E3).
Tel 12 431 03 68.

In Vino Veritas
ul. Łobzowska 26.
Map 1 B2 (5 C1).
Tel 12 606 805 51.

Polmos
ul. Starowiślna 26.
Map 2 D5 (6 E3).
Tel 12 423 11 18.

Regionalne Alkohole
ul. Miodowa 28a.
Map 4 D1 (6 F5).
Tel 533 59 33 35.

Strefa Piwa
ul. Krowoderska 37.
Map 1 B2.

Pharmacies

ul. Dunajewskiego 2.
Map 1 B4 (5 C2).
Tel 12 422 65 04.

ul. Grodzka 34.
Map 1 C5 (6 D4).
Tel 12 421 85 44.

Apteka Bonifratrów
ul. Krakowska 50.
Map 4 D2.
Tel 12 426 80 10.

Apteka Niezapominajka
ul. Starowiślna 1.
Map 2 D5 (6 E3).
Tel 12 421 08 08.

Dbam o Zdrowie
ul. Podwale 6.
Map 1 B4 (5 C2).
Tel 12 429 49 43.

Europa
ul. Karmelicka 42.
Map 1 B3.
Tel 12 632 72 57.

Pod Złotym Lwem
ul. Długa 4.
Map 1 C2
Tel 12 422 62 04.

Pod Złotym Tygrysem
ul. Szczepańska 1.
Map 1 C4 (5 C2).
Tel 12 422 92 93.

Świat. Apteka
ul. Szpitalna 38.
Map 2 D4 (6 E2).
Tel 12 422 65 34.

Ziko
ul. Dunajewskiego 2.
Map 1 C4 (5 C1).
Tel 12 687 57 47.

Florists

BeA
ul. Łobzowska 33/10.
Map 1 B3.
Tel 601 504 436.

Konwalia
ul. Zwierzyniecka 23.
Map 1 B5 (5 B4).
Tel 12 422 93 52.

Margareta
ul. Długa 74.
Map 1 C2.
Tel 12 633 78 63.

Niezapominajka
al. Krasińskiego 1.
Map 1 A5 (5 B4).
Tel 12 619 33 31.

Sofi-Flora
ul. Pawia 5.
Map 2 D3 (6 F1).
Tel 12 628 78 77.

ENTERTAINMENT IN KRAKOW

Krakow is the cultural capital of Poland, and visitors looking for entertainment may find themselves spoiled for choice. Local theatres are among the best in the country and often host leading international companies. The Szymanowski Philharmonic Orchestra and Choir and the Capella Cracoviensis have excellent reputations. There are many concerts and festivals of classical and folk music organized in the magnificent interiors of historic houses and churches. The history of Krakow's

cabarets goes back some 100 years, attracting both domestic and foreign audiences. The busy nightlife can be compared to that offered by Italian or Spanish cities. You only have to walk a couple of minutes to find a variety of music clubs, discotheques and bars. They are usually housed in Gothic or Renaissance cellars and are open until very late or even till the early hours of the morning. Theatre, film, music and ballet festivals take place throughout the year.

Useful Information

Full listings of cultural events in Krakow appear in the *Karnet – Krakowskie Aktualności Kulturalne* monthly, published by **InfoKraków** in both Polish and English. For the electronic version of the *Karnet* see their website on: www.karnet. kracow.pl. Current listings and reviews of cinemas, theatres and other events, as well as a guide to restaurants, discos and clubs (live music) are published on Friday in the *Gazeta Wyborcza* supplement entitled *Co jest grane?* (What's on?). Listings also appear in local newpapers on a daily basis. Information in English, German, French and Russian is also available on the website www.krakow.pl, under the heading "Calendar of Events". *Magiczny Kraków* is also a good source of information in English.

A theatre performance

Booking Tickets

Tickets for all major events can be purchased from the InfoKraków tourist office. This is also the best place to make enquiries about how and where to buy other tickets or to make an advanced booking. Staff at the Centre speak English, French, German and Italian. Booking is also possible through travel agents and hotel receptions.

Seats for the Philharmonic Hall and the theatres are available from their respective box offices, which also take advance bookings. Cinema tickets can be booked over the phone. Bear in mind that some performances require booking months in advance.

Ticket Prices

Ticket prices have increased considerably in recent years, but they are still cheaper than in the West. Theatre seats are more expensive in Krakow compared to anywhere else in Poland, and in greatest demand. Average prices vary from 25 to 40 zł per person. Cinema tickets cost between 13 and 20 zł. Museum tickets are good value; in some museums entrance is free on one day of the week.

Night Transport

Bus and tram day-routes stop around 11pm. Night buses and trams operate according to timetables displayed at stops or online; visit www.mpk.krakow.pl for more information. Tickets can be purchased from ticket machines at some stops and on most trams and buses.

Taxis are a better option. A radio-taxi booked over the phone is cheaper than one at a taxi-rank but you can rely on the taxis waiting at the ranks in the city centre. Most taxi drivers are honest, but it is best to

Musicians wearing costumes of the Krakow region

avoid the taxi rank by the main Railway Station. If you require a taxi while in the main Railway Station area, go to the radio-taxi rank situated at roof level above the platforms (use the platform stairway).

Festivals

The city plays host to a multitude of cultural festivals; the only problem is how to choose the most interesting. The International Festival of Alternative Theatre will appeal to theatre fans, the Krakow Film Festival to film lovers, the Krakow Spring Ballet Festival to ballet aficionados, the International Festival of Music in Old Krakow to admirers of classical music, while enthusiasts of brass instruments may enjoy the International Music Festival of Military Bands.

Walks and Open-Air Events

The tradition of open-air fairs in Krakow goes back to at least the early part of the 19th century when folk festivals were organized on the Błonia fields, then located out of town. One of the attractions was to try to climb a pole smeared in soap, a flask of alcohol and sausages attached to the top of the pole awaiting the successful climber. The event has since disappeared but the Błonia is still a venue for public events, of either a traditional or light entertainment nature. Two great cavalry parades in the inter-war years, attended by Marshals Józef Piłsudski and Edward Rydz Śmigły respectively, took place here. The masses celebrated on these fields by Pope John Paul II, and attended by millions of the faithful, are commemorated by a granite block brought here from the Tatra Mountains.

All kinds of concerts, festivals and fairs also take place at the Błonia.

The Jordan Park, situated opposite the Błonia fields, is very popular with mothers with toddlers. Doctor Henryk Jordan, a Krakow physician, introduced the idea of playing fields which are now found throughout the country and are named after this celebrated physician. The Jordan Park in Krakow was the first-ever public playground for small children.

A pillar advertising cultural events

The Wolski Wood (Las Wolski) is not far from Krakow and offers many walking routes (see pp172–3). For Krakovians it is one of the favourite destinations for a day out, though the zoo (see p173) is also popular. At weekends and on public holidays there is no access to the zoo by car, so use bus or taxi services. On weekdays a charge is made to enter the zoo by car.

Summer concerts in the open air are organized in the Wawel Castle courtyard, in the gardens of the Archaeological Museum and in Radio Kraków's amphitheatre as well as in the courtyard of the Collegium Iuridicum and on a temporary stage in Market Square.

The cosy interior of the Pod Baranami cinema

Out of Town Trips

A number of appealing sights are located within close proximity to Krakow. A trip to the Ojców National Park (see p158), one of the smallest but most beautiful of Polish national parks, is an unforgettable experience. White limestone rocks, such as Hercules's Club, have very unusual shapes.

The Salt Mines at Wieliczka (see p158) have been included by UNESCO on their World Heritage List. The mines and the underground sanatorium housed here are unique. Niepołomice (see p157) has a 14th-century castle and the remnants of an ancient forest where bison are bred. The Benedictine Abbey in Tyniec (see p159) is beautifully located on the Vistula and worth visiting, as is Schindler's Factory (see p158), in the former industrial district of Zabłocie.

Krakow Opera House (Opera Krakowska), incorporating the former riding school building

Theatre, Music, Nightlife and Sports

Krakow is famous for its cultural traditions. The renowned Stary Theatre gained its fame through productions directed by Konrad Swinarski and counts as one of Europe's leading theatre companies. The city resounds with music of every kind, ranging from classical concerts and opera to hip-hop, techno, rock and jazz in the lively clubs. Cabarets continue the best of traditions that go back to the beginning of the 20th century. As well as myriad cultural events, Krakow also offers good sporting facilites for those who like to keep active.

Foreign-Language Performances

Krakow does not have a theatre company that performs in a foreign language on a permanent basis. The annual Festival of French-speaking Theatre takes place in May and attracts many companies from French-speaking countries. The city occasionally hosts foreign theatre companies from all parts of the world who perform in their own languages.

A number of bodies, such as the **Institut Français**, the **Goethe Institut**, the **Instituto Cervantes de Cracovia**, the **Istituto Italiano di Cultura** and the **Manggha Japanese Centre of Art and Technology**, are all actively involved in artistic patronage. They usually organize events in the language of their country, and information about these events can be obtained from **InfoKraków**.

Theatre

The first professional theatre company was established in Krakow in 1781, and today there are many theatres. The most renowned is **Stary Teatr** (Old Theatre). The best actors, directors and set designers work for the Stary Teatr whose performances are mostly based on Polish and other Eastern European classics and Romantic literature.

The **Teatr im. Juliusza Słowackiego** shares the same traditions and types of plays. The building, modelled on the Opéra Garnier in Paris, opened in 1893. Its splendid Art Nouveau interior features a curtain designed by the painter Henryk Hektor Siemiradzki. As an added bonus, spectators may watch the performance from the box originally used by the Austro-Hungarian Emperor, Franz Joseph and his wife Sissi.

The **Krakowski Teatr Scena Stu** gained fame through unconventional performances, sometimes staged in the open air, and other grand productions. In their main venue in aleja Krasińkiego, their performances are predominantly of the classics. Benefit performances celebrating theatre stars take place here, and are broadcast by television. These have became classics in their own right.

The **Ludowy Theatre** in Nowa Huta has a young cast who perform not only in Nowa Huta but also in two other venues in Krakow – in the cellars beneath the Town Hall and in Kanonicza Street.

The **Bagatela Theatre** specializes in light satirical productions. The **Teatr Lalki i Maski Groteska** generally performs for children but has also staged a number of plays for adults.

The experimental productions of the world-famous Cricot 2 theatre ceased following the death of its radical founder and director, Tadeusz Kantor, in 1990. The **Cricoteka** is a museum that documents the history of this major theatre and the art of Tadeusz Kantor, and includes photographs and set designs.

Opera and Ballet

After many years without a permanent venue, the **Opera Krakowska** moved into its premises on ul. Lubicz in 2008. It continues to stage occasional performances at various venues across the city, including the courtyard of Wawel Castle and underground at the Wieliczka Salt Mines. The productions here include Galician all-time favourites by Kalman, Lehar and the Strausses.

For many years, ballet was rather unpopular in Krakow, but regular performances now take place at the Opera Krakowska building. Two festivals, the annual Krakow Spring Ballet Festival, which takes place in May and June, and the International Ballet Festival have played an important role in increasing the popularity of ballet.

Cabaret

Cabaret artists are much in demand in Krakow and can always rely on good audiences and sell-outs. Opened in 1956, the literary **Piwnica Pod Baranami**, is the longest-running cabaret in Krakow and is famous throughout Poland. Despite the death of its founder Piotr Skrynecki in 1997, the cabaret continues and is very popular.

The **Loch Camelot** is artistically affiliated to the Piwnica and also performs in cellars. Very popular is the **Kabaret Pod Wyrwigroszem**, which puts on shows in various venues across town.

Lovers of the classic, satirical texts of the **Jama Michalika** Cabaret may still attend a performance here. In surroundings which include Art Nouveau objects and caricatures dating from the early 20th century, they may listen to Tadeusz Boy-Żeleński's verses. The original decadent ambience of this place is, however, difficult to recreate today, the menu lacks absinthe and there is a total ban on smoking.

Cinemas

Krakow has many multiplex cinemas, but the largest and best independent cinema is **Kijów.Centrum**. Besides its regular programme, it is also a venue for a number of festivals, including the Krakow Film Festival and one dedicated to commercials. Food and drinks are available on the first floor. A truly Parisian-style multiplex, the **Kino ARS**, is situated at the junction of św. Jana and św. Tomasza. It comprises several auditoria named after historic cinemas, such as Gabinet, Kiniarnia, Salon, Aneks and Reduta. Cafés can be found in all of them.

The small **Pod Baranami** cinema, housed in the Palace of the Rams, is very popular with those seeking independent and art-house films from around the world. Its prime location is an added bonus. After a show, walk a few steps to enjoy a drink in the Piwnica Pod Baranami bar. Among other cinemas worth recommending are the **Kika** and **Mikro**.

Classical Music

The most prestigious concert hall in Krakow is the Szymanowski Philharmonic Hall, home of the **Filharmonia**. Classical music is, however, best enjoyed in the more informal setting of one of the city's many historic houses. Among the many venues are the Wawel Castle, the National Museum in the Cloth Hall and the **Akademia Muzyczna** (Music Academy), as well as churches, such as St Mary's (see pp94-7), St Catherine's (see p128) and the Holy Cross (see p117). In summer, concerts are also organized outside in such open-air venues as the arcades of the Wawel Castle, Collegium Maius's courtyard, in the former prison of St Michael (now the Archaeological Museum), and in the Radio Kraków amphitheatre, housed in the former Tarnowski Palace. For those prepared to travel a little, then there are the renowned organ recitals in the Romanesque Benedictine Abbey in Tyniec near Krakow (see p159).

Music Clubs

Any jazz fan visiting Krakow should seek out the **Jazz Club u Muniaka**. Here on Fridays and Saturdays Janusz Muniak, one of Poland's most celebrated jazzmen, plays to the accompaniment of other musicians. Jazz concerts take place at the **Harris Piano Jazz Bar, Mile Stone Jazz Club**, and **Jazz Club Kornet** (traditional jazz) as well as Piwnica pod Baranami. Apart from jazz, **U Louisa** provides blues music and during the break you can surf the Internet using one of several terminals provided.

The **Rotunda-Orlik** and **Pod Jaszczurami** student clubs are also venues for rock groups, blues bands and student cabaret songs. Live music, and rock in particular, can be heard in a number of pubs such as **Alchemia, Klub Piękny Pies** and **Jazz Rock Café**.

Nightclubs and Discos

The best venue for techno music, experimental music and drum and bass is the barrel-vaulted **Krzysztofory**. **Afera Club, Pod Papugami, Społem, Frantic** and **Prozak 2.0** discos are also popular, with a good party atmosphere.

Drukarnia caters for fans of avant-garde hip-hop, grunge and acid jazz music. Lovers of music of the sixties will enjoy the **Bosto** club, which offers a retro atmosphere on its small dance floor. The front end of a Syrena car, mounted in the wall, is a reminder of this unforgettable period.

If you feel exhausted after having a wild time in a disco, **Kitsch, Free Pub** and **Black Gallery** are good places to go to to relax. Krakow's nightclubs do not have any specific hour at which they close. In summer, especially, a club-goer may simply leave a club and go straight to work.

Sports

As far as sports facilities are concerned, Krakow has much to offer. Two neighbouring sports clubs, **KS Cracovia** and **TS Wisła**, are the oldest and most popular in the city. Both clubs have their own swimming pools, which are open to the public.

The artificial lake in Kryspinów has clean water and is a good place for both beach lovers and windsurfers. A supervised swimming area can be found in the **Nad Zalewem Recreation Centre**. However, here there is a charge for the use of the centre and the lake's beaches. The sports grounds in the Jordan Park (see pp212–13) are a good place for badminton players. Other sports clubs include **Korona, Olsza** and **Zwierzyniecki**.

Tennis courts are available at **Centrum tenisowe, Klub tenisowy "Kosłówek"** and **Hotel Crown Piast**. The courts at the Olsza and Zwierzyniecki sports centres are open all year round.

Horse-riding facilities are available at the University Riding Club, as well as at a number of stables located on the outskirts of the city and further afield.

Increasingly, Krakovians have shown an interest in healthy living. Sauna, sun bed and health and beauty clinics have opened in all parts of the city, as have fitness clubs such as **Relax Body Club** and **Fit-Styl**. The **Korona Club**, which is attached to the hotel of the same name, offers a covered swimming pool (filled with sea water), fitness centre and sauna facilities.

If you want to go for a run during your visit, take advantage of Błonia Fields (see p149), the expansive meadow in the middle of the city.

Billiards can be played in a number of venues throughout Krakow. Billiards and snooker clubs include **Daddy's Bilard, Frame Snooker & Bilard** and **Prominent**.

DIRECTORY

Booking Tickets

InfoKraków
ul. Św. Jana 2.
Map 1 C4 (6 D2).
Tel 12 421 77 87.

Foreign and International Institutes

The British Council
Rynek Główny 6.
Map 1 C4 (6 D3).
Tel 12 428 59 30.

Goethe Institut
Rynek Główny 20.
Map 1 C4 (6 D3).
Tel 12 422 58 29.

Institut Français
ul. Stolarska 15.
Map 1 C5 (6 D3).
Tel 12 424 5350.

Instituto Cervantes de Cracovia
ul. Kanonicza 12.
Map 1 C5 (6 D4).
Tel 12 421 32 55.

International Cultural Centre
Rynek Główny 25.
Map 1 C4 (6 D3).
Tel 12 424 28 11.

Istituto Italiano di Cultura
ul. Grodzka 49.
Map 1 C5 (6 D4).
Tel 12 421 89 46.

Manggha Japanese Centre of Art and Technology
ul. Konopnickiej 26.
Map 3 B1.
Tel 12 267 27 03.

Theatre

Bagatela Theatre
ul. Karmelicka 6.
Map 1 B4 (5 C2).
Tel 12 424 52 12.

Cricoteka
ul. Kanonicza 5.
Map 1 C5 (6 D4).
Tel 12 422 83 32.

Krakowski Teatr Scena Stu
al. Krasińskiego 16–18.
Map 1 A5 (5 A4).
Tel 12 422 27 44.

KTO
ul. Gzymsików 8.
Tel 12 623 73 00.

Ludowy Theatre
Os. Teatralne 34.
Map 1 B4 (5 C2).
Tel 12 680 21 16.

Opera Krakowska
ul. Lubicz 48. **Map** 2 F3.
Tel 12 296 62 60.

Stary Teatr
ul. Jagiellońska 5.
Map 1 C4 (5 C2).
Tel 12 422 90 80.

Stowarzyszenie Teatralne „Łaźnia"
ul. Paulińska 28. **Map** 3 C2. **Tel** 12 680 23 41.

Teatr im. J. Słowackiego
Pl. Świętego Ducha 1.
Map 2 D4 (6 E1).
Tel 12 424 45 26.

Teatr Lalki i Maski Groteska
ul. Skarbowa 2.
Map 1 B4 (5 A2).
Tel 12 632 92 00.

Zależny
ul. Kanonicza 1.
Map 1 C5 (6 D4).
Tel 12 628 24 88.

Cabaret

Jama Michalika
ul. Floriańska 45.
Map 2 D4 (6 E2).
Tel 12 422 15 61.

Kabaret Pod Wyrwigroszem
Tel 609 45 11 05.

Loch Camelot
ul. Św. Tomasza 17.
Map 1 C4 (6 D2).
Tel 501 426 404.

Piwnica Pod Baranami
Rynek Główny 27.
Map 1 C4 (6 D2).
Tel 12 421 25 00.

Cinema

Agrafka
ul. Krowoderska 8.
Map 1 C3.
Tel 12 430 01 79.

Cinema City
ul. Podgórska 34
(Galeria Kazimierz).
Map 4 F1.
Tel 12 254 54 54.

Kijów.Centrum
al. Krasińskiego 34.
Map 1 A5 (5 A3).
Tel 12 433 00 33.

Kika
ul. I. Krasickiego 18.
Map 3 C4.
Tel 12 296 41 52.

Kino 18
ul. Floriańska 18.
Map 2 D4 (6 E2).
Tel 882 041 881.

Kino ARS
ul. Św. Jana 6.
Map 1 C4 (6 D2).
Tel 12 421 41 99.

Mikro
ul. J. Lea 5. **Map** 1 A3.
Tel 12 634 28 97.

Paradox
ul. Krupnicza 38.
Map 1 B4.
Tel 12 430 00 15.

Pod Baranami
Rynek Główny 27.
Map 1 C4 (6 D2).
Tel 12 423 07 68.

Sfinks
Os. Górali 5.
Tel 12 644 27 65.

Świt
Os. Teatralne 10.
Tel 503 021 896.

Wrzos
ul. J. Zamojskiego 50.
Map 4 D3.
Tel 12 656 10 50.

Classical Music

Akademia Muzyczna
ul. Św. Tomasza 43.
Map 2 D4 (6 E2).
Tel 12 422 04 55.

Capella Cracoviensis
ul. Zwierzyniecka 1.
Map 1 B5 (5 C3).
Tel 602 620 698.

Centrum Kultury „Dworek Białoprądnicki"
ul. Papiernicza 2.
Tel 12 420 49 50.

Filharmonia
ul. Zwierzyniecka 1.
Map 1 B5 (5 C3).
Tel 12 619 87 33.

Radio Kraków SA
al. Słówackiego 22.
Map 2 D2.
Tel 12 630 60 00.

Sinfonietta Cracovia
ul. Papiernicza 2.
Tel 12 416 70 75.

Willa Decjusza
ul. 28 lipca 17a.
Tel 12 425 36 44.

Music Clubs

Alchemia
ul. Estery 5.
Map 4 D1.
Tel 12 421 22 00.

Harris Piano Jazz Bar
Rynek Główny 28.
Map 1 C4 (6 D2).
Tel 12 421 57 41.

Jazz Club u Muniaka
ul. Floriańska 3.
Map 1 C4 (6 D2).
Tel 12 423 12 05.

Jazz Klub Kornet
al. Krasińskiego 19.
Map 1 A5 (5 A4).

Jazz Rock Café
ul. Sławkowska 12.
Map 1 C4 (6 D2).
Tel 511 433 506.

Klub Piękny Pies
ul. Bożego Ciała 9.
Map 4 D2.

Mile Stone Jazz Club
ul. Nadwiślańska 6.
Map 4 E2.
Tel 12 374 5100.

Pod Jaszczurami
Rynek Główny 8.
Map 1 C4 (6 D3).
Tel 12 429 45 38.

Rotunda-Orlik
ul. Oleandry 1.
Map 1 A4.
Tel 12 634 34 12.

U Louisa
Rynek Główny 13.
Map 1 C4 (6 D3).
Tel 12 617 02 22.

Nightclubs and Discos

Afera Club
ul. Sławkowska 13/15.
Map 1 C4 (6 D2).
Tel 12 421 17 71.

Black Gallery
ul. Mikołajska 24.
Map 2 D4 (6 E2).
Tel 724 630 154.

Bosto
ul. Floriańska 33.
Map 2 D4 (6 E2).
Tel 12 421 16 93.

Drukarnia
ul. Nadwiślańska 1.
Map 4 E3.
Tel 12 656 65 60.

Frantic
ul. Szewska 5.
Map 5 C2.
Tel 12 423 04 83.

Free Pub
ul. Sławkowska 4.
Map 1 C4 (6 D2).
Tel 080 290 82.

Kitsch
ul. Dajwor 16.
Map 4 E1.
Tel 518 879 055.

Krzysztofory
ul. Szczepańska 2.
Map 1 C4 (6 D2).
Tel 12 421 36 02.

Pod Papugami
ul. Św. Jana 18.
Map 1 C4 (6 D2).
Tel 12 422 82 99.

Prozak 2.0
pl. Dominikański 6.
Map C5 (6 D3).
Tel 733 70 46 50.

Społem
ul. Św. Tomasza 4.
Map 1 C4 (6 D2).
Tel 12 421 79 79.

Sports Clubs

Korona
ul. Kalwaryjska 9/15.
Map 4 D3.
Tel 12 656 13 68.

KS Cracovia
ul. Kałuży 1.
Map 1 A5.
Tel 12 294 66 05.

Olsza
ul. Siedleckiego 7.
Tel 12 421 10 69.

TS Wisła
ul. Reymonta 22.
Tel 12 630 45 52.

Zwierzyniecki
Na Błoniach 1.
Tel 12 425 18 46.

Tennis Courts

Centrum tenisowe
Na Błoniach 1.
Tel 12 425 29 98.

Gołaski Sport
ul. Królowej Jadwigi 220.
Tel 12 425 39 00.

Hotel Crown Piast
ul. Radzikowskiego 109.
Tel 12 683 26 00.

Klub tenisowy „Kozłówek"
ul. Spółdzielców 13.
Tel 12 655 55 54.

KS Wieczysta
ul. Chałupnika 16.
Tel 12 442 42 70.

Nadwiślan
ul. Koletek 20. **Map** 3 C1.
Tel 12 422 21 22.

Olsza
ul. Siedleckiego 7.
Tel 12 421 10 69.

Tenis servis
al. Jana Pawła II 37.

Swimming Pools

Clepardia
ul. Mackiewicza 14.
Tel 12 415 16 74.

Krakowianka
ul. Bulwarowa 1.
Tel 12 644 14 21.

Park Wodny
ul. Dobrego Pasterza 126.
Tel 12 616 31 90.

Polfa
ul. Eisenberga 2.
Tel 12 411 40 88.

Wisła
ul. Reymonta 22. **Map** 1
A4. **Tel** 12 630 45 00.

Billiards and Snooker Clubs

Daddy's Bilard
ul. Krowoderska 28.
Map 1 C3.

Frame Snooker & Bilard
ul. Smolki 11A.
Map 4 D3.
Tel 12 423 57 06.

Prominent
ul. Kamienna 17.
Map 2 D1.
Tel 12 632 10 58.

Horse-Riding

Decjusz
al. Kasztanowa 1.
Tel 12 425 24 21.

Krakowski Klub Jazdy Konnej
ul. Kobierzńyska 175.
Tel 12 262 14 18.

Krakus
ul. Kąpielowa 51.
Tel 12 654 72 10.

Pegaz
ul. Łowińskiego 1.
Tel 12 425 80 88.

Pod Żubrem
Niepołomice,
Targowa 5.
Tel 12 281 19 96.

Stadnina Podskalany
ul. Podskalany 61.
Tel 606 91 50 09.

Stary Młyn
ul. Wilczkowice 50.
Tel 12 411 10 91.

Health, Fitness and Sauna Clubs

Fit-Styl
ul. Miodowa 21.
Map 4 D1.
Tel 12 421 95 34.

Forteca Climbing Centre
ul. Racławicka 60.
Tel 12 632 83 33.

Korona Club
ul. Kalwaryjska 9–15.
Tel 12 656 53 89

Nad Zalevem Recreation Centre
ul. Bronowicka 19.
Tel 12 292 75 53.

Relax Body Club
ul. Mogilska 70.
Map 2 F3.
Tel 12 411 03 60.

Tribal Fitness
ul. Św. Filipa 9a.
Map 2 D3.
Tel 12 632 68 48.

Yoga International
ul. Św. Marka 34
Map 6 E2.
Tel 692 41 41 47.

PRACTICAL INFORMATION

Krakow attracts more tourists than any other Polish city, and visitor facilities are generally first class. Points of arrival such as the main railway and bus stations have been thoroughly modernized in recent years, and the John Paul II Airport at Balice boasts a speedy rail link to the city centre. Tourist signage makes it easy to find your way around on foot and many of the city's sights are within walking distance from each other. The increased use of bicycles is a sign that Krakow is becoming much more eco-friendly. The communications system is good: postal services are easy to use, and the provision of Wi-Fi access is increasingly widespread. The tourist season lasts all year round in Krakow, but summer is particularly busy thanks to the warm weather.

When to Go

Krakow is a popular destination for visitors throughout the year and tourist facilities are open for business during every season. Spring and summer bring warm, dry weather, when the city is filled with visitors and café tables cover the pavements. Autumn and winter, although cold, can also be a magical time, with Advent markets on the main city squares and an atmosphere of celebration in restaurants and bars.

Hotel prices are at their highest from Easter to August and around Christmas and New Year. It is best to travel outside these times if you want to enjoy an inexpensive holiday without the crowds.

Culture-lovers should take note that most theatres and classical-music venues take an annual break from June to mid-September.

Visas and Passports

Citizens of the European Union, USA, Australia, Canada and New Zealand can enter Poland without a visa, on production of a valid passport for stays of up to 90 days. Citizens of other countries should check the latest visa regulations with their local Polish embassy. Poland is a member of the Schengen group of European Union countries, which means that there are unlikely to be any border controls at immigration when entering Poland from another Schengen-zone country.

Façade of InfoKraków

Customs Information

If you are travelling to or from another EU country there are few restrictions on items brought in and out of Poland for personal use.

Visitors from outside the EU should check the customs regulations of their home country – there are likely to be limits on the amount of cigarettes, alcoholic beverages, toiletries and gifts that can be taken home. The maximum value of currency that can be brought into or taken out of Poland is €10,000 (or equivalent). Sums in excess of this must be declared to the customs authority. A licence is required to export any item more than 100 years old or any artwork over 50 years old and exceeding more than 16,000zł in value. For more information contact the **Ministry of Culture and National Heritage**. Value Added Tax (VAT) can be claimed back on goods totalling 200zł or more and that are taken out of the country within 30 days of purchase.

Tourist Information

Krakow's municipal tourist office operates information centres at several locations around the city centre. Their locations are shown on the Street Finder maps towards the end of this book (see pp232–7). The main office is situated in the **Cloth Hall** on Market Square. There is also a branch at **Planty Park** and at **John Paul II Airport**. All offices offer brochures with museum and gallery opening times, and lists of accommodation.

Electronic displays with information on the availability of hotels can be found at the main railway station and John Paul II Airport. **InfoKraków**, just off the Market Square on ul. Św. Jana, provides information on upcoming concerts and shows. Hotel and hostel reception desks can be useful sources of information, although they sometimes only advertise tourist companies with whom they have a commercial agreement.

Admission Prices

Admission charges to museums and galleries are modest but may be increased substantially for a temporary exhibition. Reduced rates are available for children, students and senior citizens. Overseas students should possess a valid international student card in order to qualify for a discount *(see p212)*.

Opening Hours

The opening hours of the museums and galleries listed in this guide are given individually for each sight. Most state museums and galleries are closed on Mondays and private galleries of contemporary art are generally closed on Sundays. Opening times vary depending on the day of the week, but late openings are normally on Thursdays.

Churches usually remain open from the first to the last service without closing at midday, but there are some variations. Food stores are open 7am–7pm, but there are no strict rules about opening hours, which are at the owner's discretion. Other shops tend to open between 10am and 7pm. For information on opening times of banks and bureaux de change *see p216*.

Restaurants are open until 11pm although there are many pubs and bars that serve food and stay open until the early hours. Twenty-four-hour bars serving cheap drinks and snacks are popular with the locals and easy to find.

Tourists in Market Square, with the Church of St Mary in the background

Language

Language learning has undergone something of a boom in recent years, and most young Krakovians speak English and maybe one other world language as well. Older-generation Poles are a bit less forthcoming when it comes to foreign languages, although they will make an attempt to communicate with the few words they may have.

Some taxi companies use drivers who speak foreign languages, so you may, for example, request an English-speaking driver. Staff at museums, hotels and restaurants generally speak English, and possibly also one other major European language. In many cases staff in shops, post offices and banks communicate in Polish only, especially outside the city centre. It is worth making an effort to learn a few words and phrases in Polish; the Phrase Book is a useful place to start *(see pp255–6)*.

Etiquette and Smoking

There are nearly 100 Roman Catholic churches in Krakow and masses take place at all times of day throughout the week. Sightseeing is allowed when there are no services taking places but visitors should refrain from making noise and use cameras discreetly. In some churches, signs banning photography are clearly visible on the door. When visiting places of worship, it is polite to dress modestly: as well as the torso, upper arms and legs should be covered.

Smoking is banned in most public places. Almost all restaurants and cafés are completely smoke-free indoors, although smoking is permitted outside at restaurants and cafés that have a pavement terrace or a garden. Only a handful of bars and clubs have retained a self-contained indoor area where smoking is still allowed.

Accessibility to Public Conveniences

There are free-of-charge public conveniences in big shopping centres such as Galeria Krakowska next to the main railway station, and Galeria Kazimierz on ul. Podgórska near the Kazimierz Quarter. Pay-to-use toilets are scattered throughout the centre and can be found in the Cloth Hall, in Planty Park by Sienna and Reformacka streets, and at the parking area by the Wawel. All restaurants, bars and cafés have facilities. Most of these are free to use if you are a customer, although one or two restaurants do charge.

Taxes and Tipping

It is common to give a tip in cafés and restaurants with waiting staff, although there are no strict rules as to how much this should be. Adding 10 per cent to the bill or rounding it up to a suitable number is considered polite.

Visitors enjoying street cafés in Market Square

Travellers with Special Needs

Facilities for people with disabilities are still limited in Krakow. Moving around in a wheelchair is not easy due to the lack of contoured pavements and the large number of cars parked in pedestrian areas. Improvements are being made: some pedestrian crossings have low kerbs, and the number which are equipped with an audio message for the blind is on the increase. Wheelchair access and lifts are available at the main railway station.

Good facilities can also be found in a number of museums, including the National Museum in Krakow's Main Building *(see pp150–51)*, most of the National Museum's other branches, and the Japanese Centre for Art and Technology *(see p45)*, as well as in some cinemas and theatres. The Main Post Office also offers easy access. All hotels four stars or above offer at least a couple of rooms for wheelchair users *(see p178)*. An increasing number of trams and buses have low-level entry floors for wheelchair access.

There are several organizations which assist the disabled in Krakow, including the **Polish Association for the Blind** and the **Polish Assocation for the Deaf**. The **Radio Taxi Partner** company operates a fleet of vehicles especially adapted for wheelchair users.

Disabled parking sign in a Krakow street

Crowds watching the annual Dragon Parade on Market Square

Travelling with Children

Krakow is an enjoyable and safe environment for children, thanks to the largely pedestrianized city centre and the extensive areas of park in the surrounding areas.

One of the best public playparks is in **Jordan Park**, west of the Old Town. The **Stanisław Lem Garden of Experiments**, east of the centre towards Nowa Huta, is an open-air, hands-on science museum that encourages children to learn about science by playing on large pieces of apparatus.

Groteska Theatre is Krakow's leading children's theatre, whose productions often mix puppets with live action. Groteska also organizes the annual Dragon Parade in June, when puppet monsters descend on Market Square followed by fireworks beside the River Wisła.

Finding child-friendly accommodation in Krakow is usually problem-free *(see p178)*.

Gay and Lesbian Travellers

Although Krakow is more liberal than many other European cities, Poland as a whole is a conservative country and the gay and lesbian scene remains discreet. Krakow has a handful of clubs specifically tailored to gay men and lesbians, and a broader choice of bars, particularly in the Jewish Kazimierz quarter in the west of the city, that encourage a mixture of all customers. The annual

Tolerance March, a gay-pride-style event that takes place in mid-May, attracts many supporters from across the social spectrum – but also draws large numbers of conservative counter-demonstrators.

An ISIC card (International Student Identity Card)

Travelling on a Budget

In comparison to other major European cities, Krakow is not that expensive and with some planning it is possible to get around on a low budget.

For young travellers, international youth and student cards such as **ISIC** (International Student Identity Card) and **European Youth Card** are worth obtaining. Both cards entitle holders to reduced rates in museums, tourist attractions, hotels, hostels and on intercity buses. A wide range of other Krakow businesses offer discounts to bearers of both cards, including car-hire firms, cafés, hairdressers, pizzerias, travel agents and theatres. The logos of the cards are displayed in the windows of those businesses offering discounts.

An ISIC card is available to anyone who is either a full-time student or who is under the age of 26. You can obtain one in your home country or through youth-tourism specialists **Almatur** in Krakow, providing you have documentary evidence of your status.

The European Youth Card is available to anyone under the age of 30 and can be bought from numerous outlets throughout Europe, or online via their website.

Time

Poland is in the Central European time zone, which means that Krakow is 1 hour ahead of Greenwich Mean Time, 6 hours ahead of US Eastern Standard Time, and 11 hours behind Australian Eastern Standard Time. From late March until late October clocks are set forward 1 hour.

Electricity

The voltage in Poland is 230 volts. Plugs are of the two-pin type, as is the case in most countries in Europe. Buy a European travel adaptor before you leave home.

Responsible Tourism

Travelling responsibly is largely a matter of common sense. Eating in chain restaurants or fast-food outlets increases the likelihood that you will be consuming cheaply supplied products that have not come from ecological sources. If you eat Polish food in Polish restaurants, it is more likely that food has been locally sourced. When shopping for your own food, aim for outdoor markets rather than the large supermarkets. Stall-holders at the Stary Kleparz market at Rynek Kleparski near Planty are far more likely to sell seasonal produce of local provenance, and will frequently advertise the fact by chalking up signs advertising the Polish origin of their vegetables. Organic food shops include Naturalny sklepik

at Krupnicza 8; and Natura at Krupnicza 21. Both sell many Polish specialities. Take a multiple-use bag of your own rather than using plastic bags.

If you have rubbish to dispose of, ask locals to direct you to the recycling bins located on many street corners. There is usually a trio of containers set aside for paper, glass and plastics.

Fresh fruit and vegetables at a Krakow food market

DIRECTORY

Embassies and Consulates

Australia
3rd floor, Nautilus Building, ul. Nowogrodzka 11, Warsaw. **Tel** 22 521 34 44. **w** australia.pl

Canada
ul. Jana Matejki 1/5, Warsaw.
Tel 22 584 31 00.
w poland.gc.ca

Ireland
ul. Mysia 5, Warsaw.
Tel 22 849 66 33.
w embassyofireland.pl

United Kingdom
ul. Św. Anny 9.
Map 1 B4 (5 C2).
Tel 12 421 70 30.
w http:// ukinpoland. fco.gov.uk

United States of America
ul. Stolarska 9.
Map 1 C5 (6 D3).
Tel 12 424 51 00.
w krakow.usconsulate. gov

Customs Information

Ministry of Culture and National Heritage
w mkidn.gov.pl

Tourist Information

Cloth Hall
Rynek Główny.
Map 1 C4 (6 D2).
Tel 12 433 73 10.

InfoKraków
ul. Św. Jana 2.
Map 1 C4 (6 D2).
Tel 12 421 77 87.
w infokrakow.pl

John Paul II Airport
Tel 12 295 58 00.

Planty Park
ul. Szpitalna 25.
Map 2 D4 (6 E1).
Tel 12 432 01 10.
w infokrakow.pl

Travellers with Special Needs

Polish Association for the Blind
ul. Dr. Józefa Babińskiego 29, blok 23/3.
Tel 12 262 53 59.
w pzn.malopolska.pl

Polish Association for the Deaf
ul. Św. Jana 18.
Map 1 C4 (6 D2).
Tel 12 422 73 45.
w pzg.krakow.pl

Polish Society for the Rehabilitation of the Disabled
al. 29 Listopada 130. **Tel** 12 312 14 00.
w pfron.org.pl

Radio Taxi Partner
Tel 196 33, 196 88.
w taxi-partner. krakow.pl

Travelling with Children

Groteska Theatre
ul. Skarbowa 2.
Map 1 B4 (5 A2).
Tel 12 633 48 22.
w groteska.pl

Jordan Park
al. 3 Maja.

Stanislaw Lem Garden of Experiments
al. pokoju. **Tel** 12 346 12 85. **w** ogroddos wiadczen.pl

Travelling on a Budget

Almatur
Rynek Główny 27.
Map 1 C4 (6 D2).
Tel 12 422 46 68.
w almatur.pl

European Youth Card
w europeanyouth card.org

ISIC
w isic.org

Personal Security and Health

Krakow is one of the safest cities in Poland. Although the number of reported crimes is generally on the increase, Krakow is a quiet place and visitors can feel safe in most parts of the city. The same safety rules apply here as everywhere, so beware of pickpockets, do not leave any property visible in a car, and use guarded car parks. The local police take a tough line on rowdy, alcohol-influenced behaviour on the streets. Anyone suffering a minor health problem should seek advice at a pharmacy, while hotels can usually arrange a doctor's visit.

Police officers patrolling Krakow's Market Square

Police

In Krakow the police are assisted by other services, including town wardens and private security guards. Serious crime should be reported to a uniformed officer at a police station. Major police stations are indicated on the Street Finder maps *(see pp232–7)*. Police are often visible, especially on weekend nights when people showing signs of bad behaviour under the influence of alcohol will usually be apprehended. Blue and silver police cars are used for patrolling the streets. Town wardens are unarmed and have no power of arrest. They tend to perform traffic wardens' duties by fining owners of illegally parked vehicles. Private security agencies are generally responsible for security in large shops and public buildings, as well as at public events. They are usually uniformed and should always carry identification badges.

Ambulance

Police car

Fire engine

What to Be Aware Of

Krakow is a popular venue for weekend party tourism. Late-night noisy behaviour is a frequent annoyance, but outright public disorder is very rare. Local police are taking an increasingly hard line on drunkenness, and anyone creating a disturbance late at night is likely to be apprehended and fined.

Ulica Szewska in the Old Quarter is at the centre of the weekend party scene. Most of the bars and clubs here are legitimate, although one or two establishments on this strip are notorious for overcharging tourists. Male visitors travelling solo or in small groups should be particularly aware of over-friendly young females suggesting a drink in a nearby bar; a hugely inflated bill will probably be the result.

Anyone found driving under the influence of alcohol will be arrested and must appear in court the following day. Be aware that cyclists riding a bicycle under the influence of alcohol will receive the same treatment as car drivers. The level of alcohol in the blood for both car drivers and cyclists is so low that it is advisable to not drink and drive at all. In the event of a serious road accident you are required by law to call an ambulance, the fire brigade and also the traffic police – *see Directory opposite*.

Petty thieves and pickpockets are active in crowded bars, on public transport and at busy markets. Keep a close eye on your bag or rucksack, and carry it securely fastened across your body. Passports, wallets and other valuable items should never be carried in a back pocket or in the external pockets of a rucksack. Pickpockets frequently operate in gangs, and a sudden push or other distraction caused by them will hardly ever be accidental.

Valuables should never be left unattended in a car. Car break-ins are a big problem in Krakow. If you can remove the radio and take it with you, you may save your windows from being smashed. A car alarm offers no protection against professional thieves, so guarded parking may be a good option. A number of guarded car parks are available in the centre.

In an Emergency

Call 112 for emergencies requiring medical, police or fire services. An operator will answer (most speak English) and will direct your call. Minor health problems can often be dealt with in a pharmacy, where trained staff can provide advice on remedies. Prominent pharmacies are listed in the directory below. For more serious injury or illness, head for the casualty unit of one of the big city-centre hospitals.

Police sign

Lost and Stolen Property

If you lose something at a venue in Krakow there is a good chance that staff will keep it for a day or two, in the expectation that you will return. It is a good idea to write your mobile phone number inside bags or wallets – in the event of loss, a good citizen or conscientious policeman may call to inform you that it has been found.

There are several lost property offices in Krakow, one for property lost on public transport and one for items misplaced elsewhere in the city. Items left on aeroplanes, intercity trains or buses will be kept at lost property offices at the airport, railway and bus station respectively. Never leave luggage unattended in public, as this can lead to theft or security alerts.

Hospitals and Pharmacies

Both state and private health care are available in Krakow. First aid is provided free of charge. Other treatment may be subject to a fee, which is usually required in advance, along with showing a passport for identification. It is very important to obtain a receipt for any payment made and it is advisable to take out insurance cover before you travel.

A typical pharmacy window in Krakow

Treatment for minor problems is available at pharmacies located throughout the city. If you require treatment after normal opening hours visit a 24-hour pharmacy. Their addresses are usually displayed in any pharmacy window *(see p199)*. The ambulance service is on call day and night and should be contacted in case of an accident or emergency. There are several hospitals in Krakow including **Szpitzal Wojskowy**, north of the city centre. Hospitals with casualty units are shown on the Street Finder maps *(see pp232–7)*.

Travel and Health Insurance

Travel insurance that includes provision for health care is highly recommended. The longer you stay abroad, the more important it is to ensure that you have substantial cover in case of loss, theft, or medical emergencies that will require repatriation help.

Many airlines and travel agents offer you insurance when you book your ticket. The Australian-based **World Nomads** is a reputable service that offers travel insurance to citizens of 150 countries.

All EU nationals are entitled to state healthcare in Poland on production of a valid **European Health Insurance Card** (EHIC). In the UK, this can be obtained from a post office or online from the EHIC website. It includes a booklet that details what healthcare you are entitled to, and where and how to claim. You may still have to pay in advance to obtain treatment, and then reclaim the money back later. As not all treatments are covered, it is advisable to take out additional insurance.

Make sure you travel with all relevant insurance documents. Keep a copy in your hotel room or with a reliable family member or friend back home, and itemize any valuables you are taking with you.

Banking and Local Currency

Financial transactions are easy in Krakow. ATMs accepting all major cards are located throughout the city. Foreign visitors will find many bureaux de change in the city centre, offering more favourable exchange rates than the banks. Credit and debit cards are accepted by most of Krakow's shops and restaurants. Signs displayed by the entrance to the establishment indicate which cards are accepted.

Banks and Bureaux de Change

Banks can be found throughout the city, both in and around the centre, as well as on the outskirts. They are usually open 9am–5pm Monday–Friday and many are open until 1pm on Saturday. Banks are often busy so expect to queue. Some branches have a ticketing system – take a numbered ticket at the entrance and wait until the number is displayed before approaching the counter.

Most banks have their own exchange service but better rates are offered by the independent bureaux de change (*kantor*), which do not charge commission. In Krakow these include **Dukat**, **Euro-Kantor**, **JPJ, Kantor Exchange** and **Pod Arkadami**. Foreign currency can also be changed at hotels, but rates are more expensive.

Large Polish banks with branches in Krakow include **PKO** and **Pekao**. International banks include **ING**, **HSBC** and **Raiffeisen**.

Bankomat automated teller machine (ATM) for dispensing cash

ATMs

ATMs (*bankomat*) are easy to find in Krakow and instructions are usually available in a choice of languages. The types of card accepted will be displayed on the ATM itself. Check these carefully before inserting your card – the vast majority accept Visa, Maestro and MasterCard. ATM withdrawals will be marginally more expensive than changing cash. The exchange rate for the amount withdrawn in złoty is slightly less advanta-geous than the one you will receive in a bank or bureau de change. A small fee will be charged by your bank for each ATM transaction carried out when abroad.

Be aware of your surroundings when using an ATM and always shield the keypad when entering your PIN.

Credit and Debit Cards

Credit and debit cards payments are accepted in most hotels, museums, restaurants, and shops. There may be a minimum expenditure in some

Entrance to the PKO Bank in Market Square

restaurants and shops, below which they will not accept credit card payments; ask first. Cards are unlikely to be accepted in markets, suburban railway stations, and in smaller shops and cafés in the suburbs so it is advisable to carry a small amount of Polish cash.

All major credit cards such as American Express, VISA and MasterCard are widely accepted. Establishments normally indicate which cards they accept by displaying appropriate stickers on their windows.

It is a good idea to notify your bank before you travel so that they expect your card to be used in Poland.

Currency

The Polish unit of currency is the złoty, a term that literally means golden and which dates back to the Middle Ages, when gold pieces were used. Złoty is most commonly abbreviated to zł, although you will see the abbreviation PLN in banks and on your credit or debit card statement. One złoty equals 100 groszy, abbreviated to gr.

10 złoty

20 złoty

50 złoty

100 złoty

Bank Notes

Bank notes come in denominations of 10, 20, 50, 100 and 200 zł. Each bank note bears the portrait of a Polish king.

200 złoty

5 zł

2 zł

1 zł

50 gr

20 gr

10 gr

5 gr

2 gr

1 gr

Coins

Polish coins come in denominations of 1, 2, 5, 10, 20, 50 gr and 1, 2, 5 zł. They all feature on one side a crowned eagle, the emblem of Poland.

Communications and Media

The main Polish telephone service is provided by Telekomunikacja Polska (TP), although there are numerous mobile phone operators such as Plus, Orange and T-Mobile. There are many public telephones in the centre of Krakow, and these are mainly card-operated. Some phone booths are wheelchair-accessible. Many hotels and cafés offer guests free Wi-Fi access, and international newspapers and magazines are widely available. Offices of the efficient Polish postal service (*Poczta Polska*) are located throughout the city.

International and Local Telephone Calls

To make a telephone call you may choose to use a public telephone or go through the operator service at the post office. Keep in mind that calling from a hotel room is much more expensive, so it is always better to find a public telephone at the hotel or in its vicinity.

The vast majority of public phones are card-operated. Telephone cards (*karty telefoniczne*) can be purchased from newsagents and post offices. These cards are available in units of 15 (9zł), 30 (15zł) and 60 (24zł). A local call will only use up a few units of a phone card, but for long-distance calls it is advisable to use a higher-priced card.

Mobile Phones

Most mobile phones will function perfectly well in Krakow and elsewhere in Poland. However mobile phones supplied by providers

in the US may only have limited global coverage. Contact your service provider for clarification.

To use your mobile phone abroad you will need to check with your provider that the roaming facility has been enabled. Remember that you will be charged for the calls you receive as well as the calls you make, and you will have to pay a substantial premium for the international part of the call.

If you are staying in the area for a reasonable amount of time, a popular option is to purchase a local SIM card that uses the local mobile phone networks and can be topped up with credit. You can only do this if your handset is "unlocked", as some operators lock their phones to specific networks. Some of the local/international networks are **Orange**, **T-Mobile** and **Plus**. If you are using a smart phone, beware that charges for data roaming can be high. If you want to make and

Telekomunikacja Polska – the biggest Polish telecoms company

receive calls while abroad but do not want to be charged for use of the Internet or other data, you can switch this service off and continue using the telephone functions as normal.

Check your insurance policy in case your phone gets stolen and keep your network operator's helpline number handy in case of emergencies.

A typical public telephone booth in Krakow

Public Telephones

To make a telephone call, lift the receiver and wait for a continuous dialling tone. Insert a telephone card when the words "włóż kartę" (insert card) are displayed. The display will indicate the amount of credit (*kredyt*) available. Dial the number and await connection. Note that a short, rapidly repeating tone indicates that the number is engaged. When you have finished the call, replace the receiver and remove the ejected card.

Internet Access

If you are travelling with a laptop or a smartphone, there are numerous opportunities to log on to the Internet for little or no cost. A growing number of hotels, cafés and bars provide their guests with Wi-Fi access. In most places it is free but some establishments do charge. Look out for a Wi-Fi sticker in the window. There is also a free public Wi-Fi zone on the main Market Square.

For those travelling without a Wi-Fi-enabled device, most

Telephone Directories and Dialling Codes

- Local (Krakow) directory enquiries in English can be reached on 118 811.
- National (Polish) directory enquiries dial 118 913.
- International directory enquiries dial 118 912.
- Local calls within Krakow first dial 12, the city's area code. For calls within Poland always include the area code.
- To call overseas dial 0 and wait for the tone, dial 0 again followed by the country code, followed by the area code (omit the initial 0), and then the subscriber's number.
- Country codes: UK 44; Eire 353; Canada and USA 1; Australia 61; South Africa 27; New Zealand 64.

One of many bars in Krakow offering Wi-Fi access

hotels and hostels have at least one computer with Internet access in the lobby for guests to use. There are also several Internet cafés (*Kafejki Internetowe*) scattered throughout the city, including **Garinet**, **Hetmańska** and **Nandu** offering reasonable rates for Internet use – fares rarely exceed 10zł per hour.

Postal Services

Branches of the post office are scattered liberally throughout central Krakow and the suburbs. The main post office, **Poczta Główna**, is situated at the junction of Westerplatte and Wielopole streets. It is open 8am–8pm Monday–Friday, and 8am–2pm Saturday, and offers a wide range of services. You can send letters, faxes, telegrams and parcels, as well as make international money transfers and operator-initiated calls. Stamp collectors can buy

from the philatelic counter. A *poste restante* (mail-holding) service is also available. The post office branch near the railway station has a 24-hour counter.

Stamps can be purchased at post office counters and from selected newsagents. Inland letters arrive after 2 to 3 days but international mail can take a week or maybe a little longer. Letters or cards sent via the more expensive express service will arrive sooner. Courier service is the fastest postal method, but is very costly. This service is available from larger post office branches, as well as from **DHL** and other similar courier companies.

Newspapers and Magazines

Foreign newspapers and magazines are available from the larger newsagents and bookshops. The widest choice is available at the **Empik** multimedia store in the Galeria Krakowska mall, which sells English-language and other foreign publications.

The most popular quality newspapers in Krakow are the nationals *Gazeta Wyborcza* and *Rzeczpospolita*, and the local *Dziennik Polski* and *Gazeta Krakowska*. Populist tabloid *Fakt* is the biggest-selling daily paper in the country. *Dziennik Polski* and *Gazeta Wyborcza* have the best "what's-on" information. English-language monthly *The Krakow Post* is a good source of local news and views, and can be picked up from many bars and restaurants free of charge.

A post office housed in an old palace by the main railway station

DIRECTORY

Mobile Phones

Orange
W orange.pl

Plus
W plus.pl

T-Mobile
W t-mobile.pl

Internet Access

Garinet
ul. Floriańska 18. **Map** 2 C4 (6 E2).
Tel 12 423 2233. W garinet.pl

Hetmańska
ul. Bracka 4. **Map** 1 C5 (6 D3).
Tel 12 430 01 08.
W hetmanska24.com

Nandu
ul. Wiślna 8. **Map** 1 C4 (5 C3).
Tel 12 421 03 26. W nandu.pl

Postal Services

DHL
ul. Staniątki 735, Niepołomice.
Tel 6 345 345. W dhl.com.pl

Poczta Główna
ul. Westerplatte 20.
Map 2 D5 (6 E3).

Newspapers and Magazines

Empik
Galeria Krakowska, Level -1.
Map 1 D3 (6 F1).
Tel 12 603 112 836.
W empikgroup.com

TV and Radio

Most hotels have a television in the room offering a handful of Polish-language stations and a choice of German-, English-, Italian- and French-language stations. News channels such as CNN or BBC are more common than entertainment or film channels. Polish TV stations broadcast many English-language films and drama, although the voices are usually dubbed into Polish or read by a single actor.

Popular radio stations include RMF FM (96 FM), Trójka (99.4 FM), Radio Kraków (101.6 FM) and Radio Zet (104.1 FM).

GETTING TO KRAKOW

Krakow has good connections with other Polish and European cities. Direct air routes serve John Paul II airport from Warsaw as well as an ever-increasing number of European and American cities. There are direct trains from Berlin, Prague, Warsaw and other major Polish cities. In addition, Krakow is served by intercity buses from a growing range of European cities and from most cities in Poland itself.

Driving to Krakow is relatively easy and will take you through some wonderful scenery, with plenty of roadside restaurants and petrol stations along the way. Krakow has good, fast road connections if you are approaching from the west. Road routes from the north, south and east however are not in such good condition, and journeys via these routes are generally more time-consuming.

The logo of Polish Airlines

Arriving by Air

Krakow's **John Paul II Airport** at Balice is served by direct flights from a large number of European and Polish cities. Travellers from other continents will find that connections to Krakow – usually involving a change of plane in another European city – are easy to organize.

From the UK there's a choice of **LOT Polish Airlines** flights from London Heathrow; **Ryanair** from East Midlands, Edinburgh, Leeds-Bradford, Liverpool and London Stansted; **easyJet** from Belfast, Bristol, Edinburgh, Liverpool and London Gatwick; and **Jet2** from Newcastle. From Ireland, both **Aer Lingus** and Ryanair fly direct from Dublin.

Travellers from North America will need to make at least one stop en route. LOT airlines fly from Chicago, Toronto and New York to Krakow with a transfer in Warsaw. **Lufthansa** offer flights from various North American cities to Krakow with a change of plane in either Frankfurt or Munich. Visitors from Australasia can choose between one-stop flights via a major European hub such as London, or two-stop flights with connections in Singapore or Bangkok. LOT also operate domestic flights to Krakow from Warsaw; while Eurolot

fly to Krakow from Gdańsk, Poznań and Szczecin.

Krakow also has another international airport, **Katowice**, which is served by the budget airlines Wizz and Ryanair as well as Lufthansa. These airlines fly from numerous European destinations, in particular from Eastern Europe.

John Paul II Airport

Situated 15 km (9 miles) west of the city centre, John Paul II Airport is modern, comfortable and easy to get around. Although it has all the facilities that you would expect from an international airport, including cafés, restaurants, shops, money exchange and ATMs, it is small, and doesn't offer the variety found in larger airports. The international terminal is about 1 km (0.5 miles) away from the domestic terminal. There is a regular shuttle bus that transports passengers between the two; the same bus also goes to the airport's small railway station.

There is a tourist information office in the international arrivals hall, and car rental firms operate from their desks in the nearby concourse area.

Katowice Airport

Katowice international airport is located about 80 km (50 miles) northwest of Krakow in Pyrzowice. The airport has two busy passenger terminals. Facilities include souvenir shops, money exchange, duty-free and a post office. Car rental outlets can be found on the ground floor in Terminal A.

Tickets and Fares

Ticket prices vary enormously according to time of year and how far in advance you book. Peak periods such as Easter, June–August and the festive winter season are expensive times to travel whichever airline you book with. In general, tickets booked direct from the airline's website a month in advance or earlier are cheaper than tickets booked through

Krakow-John Paul II Airport

Matusek bus connecting Katowice Airport and Krakow city centre

DIRECTORY

Arriving by Air

Aer Lingus
w aerlingus.com

easyJet
w easyjet.com

Jet2
w jet2.com

LOT Polish Airlines
w lot.com

Lufthansa
w lufthansa.com

Ryanair
w ryanair.com

Airports

John Paul II Airport
Tel 12 295 58 00 or
801 055 000.
w krakowairport.pl

Katowice Airport
Tel 32 39 27 000.
w katowice-airport.com/en

Getting into Town

Matusek
w matusek.com

Pyrzowice Ekspress
w pyrzowiceekspres.pl

travel agents or those booked near to your date of travel.

Budget airlines specialize in offering low-cost tickets and should be your first port of call if you are looking for inexpensive deals. Be aware however, that each item of hold baggage is usually charged extra.

Some airlines offer reductions for children under 12 but this is not standard practice across the whole industry. Children under 2 years old usually travel free, providing they occupy the same seat as the accompanying parent.

Getting into Town

John Paul II Airport is connected to Krakow's main railway station, Kraków Główny *(see pp222–3)*, by fast suburban trains. There is a railway station in the departure terminal of the airport. Trains run every half hour (between approximately 6am and 11pm) and take 20 minutes. Tickets (10zł) can be bought from a machine near the central exit of Terminal 1 or from the conductor on board.

There are two regular bus services from the airport to the railway station: bus numbers 208 and 292, which depart from the airport forecourt. The journey time is about 40 minutes depending on traffic, and although slower than the train, the route runs through parts of west Krakow where several hotels are situated. If you are staying in this area and you have clear directions to your accommodation, these buses are very useful. Between 11pm and 5am, there is also a night bus service, number 902.

Bus tickets (4zł) can be purchased from a newsagent stand inside the airport terminal, from the ticket machine beside the bus stop or from the driver on the bus (coins only) prior to commencing your journey. Large pieces of luggage are subject to an additional charge.

Taxis are located at the terminal's main exit. Here you will find Radio Taxis *(see p227)*. The journey into town takes about 20 minutes but can take longer in rush hour. A Radio Taxi to the centre should cost around 50zł but may cost more at night and weekends. Credit cards are accepted. Expect to pay more if you are travelling to the suburbs, or if you book with an alternative taxi company.

From Katowice Airport, **Matusek** offers a bus service to Krakow central bus station, which takes about two hours. A single ticket costs 44zł if booked in advance or 50zł if bought on board.

Alternatively, you can hire a private car with a driver through **Pyrzowice Ekspress**. For a standard car, with up to four passengers, the journey to Krakow costs 310zł (price is per trip). Cars must be booked at least five days in advance.

Train operating between John Paul II Airport and the city

Escalators to the ticket hall in Kraków Główny, Krakow's main railway station

Travelling by Rail

You can get to Krakow by train from almost any Polish city and town, as well as from many other European cities. There are stretches of high-speed track between Warsaw and Krakow, but otherwise journey times are slow and in some cases travel by road may well be faster.

The Polish rail network is operated by various different companies. Most express intercity trains are run by **PKP InterCity** (Polskie Koleje Państwowe), who operate fast and relatively expensive services, as well as the slightly slower and slightly cheaper TLK (Twoje Linie Kolejowe) services. A number of other express trains are operated by **Przewozy Regionalne** (and go under the name of InterRegio). Przewozy Regionalne also operate slower trains that stop at more stations en route.

As a rule, train tickets in Poland are cheaper than in western Europe. Prices vary widely according to class of train, however travelling by express train will be two or three times more expensive than covering the same route on a slower local train.

Tickets for one service will not be valid for travel on another. Buying tickets is relatively straightforward as each of the ticket counters at Krakow's main railway station sell tickets for all of the above companies. Tickets can be bought in advance or on the day of travel from the ticket counters in the main railway station. Queues are common, so

allow at least half an hour to buy your ticket. You can also purchase one from the train conductor, but you must inform him that you require a ticket upon boarding the train. Bear in mind that tickets bought from the conductor are 10–20 per cent more expensive than those bought from counters at the station.

InterCity and Express Trains

Trains operated by PKP InterCity offer the fastest and most comfortable way to travel. First and second class seating is available. Seat reservations are obligatory and are made at the time of purchasing the ticket. Express trains operated by InterRegio are not as fast as PKP InterCity and only offer second-class seating although they are much cheaper and also allow bicycles. A PKP InterCity train from Warsaw to Krakow takes just under 3 hours and costs 120zł one way (160zł in first class). An InterRegio train from Warsaw to Krakow takes 3 hours 15 minutes and only costs 50zł one-way.

PKP InterCity services offer a complimentary hot drink and a pastry, and also have a buffet car and trolley service offering a limited range of drinks and snacks. Other trains do not always carry a buffet car, so buy refreshments before boarding.

Railway Stations

Krakow's main railway station, Kraków Główny, is located in the heart of the city, a 10-minute walk northeast of Market Square. All international and domestic trains pass through this station, and the Krakow airport train terminates and departs from here. The main ticket hall is located under the train platforms and can be accessed from the Krakow bus station immediately to the east, the Dworzek Głowny tram stop, the Galeria Krakowska shopping mall to the west and via a covered walkway from the square in front of the shopping mall. Parking places and taxi ranks are located on the station roof, accessible by lift directly from the platforms.

Station signage is good, with digital displays notifying passengers of train departures and platform numbers. The main ticket hall contains two rows of counters for domestic departures, an information counter, and two counters (clearly marked in Polish and English) for international tickets. Queues at the international ticket counters can be very long in summer.

If catching a train outside central Krakow, beware that smaller railway stations have

An InterCity train at Krakow's main railway station

A platform at Kracow's main railway station

DIRECTORY

Travelling by Rail

InterRegio
Ⓦ interregiorail.eu

PKP InterCity
Ⓦ rozklad-pkp.pl

Train timetable information
Tel 22 39 19 757.
Ⓦ rozklad-pkp.pl

Travelling by Coach

Coach timetable information
Ⓦ rda.krakow.pl

Jordan
Ⓦ jordan.pl

PolskiBus
Ⓦ polskibus.com

Sindbad
Ⓦ sindbad.krakow.pl

Travelling by Car

Polish Automobile Association
Tel 196 37.

poor information displays. Always allow plenty of time to buy your ticket and find the right platform.

Travelling by Coach

Regular coach services to Krakow operate from many Polish and European cities. The main coach station, Dworzec Autobusowy, is located in the city centre, immediately east of the main railway station. Local, domestic and most international coach services operate from this station. The coach station is linked to the Old Town, emerging outside the Galeria Krakowska shopping mall, via the underground pedestrian concourses that connect the bus station with the train station platforms.

The coach station has good facilities and clear timetable information, however there are insufficient ticket windows to deal with demand (especially on summer weekends), and long queues soon build up. International coach tickets can be bought from the coach station or from operating agencies **Jordan** or **Sindbad**.

Coach services are operated by various companies. Those offering prime intercity routes often use more modern, comfortable coaches. Services to nearby towns and villages are also operated by mini-buses. Tickets sell out quickly, especially at weekends. **PolskiBus** runs services to and from Krakow from Warsaw as well as from other Polish and Central European cities. Tickets are sold online, *see directory*. Pick-up and drop-off points are located in the suburbs of Krakow.

Travelling by Car

Major roads into Krakow are well signposted, but you will need time and patience to find a safe parking space. Prominent car parks in the city are located on the Street Finder maps *(see pp232–237)*.

Driving licences issued in other countries are generally valid in Poland. If you drive in Poland you must carry a valid driving licence and vehicle registration document, as well as a Green Card, which is confirmation of your international insurance cover. If you drive a rental car, a hire certificate is also obligatory. A sticker identifying the country in which the car is registered must be displayed on the vehicle. The wearing of seat belts is compulsory, and children under 12 are not allowed to travel in the front of the car. Headlights must be on, day and night, regardless of the weather.

Road signs at the Polish border indicate strictly observed speed limits (in km). If ignored, foreign drivers are required to pay hefty fines on the spot.

The permitted alcohol content in blood is so low in Poland that drinking and driving should be avoided altogether.

In the event of a break-down, call the **Polish Automobile Association**.

A PolskiBus service operating between Warsaw and Krakow

GETTING AROUND KRAKOW

Central Krakow is small and compact so moving around on foot, by bike or by public transport is best. Children in particular will enjoy a sightseeing ride on one of Krakow's blue trams, and tours in a horse-drawn cab are very popular with visitors too. A small electric "meleks" vehicle can also be hired for group sightseeing, with qualified guides who speak foreign languages. Both meleks vehicles and horse-drawn carriages await passengers in Krakow's historic Market Square. If you are visiting attractions outside the city centre, using the public transport system is more environmentally friendly than hiring a car or using taxis. This guide lists the bus and tram routes which you can use to get to the sights described in the Krakow Area by Area section. Maps of Krakow's tram and bus systems can be found on the inside back cover.

Green Travel

There are a great many private cars in circulation in central Krakow, leading to traffic congestion and a shortage of parking spaces. Foreign visitors should try and refrain from adding to this pressure on the local infrastructure and consider alternative ways of getting around the city.

Krakow's centre is easy to navigate on foot and the city is also bike-friendly – the local authorities are trying to extend the number of cycle lanes in busy areas. Otherwise, the electric-powered meleks vehicles available for hire in the Market Square provide an emissions-free alternative to hiring a taxi within the Old Quarter. When exploring further afield, the public transport network is a perfectly adequate way of reaching suburbs such as Nowa Huta or recreation areas such as Las Wolski forest.

Walking

Krakow is ideal for exploring on foot. Much of the city centre is pedestrianized and distances between the main sightseeing areas are small.

Walking from the Old Town to the Kazimierz quarter takes around 20 minutes and there is much to see on the way. Planty Park runs round three sides of the Old Town, and the tree-shaded paths offer a pleasant walk from one part of the centre to another.

Pedestrians should take care at zebra crossings as drivers do not always stop.

A stop and give way road sign

Cycling

Cycling is a wonderful way to see Krakow, and the number of bike-rental outlets is increasing. Beware that marked cycle lanes are not widespread and cycling on main roads can be unnerving. It is permissible to cycle on the pavement, although pedestrians have right of way. The broad avenues of Planty Park are an ideal way of getting around the Old Town by bike.

There are several rental outlets around town and your hotel or hostel will know where the nearest one is. Prices depend on the type and age of the bike you are hiring, but you should expect to pay 40–70zł per day. A scheme called **KMK Bike** allows you to pick up rental bikes from one of 16 automated bike parks located throughout the city, although registering online is required. If you are hiring a bike for just one day or if you prefer to pay by cash, use **Eccentric Bike Rental** or **Bike Trip**.

Driving

Visitors are advised to walk, cycle or use public transport as access to the historic centre is limited to licenced taxis, delivery vans and local residents. Outside the Old Town traffic is busy and parking places are hard to find.

If you do drive, note that congestion is common during rush hours, especially on Friday afternoons. Main roads into the city have numerous traffic lights and junctions causing frequent tailbacks. A ring road runs around the west and south sides of the city, but is yet to be extended all the way round.

Tourists cycling by the Vistula River

Popular excursion routes in the environs of Krakow are well serviced by public transport, although you will need a car in order to explore the countryside in depth. Car hire in Krakow is problem-free, with several car-hire counters in the international arrivals hall of John Paul II airport, and car-hire deals offered by virtually all of the city's hotels and hostels *(see p223)*. Major car hire companies include **Avis**, **Europcar**, **Hertz** and **Sixt** and the Polish car rental company, **Joka**.

Parking

Parking areas are divided into zones. Most of the Old Town (zones A and B) is a no-parking zone for non-residents, although there is a limited amount of space available for hotel guests – you should enquire about availability when booking your room. Street parking is possible in a belt of territory surrounding the Old Town (zone C), but places are hard to come by. Parking in zone C costs 4zł per hour, payable at roadside parking meters, between 10am and 6pm Monday–Friday, but is free outside that time.

The most convenient car park for the Old Town is at Starowiślna 13 (6–8zł per hour). The largest underground parking garage is near Wawel Castle at Na Groblach (8zł per hour).

Illegally parked vehicles are prone to clamping. Details of where to pay the fine and get the clamp removed will be posted on the windscreen.

A water tram on the Vistula River

Water Trams

Water trams (*tramwaj wodny*) run during the tourist season from May to October. One service runs between Flisacka (in the suburb of Zwierzyniec) and Kazimierz, passing Wawel Castle on the way. Another less frequent service sails from Flisacka to Tyniec Abbey on the western fringes of Krakow. They function very well as scenic excursions, but are slower than other modes of public transport and should not be used to travel anywhere if you are in a hurry.

Tickets are bought on the boat and cost 8zł one-way on the Flisacka-Kazimierz route and 25zł one-way on the Flisacka-Tyniec route. Buying return tickets works out about 20 per cent cheaper than buying two singles.

Guided Tours

Guided sightseeing tours of Krakow are strongly recommended. The multi-lingual meleks drivers are situated by the Church of St Adalbert in Market Square. Bike-hire and horse-drawn cabs can also be found here.

Top sightseeing spots, such as **Wawel Castle** have their own guides, and many local travel agencies also offer specialist sightseeing tours. **Crazy Guides** focus on the communist past, frequently using old style Trabant cars as transport. **Krakow City Tours** operate themed tours such as Jewish Krakow and ghost walks, as well as organizing trips to the Auschwitz-Birkenau memorial site. **Discover Krakow** arrange tailor-made city centre and John Paul II tours.

DIRECTORY

Cycling

Bike Trip
ul. Zwierzyniecka 10.
Tel 667 712 054.
w biketrip.pl

Eccentric Bike Rental
ul. Grodzka 2. **Map** 1 C5 (6 D3). **Tel** 12 430 20 34.
w krakowbiketour.com

KMK Bike
w kmkbike.pl

Driving

Avis
ul. Lubicz 23. **Map** 2 E4.
Tel 12 629 61 08.
w avis.pl

Europcar
ul. Nadwislanska 6.
Map 4 E2.
Tel 12 374 56 96.
w europcar.pl

Hertz
Al. Focha 1. **Map** 1 A5.
Tel 12 429 62 62.
w hertz.com.pl

Joka
ul. Zacisze 7.
Map 2 D3 (6 E1).
Tel 12 429 66 30.
w joka.com.pl

Sixt
John Paul II Airport.
Tel 12 639 32 16.
w sixt.pl

Water Trams

**Water Tram
(Tramwaj Wodny)**
w ktw.krakow.pl

Guided Tours

**Crakow City
Tours**
ul. Floriańska 44.
Map 2 D4 (6 E1).
Tel 12 421 13 33.
w cracowcitytours.
com

Crazy Guides
ul. Floriańska 38.
Map 2 D4 (6 E1).
Tel 500 091 200.
w crazyguides.com

Discover Cracow
Rynek Główny 7–10b.
Map 1 C4 (6 D3).
Tel 12 346 38 99.
w discovercracow.eu

**Wawel Castle Guide
Service**
Wawel 5.
Map 3 C1 (6 D5).
Tel 12 422 51 55.
w wawel.krakow.pl

Buses, Trams and Taxis

Krakow is covered by an extensive public transport network. Trams and buses are frequent on weekdays, with rush hours between 7 and 8am and 2 and 5pm, but less so at weekends and on public holidays. A few trams and buses operate at night. Tickets, valid for both buses and trams, are inexpensive, especially if you opt for a 24- or 48-hour travel pass. A number of private firms operate minibus services, which will stop on request within the inner and outer city. Taxi ranks are located around the Old Town, and their prices are reasonable.

Ticket machine

Tourists planning a route at a Krakow tram stop

Tickets and fares

One type of ticket is used for both trams and buses. Tickets can be purchased from kiosks on the street, from ticket machines at some stops and on most trams and buses. There are two zones: zone 1 covers the city of Krakow and includes all tram and bus routes numbered 100 to 194. Zone 2 covers the outer suburbs, outlying villages and John Paul II Airport.

Several types of ticket are available: in zone 1, a ticket for a single journey by tram or bus is 3.80zł, a ticket for two journeys by bus or tram costs 7.20zł. Tickets valid for unlimited travel within a specific time period include the 20-minute ticket, which costs 2.80zł (useful if you're only travelling a few stops), as well as a 40-minute (3.80zł), 60-minute (5zł), 90-minute (6zł), 24-hour (15zł), 48-hour (24zł) and 72-hour (36zł) ticket. A weekly ticket is also available, which costs 48zł. Family tickets, allowing for unlimited travel for two adults and two children at weekends, cost 16zł. A group

ticket for up to 20 people costs 36zł. If you are travelling to zone 2, a single ticket is priced at 4zł and a ticket for two journeys is 7.60zł. Children under 4 and senior citizens over 70 travel for free.

After boarding, passengers must validate each ticket (even those purchased on board) by inserting it in one of the orange machines. Weekly tickets require the holder to carry identification.

Ticket Inspectors

Tickets are subject to regular checks on Krakow's trams and buses. Ticket inspectors operate in plain clothes but carry ID bearing an MPK symbol and a photograph. A passenger without a valid, punched ticket is liable to pay a fine, which is up to 250zł. Fines may be paid on the spot or at a post office with a penalty ticket. Foreign visitors, however, must pay on the spot.

Machines for checking the validity of your ticket are located throughout the city.

Travelling by Bus

Krakow is well served by buses that take passengers to all parts of the city. Bus routes numbered from 100 to 194 operate in the city centre and those numbered 201 to 297 link the city with outer suburbs and villages. Express buses, which do not go to every stop, begin with a 3 or a 5 and are three digits long. The frequency of buses varies from every few minutes to approximately every 20 minutes Monday–Friday, but they are less regular at weekends and on public holidays.

Bus stops are marked by a blue sign with a picture of a bus on it. When boarding the bus remember to validate your ticket. Approaching stops are read out by a pre-recorded voice and – in the newer vehicles – displayed on an electronic sign. To request a stop, push one of the red buttons near the doors. Some of the more modern buses have low floors, which allow easier wheelchair, pram and pushchair access.

Bus routes beginning with a 6 or a 9 are night buses. These

Interior of main bus station in Krakow

buses run about once an hour and cross the city in all directions. The fare is the same as for any other bus journey.

Private minibus services operate on many routes within the city and in the suburbs. You can purchase a ticket directly from the driver which costs approximately twice the fare of the MPK public transport. Most of these minibuses depart from the main railway station or nearby.

A Krakow tram operating in the city centre

Travelling by Tram

Trams are the main form of public transport in central Krakow, running round either side of the Old Town and fanning out towards outlying suburbs. They are the best means of travelling between the major bus and rail stations, and they are also the quickest way of reaching outlying attractions in the suburbs of Podgórze, 3 km (2 miles) south of the centre and Nowa Huta, 7 km (4 miles) east. Trams run from around 5:15am–11:15pm daily. Most tram routes operate every 10–15 minutes in the middle of the day, and every 20–25 minutes early in the morning and in the evening. Many vehicles have low floors enabling easy wheelchair access,

but it is not always possible to tell when one of these trams is due at your stop.

Taxis

Taxis are easy to locate in central Krakow and rates are reasonably low. Various taxi companies are in operation – vehicles vary in colour and make, and have different signs, depending on which company they belong to. All have an identification number clearly marked on the side of the car, as well as an illuminated "taxi" sign on the roof displaying the name of the company.

Taxis wait in taxi ranks rather than driving round the city looking for custom, so it is highly unlikely that you will be able to hail a taxi on the street. Those ordered by phone are usually cheaper than those picked up at a taxi rank.

Taxi ranks can be found all around the Old Town area. The biggest are on ul. Sienna, a short walk east of the main Market Square, and pl. Wszystkich Świętych, close to the Franciscan and Dominican churches. There are also plenty of taxis on or near pl. Nowy in the Kazimierz quarter. The

taxi rank for the main railway station is located on its roof – take the escalator or lift up from the platform.

There is an initial charge of 7zł, followed by 3zł per kilometre. Rates rise by 50 per cent between 11pm and 5am. Bear in mind large items of luggage will increase the fare.

Radio Taxi-Partner runs a fleet of taxis for disabled passengers. Fares are cheaper than those of regular taxis. These must be booked in advance.

Useful Tram Routes

This map shows the best tram routes for sightseeing in Krakow. The locations of major sights are marked, as well as the nearest useful stop. Sights should then only be a short walk away.

Krowodrza Górka 18
3 Krowodrza Górka
2 Cmentarz Rakowicki
Main Rail Station
Teatr Bagatela
Czartoryski Museum
Dworzec Główny
National Museum in Krakow
Church of St Anne
Cloth Hall
Collegium Maius
Church of St Mary
20 Cracovia
Cichy Kącik
Filharmonia
Dominican Church
Poczta Główna
Św. Gertrudy
6 2
Franciscan Church
Church of Saints Peter and Paul
Wawel
Salwator Pętla
Krakow Cathedral Wawel Royal Castle
Miodowa
Vistula
Orzeszkowej
Szeroka Street
Japanese Centre of Art and Technology
Ethnographic Museum
Zabłocie
Czerwone Maki 18
Paulite Church "On the Rock"
Plac Wolnica
Vistula
Most Grunwaldzki
Pl. Bohaterów Getta
20
Key
Schindler Factory
Mały Płaszów
■ Major sight
Limanowskiego
— Tram route
Ⓞ Stop (selected stops only)
Kurdwanów 6
3 Nowy Bieżanów

STREET FINDER

Map references, given for each sight within its individual entry in this guide relate to the map on the following pages only. The same applies to the hotels *(see pp180–83)* and restaurants *(see pp190–93)* listed. The first figure indicates the map number, while the middle letter and the last number refer to the relevant grid. The key map on the right shows Krakow divided into six parts which correspond to the maps that follow. All symbols used are explained in the key. You will find the Street Finder Index on pp230–31. Note that Polish is an inflected language and street names require different name endings (Jan Kowalski but Jana Kowalskiego Street).

Top sights and attractions are indicated on the maps.

Key to Street Finder

- Major sight
- Other sight
- Railway station
- Coach terminal
- Tram stop
- Tourist information
- Hospital
- Police station
- Boat pier
- Church
- Synagogue
- Railway line
- Pedestrian street
- City wall

Scale of Maps 1–4

| 0 metres | 200 | |
| 0 yards | 200 | 1:13,000 |

Scale of Maps 5–6

| 0 metres | 150 | |
| 0 yards | 150 | 1:8,500 |

A hurdy-gurdy man in Market Square

Stairs leading to the Decius Villa

Church of St Adalbert in Market Square

1

WROCŁAWSKA

PRADNICKA

AL. JULIUSZA SŁOWACKIEGO

DŁUGA

WARSZAWSKA

AL. 29 LISTOPADA

PRANDOTY

2

RAKOWICKA

BELINY-PRAŻMOWSKIEGO

5

BASZTOWA

6

*Piasek and
Nowy Świat*

PODWALE

*Old
Quarter*

DOMINIKAŃSKA

WESTERPLATTE

*Wesoła, Kleparz
and Biskupie*

AL. POWSTANIA

WARSZAW-KIEGO

AL. Z. KRASIŃSKIEGO

*Okól and
Stradom
Quarters*

3

TADEUSZA KOŚCIUSZKI

*Wawel
Hill*

J. DIETLA

4

*Kazimierz
Quarter*

MONTE CASSINO

Vistula

MARII KONOPNICKIEJ

B. LIMANOWSKIEGO

WADOWICKA

KALWARYJSKA

H. KAMIEŃSKIEGO

POWSTAŃCÓW ŚLĄSKICH

0 kilometres   1
0 miles   0.5

Rakowiecki
Cemetery

The Zygmunt Dome
of the Cathedral

Street Finder Index

3

A B **1** C

SENATORSKA
B. KOMOROWSKIEGO
PLAC NA STAWACH
M. BORELOWSKIEGO
WŁÓCZKÓW

Church of St Mar

1

TADEUSZA KOŚCIUSZKI
DOJAZDOWA
JASKÓŁCZA
BULWAR RODŁA

Most Dębnicki

SEE MAPS 5–6 FOR ENLARGEMENT OF THIS AREA

1

Krakow Cathedral

Royal Arsenal

PODZAMCZE

Wawel Royal Castle

STRADO

Vistula

MARII KONOPNICKIEJ

ZAMKOWA

Dragon's Lair

WAWEL

BERNARDYŃSKA

Bernardine Church

CZECHOSŁOWACKA
TYNIECKA
TYNIECKA
SKWEROWA

RYNEK DĘBNICKI

Japanese Centre of Art and Technology

Częstochowa Seminary

SMOCZA

KOLETEK

SUKIENNICA

RÓŻANA
M. BAŁUCKIEGO
BARSKA

1

SMOCZA

ŚW. STANISŁAWA
KS. A. KORDECKIEGO

PRASKA
BIAŁA DROGA
DĘBNICKA
SZWEDZKA
ZAGRODY
ROLNA
M. BAŁUCKIEGO
OBROŃCÓW POCZTY GDAŃSKIEJ

DĘBNIKI

K. PUŁASKIEGO
KONFEDERACKA
K. E. WASILEWSKIEGO
JANA KILIŃSKIEGO

Most Grunwaldzki

PAULIŃS

2

SKWEROWA
DĘBOWA

MONTE CASSINO

Paulite Church "On the Rock"

Church of St Catherin

SKAŁECZ

PIEKAR

A. NOWACZYŃSKIEGO

MITKOWSKIEGO
MIESZCZAŃSKA
TWARDOWSKIEGO
JANA BULHAKA
WYGRANA
BARSKA

BULWAR BOLESŁAWA DROBNERA
BULWAR MIKOŁAJA ZYBLIKIEWICZA

SKAWIŃS

3

BOCZNA
DWORSKA
WIERZBOWA

TWARDOWSKIEGO
DWORSKA
SŁOMIANA
SZWEDZKA
KOMANDOSÓW
BARSKA

MARII KONOPNICKIEJ

LUDWINOWSKA

ŚWIĘTEGO JACKA

KAPELANKA

SŁOMIANA

TURECKA
SWOBODA
ZATORSKA
PRZEDWIOŚ

Wilga

SZARSKIEGO
T. CZACKIEGO
SPISKA
ORAWSKA

I. KRASICK

4

LUDWINÓW

ROZDROŻE

CEGLARSKA

Wilga

ST. MIT

ZAKRZÓWEK

RYDLÓWKA

WADOWICKA

BONA

5

KOBIERZYŃSKA
KOBIERZYŃSKA

KAPELANKA

T. SZAFRANA

GEN. J. SKRZYNECKIEGO

RZEMIEŚLNICZA

A B C

General Index

Acknowledgments

Dorling Kindersley would like to thank the following people whose assistance has made the preparation of this book possible.

Managing Editor Helen Townsend
Managing Art Editor Kate Poole
Senior Managing Editor Louise B. Lang
Art Director Gillian Allan
Additional Photography Jakub Hałun, Jamie Howard, Krzysztof Kotowski, Piotr Kozłowski, Wojciech Kozłowski, Ian O'Leary, Kamil Szymaczek.
Revisions Team Claire Baranowski, Sonal Bhatt, Hilary Bird, Jonathan Bousfield, Arwen Burnett, Caroline Elliker, Eli Estaugh, Rhiannon Furbear, Lydia Halliday, Victoria Heyworth-Dunne, Elly King, Piotr Kozłowski, Ferdie McDonald, Gordon McLachlan, Casper Morris, Scarlett O'Hara, Catherine Palmi, Susie Peachey, Rada Radojicic, Simon Ryder, Sands Publishing Solutions, Sadie Smith, Jamie Stokes, Leah Tether, Conrad Van Dyk, Vinita Venugopal, Deepika Verma, Stewart J. Wild.

Dorling Kindersley wish to thank the following institutions, picture libraries and individuals for their kind permission to reproduce photographs of objects in their care and for the use of other photographic material:

Magdalena Maros the Director, and Krystyna Litewka at the Public Record State Office, Krzysztof Zamorski, Director of the Jagiellonian Library, Stanisław Waltoś the Director, Lucyna Bełtowska and Robert Springwald at the Collegium Malus, Matejko House, St Vladimir Foundation, Katarzyna Bałus, Princes Czartoryski Foundation, Jama Michalika, Prelate Janusz Bielański, Krakow Cathedral and Cathedral Museum, Church of the Bernardine Nuns, Bernardine Church, Father Mirosław Pilśniak, OP, Dominican Church, Sister Wanda Batko, Church of the Felician Nuns, Brother Bogumił Stachowicz, OFM, Franciscan Church, Father Edward Stoch, SJ, Jesuit Church in Wesoła, Capuchin Church, Father Dr Bronisław Fidelus, Church of St Mary, Father Jan Mazur, Paulite Church "On the Rock", Church of St Anne, Father Henryk Dziadosz, Church of St Barbara, Church of St Florian, Church of St Catherine, Church of the Holy Cross, Church of St Mark, Church of St Peter and St Paul, Church of St Vincent, Wieliczka Salt Mine, Father Dr Józef A. Nowobilski, the Metropolitan Curia and Archdiocesan Museum, Balice Airport, Archaeological Museum, Andrzej Szczygieł, Director of the Museum of Krakow, Anna Studnicka, National Museum, Natural History Museum, Zbigniew Święcicki the Director, and Mirosław Ciunowicz at the Polish Military Museum in Warsaw, PAP Polish Press Agency, Society of Physicians, Pieskowa Skała Castle.

Dorling Kindersley are grateful to the following individuals for their kind permission to reproduce their photographs:
Jacek Bednarczyk, Olaf Beer, Maja Florczykowska, Michał Grychowski, Stanisława Jabłońska, Dorota i Mariusz Jarymowiczowie, Beata i Mariusz Kowalewscy, Grzegorz Kozakiewicz, Wojciech Mędrzak, Stanisław Michta, Hanna i Maciej Musiałowie, Tomasz Robaczyński, Maciej Sochor, Jan Zych.

All the dishes whose photographs feature in this guide were prepared in the restaurant Pod Aniołami. We wish to thank the owner, Jacek Łodziński for his help. We are also grateful to Marcin Duszyński, Madropol for his kind assistance.

Key: a=above; b=below/bottom; c=centre; f=far; l=left; r=right; t=top.

Works of art have been reproduced with the permission of the following copyright holders: © ADAGP, Paris and DACS, London 2011

collegium Iuridicum by Igor Mitoraj 78tr. **123RF.com:** kaetana 80tl; qumrran 153tl.
AKG-Images: 20; 163cr; Ullstein Bild-KPA/HIP/Jewish Chronicle Ltd 127br. **Alamy Images:** AA World Travel Library 170bl; David Crausby 218cr; David Sanger Photography/David Sanger 187tl; Kevin Foy 126tl, 187c; Kevin George 113bc; Karolek 10cr; kpzfoto 135br; lookGaleria 11bl, 127cb; Look Studio 90tl; G Owston (Poland) 222tl; Pegaz 76, 211bl; Magdalena Rehova 166; David Robertson 74-75; Sherab 120; Paul Springett 72clb; Peter Svarc 10bl; Krystyna Szulecka 186cl; Matthew Taylor 174-175; VIEW Pictures Ltd 147br; John Warburton-Lee Photography 40; Jan Włodarczyk 208-209. **Archaeological Museum:** 22clb, 22bc, 23cr, 23cb, 23bl, 42b. **The Art Archive:** Laurie Platt Winfrey 127cra. **Art Hotel Niebieski:** 179bl, 182tr. **Auschwitz-Birkenau Memorial & Museum:** 162tr, 162cl, 162bl, 163tc, 164clb, 165cr, 164br; Ryszard Domasik 162tl, 163crb, 164cla, 165tl, 165tr; Jarek Mensfelt 164tr. **AWL Images:** Katie Garrod 58-59. **Carlsberg polska:** Chris Biggs 189c. **Cathedral Museum:** 24–5c, 26cla, 27cla, 46cl, 62ca, 64c. **Collegium Maius:** 27cb, 33b, 108–9. **Cool Tour Company:** 224bl. **Copernicus Restaurant:** 185br. **Corbis:** Bettmann 127tl; Jon Hicks 74–5; Historical Picture Archive 126tr. **Czartoryski Museum:** 43t, 45b, 114–15. **CK Dezerter:** 190bc. **Del Papa:** 184c, 192tc. **Dreamstime. com:** Artur Bogacki 225tr; Roksana Bashyrova 93tl; Dimaberkut 12tr; Jorg Hackemann 19br; Mbonaparte 128bl; Krzysztof Nahlik 2-3, 154; Neirfy 13tr; Nightman1965 160tl; Puchan 211tr; Tatiana Savvateeva 60; Jacek Sopotnicki 13bl; Simon Thomas 227cla. **FM Dutton, uk:** 213cra. **Edyta Gawron:** 126br. **Encyclopaedia Judaica:** 126cl. **Flamingo Hostel:** 178tr. **Hotel Fortuna:** 176bl. **Hotel Galaxy:** 177bc, 181tr. **Groteska Theatre:** Anna Kaczmarz 212tr. **Jagiellonian Library:** 22–3c, 26clb, 28tl, 28cra, 28b, 32b, 32crb, 30br, 34cb, 152bl. **Dariusz Jedrzejewski:** 11tr. **Kraków Airport:** 220br; 221br. **Krakow Festival Office:** 210cr. **Matejko House:** 25cr. **Metropolitan Hotel Krakow:** 177tr, 183br. **MOCAK The Museum of Contemporary Art in Krakow:** Rafał Sosin 159tl. **Museum of Krakow:** 20, 21b, 29ca, 31cb, 36b, 37ca, 37cr, 42cr, 43cbr, 94tr, 101br; Emeryk Hutten Czapski Museum 148tr. **Muzeum Historyczne Miasta Krakowa:** Ignacy Krieger 126clb, 126cb, 126crb. **National Museum:** 8–9, 24bc, 25tc, 26b, 27cr, 31br, 32bl, 32–3c, 33cr, 34tc, 34–5c, 35t, 35tr, 36cl, 36–7c, 39bl, 42tr, 42cl, 43tcr, 43c, 45t, 52tc, 53tl, 52cl, 104tr, 104c, 105, 112cl, 149l. **Natural History Museum:** 45c; **Novotel Krakow Centrum:** 177tr. **Pimiento Argentino:** 185tl, 191tr. **PKO Bank Polski:** Wojciech Czerniewicz 216c, 216bl. **Pod Baranemi:** 203tr. **Polskibus.com:** 223br. **Polski Hotel Pod Bialym Orlem:** 176cra, 180bc. **Polskie Koleje Panstwowe S.A.:** PKP InterCity 222br. **Public Record State Office:** 26–7c, 26bl. **Robert Harding Picture Library:** Bennet Dean 12bc, Henryk T. Kaiser 107tl, 130. **Secret Garden Hostel:** 178bl. **Sheraton Krakow Hotel:** The Olive 193br, SomePlace Else 184bl. **STA Travel Group:** 212cr. **SuperStock:** age fotostock / age fotostock 156tl, Henryk T. Kaiser 142. **Tel Aviv Museum of Art:** Jews Praying in the Synagogue on Yom Kippur by Maurycy Gottlieb, oil on canvas, gift of Sydney Lamon, New York 126–7c; **Telekomunikacja Polska:** 218c. **Topfoto.co.uk:** Roger-Viollet 165br. **Urzad Miasta Krakowa:** P. Krawczyk 226tr. **Hotel Wyspianski:** 179tr. **s Żywiec group:** 189cl; 189fcl.
Front Endpapers: Alamy Images: Look Studio Lclba; Pegaz Rc; Sherab Rcr. Dreamstime.com: Tatiana Savvateeva Lcrb. Robert Harding Picture Library: Henryk T. Kaiser Rtr. SuperStock: Henryk T. Kaiser / age fotostock Lcla.
Sheet Map Cover - Superstock: Travel Library Limited.
Jacket
Front main and spine t – Superstock: Travel Library Limited.

All other images ©Dorling Kindersley.
For further information see: www.dkimages.com

Phrase Book

Summary of Pronunciation in Polish

ą a nasal *"awn"* as in *"sawn"* or *"an"* as in the French *"Anjou"* but barely sounded
c *"ts"* as in *"bats"*
ć, cz *"ch"* as in *"challenge"*
ch *"ch"* as in Scottish *"loch"*
dz *"j"* as in *"jeans"* when followed by **i** or **e** but otherwise *"dz"* as in *"adze"*
dź *"j"* as in *"jeans"*
dż *"d"* as in *"dog"* followed by *"s"* as in *"leisure"*
ę similar to *"en"* in *"end"* only nasal and barely sounded, but if at the end of the word pronounced *"e"* as in *"bed"*
h *"ch"* as in Scottish *"loch"*
i *"ee"* as in *"teeth"*
j *"y"* as in yes
ł *"w"* as in *"window"*
ń similar to the *"ni"* in *"companion"*
ó *"oo"* as in *"soot"*
rz similar to the *"s"* in *"leisure"* or, when it follows **p**, **t** or **k**, *"sh"* as in *"shut"*
ś, sz *"sh"* as in *"shut"*
w *"v"* as in *"vine"*
y similar to the *"i"* in *"bit"*
ź, ż similar to the *"s"* in *"leisure"*

Emergencies

Help!	**pomocy!**	*pomotsi*
Call a doctor!	**zawołać doktora!**	*zawowach doctora*
Call an ambulance!	**zadzwonić po pogotowie!**	*zadzvoneech po pogotovee*
Police!	**policja!**	*poleetsya*
Call the fire brigade!	**zadzwonić po straż pożarną!**	*zadzvoneech po stras posarnAWN*
Where is the nearest phone?	**Gdzie jest najbliższa budka telefoniczna?**	*gjeh yest nIbleezhsha boodka telefoneechna*
Where is the hospital?	**Gdzie jest szpital?**	*gjeh yest shpeetal*
Where is the police station	**Gdzie jest posterunek policji?**	*gjeh yest posterunek politsyee*

Communication Essentials

Yes	**Tak**	*tak*
No	**Nie**	*n-yeh*
Thank you	**Dziękuję**	*jENkoo-yeh*
No thank you	**Nie, dziękuję**	*n-yej jENkoo-yeh*
Please	**Proszę**	*prosheh*
I don't understand.	**Nie rozumiem.**	*n-yeh roozoom-yem*
Do you speak English? (to a man)	**Czy mówi pan po angielsku?**	*chi moovee pan po ang-yelskoo*
Do you speak English? (to a woman)	**Czy mówi pani po angielsku?**	*chi moovee panee po ang-yelskoo*
Please speak more slowly	**Proszę mówić wolniej.**	*proseh mooveech voln-yay*
Please write it down for me.	**Proszę mi to napisać.**	*prosheh mee to napeesach*
My name is…	**Nazywam się…**	*nazivam sheh*

Useful Words and Phrases

Pleased to meet you (to a man)	**Bardzo mi miło pana poznać**	*bardzo mee meewo pana poznach*
Pleased to meet you (to a woman)	**Bardzo mi miło panią poznać**	*bardzo mee meewo pan-yAWN poznach*
Good morning	**Dzień dobry**	*jen-yuh dobri*
Good afternoon	**Dzień dobry**	*jen-yuh dobri*
Good evening	**Dobry wieczór**	*dobri v-yechoor*
Good night	**Dobranoc**	*dobranots*
Goodbye	**Do widzenia**	*do veedzen-ya*
What time is it…?	**Która jest godzina?**	*ktoora yest gojeena*
Cheers!	**Na zdrowie!**	*na zdrov-yeh*
Excellent!	**Wspaniale**	*wspan-yaleh*

Shopping

Do you have…? (to a man)	**Czy ma pan…?**	*che ma pan*
Do you have…? (to a woman)	**Czy ma pani…?**	*che ma panee*
How much is this?	**Ile to kosztuje?**	*eeleh to koshtoo-yeh*
Where is the… department?	**Gdzie jest dział z…?**	*gjeh yest jawuh z*
Do you take credit cards? (to a man)	**Czy przyjmuje pan karty kredytowe?**	*chi pshi-yuhmoo-yeh pan karti kreditoveh*
Do you take credit cards? (to a woman)	**Czy przyjmuje pani karty kredytowe?**	*chi pshi-yuhmoo-yeh panee karti kreditoveh*
bakery	**piekarnia**	*p-yekarn-ya*
bookshop	**księgarnia**	*kshENgarn-ya*
chemist	**apteka**	*apteka*
department store	**dom towarowy**	*dom tovarovi*
exchange office	**kantor walutowy**	*kantor valootovi*
travel agent	**biuro podróży**	*b-yooro podroozhi*
post office	**poczta, urząd pocztowy**	*pochta, ooZHAWNd pochtovi*
postcard	**pocztówka**	*pochtoovka*
stamp	**znaczek**	*znachek*
How much is a postcard to…?	**Ile kosztuje pocztówka do…?**	*eeleh koshtoo-yeh pochtoovka do*
airmail	**poczta lotnicza**	*pochta lotneecha*

Staying in a Hotel

Have you any vacancies? (to a man)	**Czy ma pan wolne pokoje?**	*chi ma pan volneh poko-yeh*
Have you any vacancies? (to a woman)	**Czy ma pani wolne pokoje?**	*chi ma panee volneh poko-yeh*
What is the charge per night?	**Ile kosztuje za dobę?**	*eeleh koshtoo-yeh za dobeh*
I'd like a single room.	**Poproszę pokój jednoosobowy.**	*poprosheh pokoo-yuh yedno-osobovi*
I'd like a double room.	**Poproszę pokój dwuosobowy.**	*poprosheh pokoo-yuh dvoo-osobovi*
I'd like a twin room.	**Poproszę pokój z dwoma łóżkami.**	*poprosheh pokoo-yuh z dvoma woozhkamee*
I'd like a room with a bathroom.	**Poproszę pokój z łazienką.**	*poprosheh pokoo-yuh z wazhenkAWN*
bathroom	**łazienka**	*wazhenka*
bed	**łóżko**	*woozhko*
bill	**rachunek**	*raHoonek*
breakfast	**śniadanie**	*shn-yadan-yeh*
dinner	**kolacja**	*kolats-ya*
double room	**pokój dwuosobowy**	*pokoo-yuh dvoo-osobovi*
full board	**pełne utrzymanie**	*pewhneh ootzhiman-yeh*
guest house	**zajazd**	*za-yazd*
half board	**dwa posiłki dziennie**	*dva posheewuhkee jen-yeh*
key	**klucz**	*klooch*
restaurant	**restauracja**	*restawrats-ya*
shower	**prysznic**	*prishneets*
single room	**pokój jednoosobowy**	*pokoo-yuh yedno-osobovi*
toilet	**toaleta**	*to-aleta*

Eating Out

A table for one, please.	**Stolik dla jednej osoby proszę.**	*stoleek dla yednay osobi prosheh*
A table for two, please.	**Stolik dla dwóch osób proszę.**	*stoleek dla dvooh osoob prosheh*
Can I see the menu?	**Mogę prosić jadłospis?**	*mogeh prosheech yadwospees*

Can I see the wine list?	**Mogę prosić kartę win?**	*mogeh prosheech karteh veen*
I'd like…	**Proszę**	*prosheh*
Can we have the bill, please?	**Proszę rachunek?**	*prosheh raHoonek*
Where is the toilet?	**Gdzie jest toaleta?**	*gjeh yest to-aleta*

Menu Decoder

baranina	mutton, lamb
barszcz czerwony	beetroot soup
bażant	pheasant
befsztyk	beef steak
bigos	hunter's stew *(sweet and sour cabbage with a variety of meats and seasonings)*
bukiet z jarzyn	a variety of raw and pickled vegetables
ciasto	cake, pastry
cielęcina	veal
cukier	sugar
cukierek	sweet, confectionery
dania mięsne	meat dishes
dania rybne	fish dishes
dania z drobiu	poultry dishes
deser	dessert
flaki	tripe
grzybki marynowane	marinated mushrooms
herbata	tea
jarzyny	vegetables
kabanos	dry, smoked pork sausage
kaczka	duck
kapusta	cabbage
kartofle	potatoes
kasza gryczana	buckwheat
kaszanka	black pudding
kawa	coffee
kiełbasa	sausage
klopsiki	minced meat balls
lody	ice cream
łosoś	salmon
łosoś wędzony	smoked salmon
makowiec	poppy seed cake
naleśniki	pancakes
piernik	spiced honeycake
pierogi	ravioli-like dumplings
piwo	beer
prawdziwki	ceps (type of mushroom)
przystawki	entrées
pstrąg	trout
rolmopsy	rollmop herrings
sałatka	salad
sałatka owocowa	fruit salad
sok	juice
sok jabłkowy	apple juice
sok owocowy	fruit juice
sól	salt
śledź	herring
tort	cake, gâteau
wieprzowina	pork
wino	wine
woda	water
ziemniaki	potatoes
zupa	soup

Health

I do not feel well.	**Źle się czuję.**	*zhleh sheh choo-yeh*
I need a prescription for…	**Potrzebuję receptę na…**	*potzheboo-yeh retsepteh na*
cold	**przeziębienie**	*pshef-yENb-yen-yeh*
cough (noun)	**kaszel**	*kashel*
cut	**skaleczenie**	*skalechen-yeh*
flu	**grypa**	*gripa*
hayfever	**katar sienny**	*katar shyienny*
headache pills	**proszki od bólu głowy**	*proshkee od booloo gwovi*
hospital	**szpital**	*shpeetal*
nausea	**mdłości**	*mudwosh-che*
sore throat	**ból gardła**	*bool gardwa*

Travel and Transport

When is the next train to…?	**Kiedy jest następny pociąg do…?**	*k-yedi yest nastENpni pochAWNg do…*
What is the fare to…?	**Ile kosztuje bilet do…?**	*eeleh koshtoo-yeh beelet do*

A single ticket to … please	**Proszę bilet w jedną stronę bilet do…**	*prosheh beelet v yednAWN stroneh beelet do*
A return ticket to … please	**Proszę bilet w obie strony do…**	*prosheh beelet v obye strony do*
Where is the bus station?	**Gdzie jest dworzec autobusowy?**	*gjeh yest dvozhets awtoboosovi*
Where is the bus stop?	**Gdzie jest przystanek autobusowy?**	*gjeh yest pshistanek awtoboosovi*
Where is the tram stop?	**Gdzie jest przystanek tramwajowy?**	*gjeh yest pshistanek tramvl-yovi*
booking office	**kasa biletowa**	*kasa beeletova*
station	**stacja**	*stats-ya*
timetable	**rozkład jazdy**	*rozkwad yazdi*
left luggage	**przechowalnia bagażu**	*psheHovaln-ya bagazhoo*
platform	**peron**	*peron*
first class	**pierwsza klasa**	*p-yervsha klasa*
second class	**druga klasa**	*drooga klasa*
single ticket	**bilet w jedną stronę**	*beelet v jednAWN stroneh*
return ticket	**bilet powrotny**	*beelet povrotni*
airline	**linia lotnicza**	*leen-ya lotna-yeecha*
airport	**lotnisko**	*lotn-yeesko*
arrival	**przylot**	*pshilot*
flight number	**numer lotu**	*noomer lotoo*
gate	**przejście**	*pshaysh-cheh*
coach (bus)	**autokar**	*awtokar*

Numbers

0	**zero**	*zero*
1	**jeden**	*yeden*
2	**dwa**	*dva*
3	**trzy**	*tshi*
4	**cztery**	*chteri*
5	**pięć**	*p-yENch*
6	**sześć**	*shesh-ch*
7	**siedem**	*sh-yedem*
8	**osiem**	*oshem*
9	**dziewięć**	*jev-yENch*
10	**dziesięć**	*jeshENch*
11	**jedenaście**	*yedenash-cheh*
12	**dwanaście**	*dvanash-cheh*
13	**trzynaście**	*tshinash-cheh*
14	**czternaście**	*chternash-cheh*
15	**piętnaście**	*p-yEntnash-cheh*
16	**szesnaście**	*shesnash-cheh*
17	**siedemnaście**	*shedemnash-cheh*
18	**osiemnaście**	*oshemnash-cheh*
19	**dziewiętnaście**	*jev-yENtnash-cheh*
20	**dwadzieścia**	*dvajesh-cha*
21	**dwadzieścia jeden**	*dvajesh-cha yeden*
22	**dwadzieścia dwa**	*dvajesh-cha dva*
30	**trzydzieści**	*tshijesh-chee*
40	**czterdzieści**	*chterjesh-chee*
50	**pięćdziesiąt**	*p-yFNchjeshΛWNt*
100	**sto**	*sto*
200	**dwieście**	*dv-yesh-cheh*
500	**pięćset**	*p-yENchset*
1,000	**tysiąc**	*tishAWNts*
1,000,000	**milion**	*meel-yon*

Time

today	**dzisiaj**	*jeeshl*
yesterday	**wczoraj**	*vchorl*
tomorrow	**jutro**	*yootro*
tonight	**dzisiejszej nocy**	*jeeshAYshay notsi*
one minute	**jedna minuta**	*yedna meenoota*
half an hour	**pół godziny**	*poowuh gojeeni*
hour	**godzina**	*gojeena*

Days of the Week

Sunday	**niedziela**	*n-yejela*
Monday	**poniedziałek**	*pon-yejawek*
Tuesday	**wtorek**	*vtorek*
Wednesday	**środa**	*shroda*
Thursday	**czwartek**	*chvartek*
Friday	**piątek**	*p-yAWNtek*
Saturday	**sobota**	*sobota*

Krakow Trams and Buses

KRÓLEWSKA

4-8-13-14-24-64-74

132-257-277

18-19

130-139-154-159
257-277-292-439

AL. JULIUSZA SŁOWACKIEGO

139-159-164-168-179
208-292-439-501-503-608

102

144-194

DŁUGA

608

NOWA
WIES

KARMELICKA

18-19

KLE

BASZTOWA

139-159-173
208-439-501
601-618

139-144-159-173
194-208-439-501-601-618

NAWOJKI

4-8-13-14-24-64-74

2-4-14-18-20
24-74-64-69

2-4-14-18-20
24-74-64-69

Czartoryski
Museum

102-159

AL. MICKIEWICZA

144-164-169-173
179-194-292-503
601-608-618

PIASEK

601-605-618-902

STARE
MIASTO

Church of
St Anne

Cloth
Hall

Church
of St Mary

20

2-8-13-18-20-69

National
Museum in
Krakow

Collegium
Maius

Dominican
Church

J. PIŁSUDSKIEGO   20

152-304-502-724-744
601-605-618-902

NOWY
ŚWIAT

1-6-8-13-18-69

134-152-292-902

20

Franciscan
Church

OKÓŁ

ALFOCHA

109-134-409
502-724-744

173-179-194-402-605-608

1-4-12-14-144-169

STRASZEWSKIEGO

Church of Saints
Peter and Paul

ŚW. GERTRUDY

1-2-6

Z. KRASIŃSKIEGO

609-601

Krakow
Cathedral

STRADO

109-409-605

109-409-605

T. KOŚCIUSZKI

most
Dębnicki

WAWEL

Wawel
Royal Castle

100-209-229-239
249-259-269

109-409-605

1-2-6

Vistula

MARII KONOPNICKIEJ

STRADOM

5-8-13-69

1-2-6

144-164-169-173
179-194-304-503-608

162-412

11-18-22-52-70-72-62

184-610

most
Grunwaldzki

DĘBNIKI

PRASKA

12-16

101

MONTE CASSINO

101-112
162-412

144-164-169-173-179-184-304-503-608-610

11-18-22-52-70-62-72

101-194

101

KAPELANKA

194

LUDWINÓW

| 0 metres | 500 |
| 0 yards | 500 |